SOCIAL
CONTROL

SOCIAL CONTROL

Lorne Tepperman   Laura Upenieks

OXFORD
UNIVERSITY PRESS

OXFORD
UNIVERSITY PRESS

Oxford University Press is a department of the University of Oxford.
It furthers the University's objective of excellence in research, scholarship,
and education by publishing worldwide. Oxford is a registered trade mark of
Oxford University Press in the UK and in certain other countries.

Published in Canada by
Oxford University Press
8 Sampson Mews, Suite 204,
Don Mills, Ontario M3C 0H5 Canada

www.oupcanada.com

Library and Archives Canada Cataloguing in Publication
Tepperman, Lorne, 1943-, author
Social control / Lorne Tepperman and Laura Upenieks.

(Themes in Canadian sociology)
Includes bibliographical references and index.
ISBN 978-0-19-901858-1 (paperback)

1. Social control–Canada. I. Upenieks, Laura, author
II. Title. III. Series: Themes in Canadian sociology

HM661.T46 2016   303.3'30971   C2015-908518-7

Cover image: © iStock/zodebala

Part-opening photos—Part I: ©zeber/Shutterstock.com; Part II: ©Corepics VOF/Shutter-
stock.com; Part III: ©sakhorn/Shutterstock.com.

Oxford University Press is committed to our environment.
Wherever possible, our books are printed on paper which comes from
responsible sources.

Printed and bound in Canada

1 2 3 4 — 19 18 17 16

Contents

Preface

We wrote this book for use in undergraduate college and university sociology courses, in any of three venues. First, the book can be used in one-semester second- or third-year courses on *social control* (or *deviance and control*); or it can be used in two-semester courses if accompanied by an appropriate set of readings. Second, it can be used in one-semester courses on *social institutions*; or in two-semester courses on that topic, if accompanied by an appropriate set of readings. Finally, it can be used in any *introduction to sociology* course in conjunction with an appropriate textbook on social inequality.

Most sociologists would agree that sociology has historically been concerned with two central questions:

1. What are the forms/causes of social inequality and diversity?
2. What are the bases of social order?

This book is concerned with the second question: with the institutions, practices, and performances that reproduce social order from day to day and year to year.

Why is the separate study of social control so crucial to the study of sociology? The answer to this question is surprisingly simple, given that many sociology departments do not offer a course titled "Social Control." The answer is, social control is absolutely fundamental to the study of social life—indeed, to every aspect of social life. As we will see in this book, you cannot understand social order, social inequality, socialization, the formation of social institutions, or change and conflict—let alone crime and punishment—if you don't understand social control.

To say this a slightly different way, social control is implicated in all of society's main institutions and social processes. You could no more have social life without social control than you could have social life without social interaction—another fundamental concern of sociology. So, in that sense, the study of social control is a general introduction to all the core concerns of sociology, past and present. As noted, you cannot understand social order without understanding social control. In relation to *social control*, this question of order has been raised historically in two different ways. From Durkheim onward, the question of order and control has been viewed as a matter of social integration and solidarity. Accordingly, it has focused on issues of culture, consensus, religion, ritual, socialization, education, and the like. From Marx and Weber onward, the question of order and control has been viewed as a matter of social regulation. Accordingly, the discussion of order has been concerned with issues of coercion, power, ideology, law-making, and law-enforcement.

The criminological approach to control has focused on this latter tradition: on why certain laws are made and enforced by the state, for example. This approach has included a concern with the effectiveness of strategic law-making and law-enforcement, policing, and imprisonment, among other things. On the other hand, classical, functionalist, and critical approaches have tended to focus on broader issues: for example, on the role played by families, schools, religions, and the mass media in propagating control and self-control (e.g., through notions of duty and normality.)

In addition to these macro-sociological approaches, micro-sociological approaches to control have focused on strategies and tactics of seeking compliance: for example, on the interpersonal uses of reward, threat, blame, shame, and stigma. These micro-sociological approaches are evident in the dramaturgical analyses of Erving Goffman and other symbolic interactionists. More recent social constructionist approaches extend these analyses of strategic persuasion to the societal sphere, asking questions like this: How do claims-makers shape (i.e., control and manipulate) people's opinions about particular social, moral, or political issues?

In short, then, the topic of social control covers a wide variety of subtopics from a wide variety of perspectives; and it is the goal of this book to examine all of these approaches. Here's how the book is laid out.

Part I: Describing the Social World

In Chapter 1, we examine the history of thinking about social control, including both the functionalist and critical approaches outlined above. In the next two chapters, we briefly contrast discussions of the micro- and macro-strategies of control, using specific cases to do so. In Chapter 2, "Micro-Strategies of Control: Appearance Norms," we use the examples of beauty, tattooing and piercing, styles of dress, and obesity and eating disorders (among other things) to illustrate interpersonal and cultural strategies of shaming and stigmatization in social control. In Chapter 3, "Macro-Strategies of Control: Laws against Substance Abuse," we examine societal attempts to use law-making and law-enforcement strategies as well as health promotion strategies to control alcohol and drug abuse.

Thus, Part 1 of the book is an introduction to the idea of social control, its history, and its application to two very specific cases: a micro-sociological example (control of appearances through the use of shame) and a macro-sociological example (control of substance use through the use of legislation). These two cases represent the two main varieties of social control discussed in the book, and the two main views of social control: as a means of integration and as a means of regulation.

Part II: Sources of Control

In this part of the book, we discuss four main social institutions that exercise social control in our society. Chapter 4, "Socialization and Culture," discusses attempts to control people's behaviour by socializing them into certain culturally defined notions of propriety and normality. Chapter 5, "Religion and Religious Institutions," discusses the role of religious institutions in defining and enforcing normative and moral standards, thereby ensuring social control. Chapter 6 is titled "Media and Mass Communication" and considers the ever-growing role of the mass media in promoting a secular set of ideas and rules for behaviour. Finally, Chapter 7, "Government, Politics, and Ideology," considers the role of the state as a source of laws and law enforcers; the associated concepts of authority, ideology, and legitimacy are also discussed here.

Part III: Process of Formal Control

In this part of the book, we discuss formal social control in its various manifestations, and we examine how this formal control relates to social inequality. In Chapter 8, "Unequal Opportunities and Crime Prevention," we look at the economic dimension of social control, focusing on the unequal impact of social class on crime and punishment and, conversely, on the role of economic opportunity in channelling (and thereby controlling) unwanted behaviour. Chapter 9, "Sources of Control: Force and Punishment," examines some of the traditional criminological topics around policing, prison, parole, and, generally, the purposes of punishment. In Chapter 10, "Social Control and Victimization," we return to the starting theme of the book—the duality of control—by considering (on the one hand) the price of rule-breaking for people who are victimized by criminal rule-breakers; and (on the other hand) the price of conformity for people who are victimized by too strict ideas about propriety and normality.

These topics—the definition and history of social control, the institutions that exercise control, and the relationship of social control to inequality and power—are all topics that one would expect to find in a book on social control. If space allowed, we would present a fuller discussion of all of these topics and of their relationship to families, workplaces, political ideologies, policing, and class systems, for example. There are a great many sociological topics that connect to social control, as we have already noted. This means that, in a short book, a great many have to be left out or noted only in passing.

Here's what this book will argue: there is no group, community, or society without social control; in that sense, social control surrounds and shapes all of our social life. There could be no societies without both informal and formal controls.

For these reasons, all of the founding figures of sociology have had something to say about social control. Consider just a few. For Durkheim, the integration and regulation provided by social control is something all humans require, if they are to survive; he says so in his work on suicide. For Weber, we are all complicit in social control through our legitimation of authority. That is, we generally acquiesce in the state's control of ourselves and others. For Marx, on the other hand, social control is part of a larger apparatus of class domination, largely accomplished through the state. For Foucault, social control is largely accomplished through the colonization of our selves by major institutions and their "experts." For Gramsci and members of the Frankfurt School of critical theory, social control is largely accomplished through ideology and media manipulation.

In our view, it is fruitless to study criminology and criminological theories without first receiving a general grounding in the topic of social control. Criminological theories of crime and punishment represent a special case of theories about social control, and this book attempts to contextualize these theories. It is true that, by now, criminology is a multidisciplinary field with its own history of important scholarship; but there is no escaping the social context of crime and punishment, whatever one's approach to criminology.

In taking on the general topic of social control, we have taken on a lot to cover in only 250 pages. However, we think this book will give you a taste of important topics and make you want to dig further into these topics, in other books and other courses. We hope you agree.

Acknowledgements

We are grateful to the wonderful undergraduate research assistants who helped us find and prepare material for inclusion in this book. They include Emily Berry, Kimberley Enarson, Bastian Leones, Amir Fleischmann, Richard Kennedy, Dasha Kuznetsova, Amy Lin, Shaina McHardy, Hamdi Moalim, Ashley Sewrattan, and Koet Wu. Amir Fleischmann also provided valuable assistance in creating pedagogical materials for each chapter. We are also grateful to our undergraduate students in Sociology 313, "Social Control," who heard lectures on this material during the summer and fall of 2014. Their reactions to the course lectures (and tests) helped us refine the manuscript and hone it more precisely to the instructional task at hand.

At Oxford University Press, we are grateful to developmental editor Tanuja Weerasooriya, who set up our work plan and schedule, and to developmental editor Amy Gordon, who reviewed our manuscript, suggested improvements, raised useful questions, and proposed helpful cuts in the manuscript. Most important of all was the help we received from copy editor Colleen Ste. Marie. We are indebted to her clear thinking and writing, which pushed us to think and write even more clearly than we had already done. Thank you, Colleen.

Finally, we would like to give thanks to the reviewers: Heidi Rimke, University of Winnipeg, and Camilla Sears, Thompson Rivers University. We also thank the anonymous reviewers who provided feedback on the manuscript.

Lorne Tepperman,
Laura Upenieks,
September 2015

Part I

Describing the Social World

1 What Is Social Control?

Learning Objectives

◎ To understand the purpose of social control

◎ To examine how integration and regulation are achieved and to distinguish between formal and informal social control

◎ To become familiar with different theories regarding the two sides of social control: social norms and strict enforcement of written rules

◎ To distinguish between micro-sociological and macro-sociological approaches to social control

◎ To identify agents of social control and the strategies they use

Introduction

Imagine this: Here you are, in school for another year, plowing through seemingly endless assignments, tests, readings, and quizzes. And now, to cap it all, your teacher has insisted that you must give a classroom presentation lasting not less than 10 minutes on a topic related to the course material. Oddly, you are terrified by the prospect and can't figure out why.

Well, here's the reason. Repeated studies have found that a majority of people fear public speaking—indeed, fear it more than death, spiders, darkness, heights, enclosed spaces, and a variety of other common fears. But consider for a moment why someone like you might be afraid to stand up in front of others and say what you think. The likely reason is that you fear making a fool of yourself.

But why do you fear making a fool of yourself? The answer to this question goes to the heart of this book. For we will see that all people are terrified by, and therefore controlled by, the opinions other people hold of them. As a result, when they think of humiliating themselves in front of others, they feel shame, fear, and even some anticipated guilt.

Shame, guilt, and fear are just a few of the things we will discuss in this book. The example of public speaking illustrates the "social psychology" of social control, but there are other forms of control we will consider as well. Imagine, for example, that you are 12 years old and have just moved to a new neighbourhood in a new town or city. You don't know anyone at your new school and no one wants to talk to you. The few who even notice you at all seem to hold you in contempt and make cracks about the way you are dressed. Eventually, you discover that most of the students in this school belong to one of seven cliques, and each of these cliques has a leader. In gym class yesterday, you traded jokes with Jennifer, one of those leaders, and felt a spark of friendship. Suddenly, friends of Jennifer are willing to speak to you and students in other cliques are starting to notice you exist.

What does this example mean? A few key students—Jennifer and a half-dozen other clique leaders—are the key to your social acceptance at school. You have to please at least one of these students to gain social acceptability in the school. This is another example of social control.

In another example of social control, think about your younger brother, Tim. He's in grade 5 and he's been getting into a lot of trouble at school. Sometimes, he shouts out answers in class and refuses to stay seated, moving around the room freely to talk and joke with his friends at their desks. Other times, he seems to be in another world entirely, half asleep, staring out the window, or secretly playing video games. His teacher, Mrs Jones, insists that Tim receive an assessment from the school psychologist. The psychologist calls in your parents and tells them that Tim has borderline symptoms of attention deficit hyperactivity disorder (ADHD) and that, if action is not taken, Tim may have to go into a class for "special learners." Your terrified parents agree to sign up Tim for a series of additional tests and counselling sessions, at their own expense. Eventually, they agree to put Tim on Ritalin for a trial period of not less than a year.

In this instance, control over Tim's inclusion in regular school classes—and perhaps his education and occupational future—rests on the diagnosis provided by a school psychologist. Because of her expertise, the school psychologist holds enormous power over Tim and thousands of other students with supposed "behaviour problems."

In this chapter, we will provide an overview of all of these mechanisms of control, as well as others. We will briefly review the history of the concept of social control. As we will see, this concept is central to the study of sociology: indeed, some would say that understanding social control is central to understanding everything about social life.

So, learning about social control will help you understand why you behave the way you do and why you fear what you fear: why you feel nervous addressing a large group of people, going to a job interview, asking someone out on a date, dressing in an unusual fashion, voicing an unpopular opinion among friends, or standing up for your rights against family members or people in authority. Learning about social control will also help you understand how cliques, groups, and communities sometimes influence us to behave in ways we never would have imagined. Finally, learning about social control will help you understand how and why modern institutions—especially schools, workplaces, and hospitals—exercise such a powerful influence over us.

The *Oxford Dictionary of Sociology* defines *social control* as

> [t]he social processes by which the behaviour of individuals or groups is regulated. Since all societies have norms and rules governing conduct (a society without some such norms is inconceivable) all equally have some mechanisms for ensuring conformity to those norms and for dealing with deviance. Social control is consequently a pervasive feature of society, of interest to a broad range of sociologists having differing theoretical persuasions and substantive interests, and not just to sociologists of deviance.

In other words, social control is devised by society—by people acting together to invent and enforce rules. People also learn to obey the rules of society—to control themselves—through socialization, another social activity. And because social control is *social*, the rules and practices of social control vary from one group, community, and society to another, and they change over time; they are *not* natural, permanent, or genetically given.

Moreover, no human community, and no human beings, exist without social control. Even pirates—those violent, nasty, anti-social demons of the sea—devise and live by rules. We know this because historians have recovered the laws that pirates agreed to on joining a crew, and they make pretty good sense.

For example, according to Alexandre Exquemelin's (1678) book *The Buccaneers of America*, common pirate rules guaranteed the following: every person was to have a vote in important ship affairs; they were also to have equal rights to the fresh provisions or strong liquors that had been seized and were free to use them as wished, unless a scarcity made it necessary, for the good of all, to do otherwise. No person was to play card games or roll dice for money. The lights and candles were to be put out at 8:00 p.m., and if any of the crew stayed up late to drink, they were to do it on the open deck. Crew members were to keep their swords, knives, and pistols clean and fit for service.

The pirate rules prescribed a variety of punishments for infractions of particular rules. So, for example, if crew members hid stolen property from the others, marooning was their punishment. If a crew member robbed another, the crew would slit the ears and nose of the guilty party and set him on shore somewhere where he was sure to encounter hardships. And if a crew member deserted the ship or his quarters in battle, he was punished with death or marooning. And no boy or woman was to be allowed on board. Any crew member who seduced a woman and carried her to sea, disguised as a man or boy, was to suffer death. In short, even pirates controlled themselves—and so do we.

This book will argue that we all control one another in everyday life—as students, family members, workers, citizens, and otherwise. All groups and

institutions—families, classrooms, and workplaces, among others—use social control to maintain their boundaries, regulate member activities, and preserve order. The major institutions of society are particularly important sources of social control through a process Michel Foucault has called "governmentality," which we discuss later. As we will see, the most effective social control works through socialization and indoctrination—not through threat and coercion.

In short, this book is concerned with the institutions, practices, and performances that reproduce **social order** from day to day and year to year. Said another way, social order is concerned with showing how the various institutions of society—education, religion, mass media, government, and the law, for example—get us to conform to social rules, often without our awareness.

How to Achieve Integration and Regulation in Society

Let us begin by noting that there are two main types of social control:

1. *Informal social control*: The regulation of people's behaviour by other people in ordinary social settings—homes, schools, churches, workplaces
2. *Formal social control*: The regulation of people's behaviour through the use of laws, police officers, courts, jails, and other formal (rational-legal, often bureaucratic) procedures

Both of these types of social control contribute to the achievement of **integration** and **regulation** in society.

In sociology, the concept of social control has evolved through many formulations. In present-day society, social control is often understood as the enforcement of law and the subsequent control of crime and criminal behaviour (i.e., formal social control) (Deflem, 2007). From the nineteenth century onwards, social control has been used to describe the ability of a society to regulate itself without the use of force. Deflem (2007) notes that this approach to the study of social control lends itself to a focus on *social integration* in society. Social integration is assumed to come about through the **socialization** of people into a common set of values (i.e., informal social control).

This way of thinking first became evident in Durkheim's classic work *Rules of Sociological Method* (1982). Each individual, according to Durkheim, is born into a socially organized community that demands conforming beliefs and behaviours. From this standpoint, laws and punishments, politics, language, religion, economics, and professions are all concerned with reproducing the social facts that characterize a society and shape people's behaviour. These social institutions push people into predictable forms of behaviour; but these people do not usually feel or recognize these informal social controls as coercion. Instead, they usually attribute their behaviour to their own values and beliefs and, in turn, attribute their values and beliefs to personal insight.

Even suicide—a profoundly personal behaviour—is an indicator of informal social control. That's why changes in social integration and regulation predict changes in the suicide rate of a community and the suicide chances of an individual. To illustrate this, Durkheim (1979) shows that Protestants are more likely to commit suicide than Jews or Catholics. He theorizes that this is because of a lack of integration of the Protestant community's norms and values (Durkheim, 1979). Protestantism is simply less cohesive and less integrative, hence less controlling, than the other religions—especially, Catholicism and Judaism. As Durkheim points out, "when society is strongly integrated it holds people under its control, considers them at its service and thus forbids them to dispose willingly of themselves" (1979, p. 209).

However, integration isn't the whole story; people and societies also need regulation. To regulate human passions, laws, social codes, and rules come into being. Durkheim (1979) proposes that societies with strongly stated and strongly enforced legal and social codes have lower suicide rates than societies without these things. As social regulation declines, due to rapid social change, to a lack of political will, or to other kinds of disorganization, suicide rates rise.

Because suicide rates are affected by *both* integration and regulation, four types of suicide are logically possible. The first type of suicide, *egoistic suicide,* occurs when low social integration leads to a sense of meaninglessness among people. The second type of suicide, *altruistic suicide,* results when the level of social integration is too high and the individual is forced into giving up his or her life in the interest of his community. Examples of altruistic suicide include the following: self-sacrifice for military objectives in wartime, suicide bombers, people who see the social world as meaningless and would sacrifice themselves for a greater ideal—essentially people who feel their death would bring great benefit to society. A third type of suicide Durkheim (1979) describes is *anomic suicide,* which results from the breakdown of regulative standards and values. In short, people can't handle all that freedom. Finally, a fourth type of suicide, and the opposite of anomic suicide, is *fatalistic suicide,* characterized by regulation that is too strong. In this instance, the individual sees no way that his or her life can be changed and improved.

Throughout this book, we will consider how both integration and regulation control people in the social world. Out of the mix of these two elements we get a vast variety of theories about social control.

Theories Regarding the Two Sides of Social Control

As noted earlier, in its original sense, **social control** referred to the ability of a group, community, or society to regulate itself. Sociology has always explored the conditions and variables that influence the attainment of this collective goal. Janowitz reminds us that the pursuit of social control rests on a commitment to both "the reduction of coercion and the elimination of human misery" (1975, p. 88). Social control, as enforced through social norms (one side of social control) and as defined by classical sociologists, is different from coercive control (the other side of social control), which relies heavily on both the threat and application of force. Some level of coercion may be necessary, but Janowitz (1975) notes that coercion is minimal in a well-functioning society and is embedded in a larger system of legitimate norms.

At the end of the nineteenth century, E.A. Ross first used the idea of social control to understand how people "live closely together and associate their efforts with that degree of harmony we see about us" (Janowitz, 1975, p. 89). He focused on the role of interpersonal and institutional persuasion, through face-to-face interactions, public opinion, and legal control, and how such persuasion guided "the will or conscience of the individual members of the society" (Janowitz, 1975, p. 89).

In this respect, Ross (1926) saw the law as only one institution (of many) through which social control was exercised; others included education, public opinion, and religion. Ross understood social control as applying to all members of society, and he thought that consensus, not coercion, is the goal or function of social control. Like Durkheim, Ross proposed that under conditions of increased individualism and specialization, societies have to take extra measures to achieve consensus. Moreover, social control, for Ross, is only achieved when multiple institutions work together. Social control thus contributes to social order and social integration, based largely on peaceful social relations and harmony achieved by the collective.

Charles Horton Cooley and W.I. Thomas, who were other early figures in sociology and who were social interactionists, also addressed the concept of social control in their writings. Cooley proposed that social control was important for the development and growth of the "self," which people achieved through the process of interaction. For his part, W.I. Thomas focused his attention on "rational control in social life." Thomas looked at the impact of "rational thought" in weakening the "social fabric" of society. Thomas imagined society as consisting of many diverse social groups, from simple primary groups like the family to larger, more complex bureaucratic institutions. Social control, from this angle, depended on the creation of a civil society that knit together all of social life—all of society's major institutions. Without this, social disorganization resulted.

George Herbert Mead, another symbolic interactionist, proposed that social control depended on the ability of people "to assume the attitudes of the others who are involved with them in common endeavor" (1925, p. 275). In this way, social control was seen as overlapping with self-control: "Self-criticism is essentially social criticism, and behavior controlled by self-criticism is essentially behavior controlled socially." Hence social control, "so far from tending to crush out the human individual or to obliterate his self-conscious individuality, is, on the contrary, actually constitutive of and inextricably associated with that individuality" (Mead, 1934, p. 255).

Sociologists writing during in the first half of the twentieth century did not view social control as a tool of oppressive conformity. Rather, the health of society itself was wrapped up in problems of social control and social disorganization. Later, the European sociologist Karl Mannheim (1940) addressed the concept of social control in his book *Man and Society in an Age of Reconstruction*. Mannheim (1940) focused his work on government institutions. For Mannheim (1940), freedom was an essential element of social control—not a matter of either/or; and this was especially important in wartime, to assure the prevention of authoritarian rule.

The most important later work on social control was done by French sociologist Michel Foucault. His work locates the power of social control neither in **the state** nor in interpersonal (dyadic) interactions but, rather, in society's main institutions: in its families, schools, and workplaces, for example. The name he gives to this kind of social control is governmentality.

As Foucault (1977) points out, all modern institutions are complicit in the business of social control. It was to capture this idea that Foucault coined the concept of governmentality. The *Oxford Dictionary of Sociology* defines *governmentality* as

> a complex set of processes through which human behaviour is systematical-ly controlled in ever wider areas of social and personal life. For Foucault, such government is not limited to the body of state ministers, or even to the state, but permeates the whole of a society and operates through dispersed mechanisms of power. It comprises both sovereign powers of command, of the kind that figure in traditional political science and political sociology, and disciplinary powers of training and self-control.

As we will see in a later chapter, the power of the state is largely coercive and repressive, involving exclusion through external controls and induce-ments, thanks to a monopoly on the use of force. By contrast, *non*-state disciplinary power operates by shaping the motives, desires, and character of individuals. This it does through what Foucault (1977) calls "techniques of the self." Through childhood socialization, for example, we are not merely taught—we are disciplined into habits and skills that lead us to act in socially appropriate ways without requiring external, coercive power.

As we will soon see, disciplinary power in modern societies is exercised through experiences in families, schools, and workplaces; also, in hospi-tals, military barracks, and prisons, and other so-called **total institutions** (Foucault, 1977). The family is especially important in creating and dis-ciplining selves and bodies at a personal, intimate level. Assisting in this massive task of discipline and control is the rise of an army of highly trained "experts" who use scientific knowledge to legitimate the discipline of individuals. An example is the school psychologist we discussed earlier. In short, social control by governmentality takes place through all of these mechanisms.

The Variety of Social Norms

As Foucault (1977) points out, despite the large number of laws and written or formal rules governing a modern society, most of the time we are guided by **social norms**, or *informal controls*: a collection of unspoken rules, guides, and standards of behaviour that prevail in any society or organization (see Box 1.1). People base their opinions of themselves largely on how they believe other people view them, so they are likely to feel punished—bruised

Box 1.1 — The Unwritten Rules of Christmas

In a classic study of "Middletown, America," Theodore Caplow (1984) examined the informal control of the practices of Christmas gift giving in "Middletown," the pseudonym for a small American city. From people's practices, Caplow was able to deduce eight "Unwritten Rules of Christmas." Consider, for example, the following rules:

The Gift Selection Rule: A Christmas gift should demonstrate the giver's familiarity with the receiver's preferences, surprise the receiver, and be priced in accordance with the emotional value of the relationship (Caplow, 1984, p. 1313).

The Reciprocity Rule: People should give at least one Christmas gift every year to their mother, father, spouse, son, daughter, and to the current spouses of these children (Caplow, 1984, p. 1315).

The Scaling Rule: The most money should be spent on a gift for one's spouse, then on child(ren) and their spouses (equally). Parents with several children should value the children equally throughout their lives, as exemplified by the value of gifts they give (Caplow, 1984, p. 1313).

Now, this set of practices illustrates "social control without visible means." This unwritten rule controls people's behaviour, but the source of control is invisible. There are no prescribed responses to people who break any of these rules. But just imagine what would happen if a husband gave his youngest daughter a better gift than he gave his wife, his oldest daughter, or his son. At the very least, feelings would be hurt. Likely, that husband would find himself sleeping on the couch for at least a few nights.

even—when other people disapprove. That, ultimately, is why people trouble themselves to learn the norms and follow them.

In groups large and small, we create these rules for ourselves and also enforce them ourselves. We also create these as experts, managers, and administrators. People obey these norms because they value the good opinion of others and believe that obeying the rules is normal and legitimate.

Ridicule, shame, sarcasm, criticism, and ostracism are some of the informal controls people use to punish others who stray from these informal rules. In this respect, shaming is a particular potent means of control that everyone uses from time to time and that everyone has endured. Besides shaming, ostracism, or exclusion, may be used against people who violate social norms. This is the expulsion of people from a social group or the refusal to let a certain individual join the group. Sometimes, entire groups are ostracized. Like shame, however, exclusion is a type of social control that can backfire. For example, consider the angry, destructive violence of minority people who live in modern-day ghettos.

Control of Crime and Deviance: The "Narrow" Nature of Social Control

Now consider the second side of social control and a stark contrast to social norms: the criminological approach to social control, which focuses on regulation through formal means—that is, based on the strict enforcement of written rules.

Deflem (2007) notes that, after World War II, a shift occurred in how social control was defined and studied as a concept. Partly as a result of the atrocities and the rise of Nazism, "social control" came to take on a more coercive meaning than it had in the past. Power and force came to occupy a more important place in sociological thinking. Institutions also became viewed as much more controlling. From the 1950s, social control was defined more "narrowly" than before, and sociologists placed an increasing emphasis on social control's relationship to crime and **deviance**. The present-day definition of social control extends this pattern, considering how major social institutions both define and respond to crime and other deviant acts.

Consider white collar or business crime, a topic of interest to sociologists ever since the early work of Edwin H. Sutherland. Sutherland (1939, 1973), for his part, viewed rule-breaking as a result of social imitation, and he proposed **differential association theory** to understand criminal behaviour. Specifically, he proposed that criminal behaviour is learned behaviour, the result of repeated interaction with peers who are deviant (Sutherland, 1939; 1973). Through this association, people learn the techniques of committing certain crimes but also specific motives and justifications for such offences.

Sutherland's (1939, 1973) principle of differential association asserts that a person becomes deviant because of an "excess" of definitions that

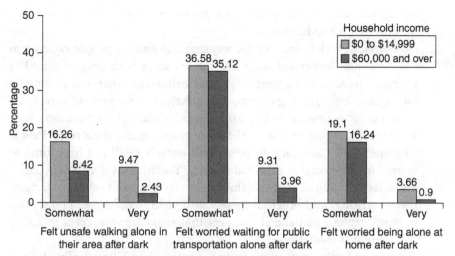

1. No statistically significant differences between individuals from households with incomes of $0 to $14,999 and those from households with incomes of $60,000 and over.

Figure 1.1 Canadians from Low Income Households More Fearful of Crime in Certain Situations
Source: Statistics Canada (2009).

are favourable to the violation of the law over definitions unfavourable to the violation of the law. Stated otherwise, criminal behaviour results when a person is exposed to more social messages that favour rule-breaking behaviour than those that favour rule-abiding behaviour. So, the focus is on social and cultural organization, not disorganization; and it is on social approval and support, not poverty and disadvantage. People living in close proximity to areas in which these messages resound are also affected by them (see Figure 1.1).

When people become criminals, according to this theory, they do so from exposure to deviant peer groups. But how can we explain why two people exposed to the same criminal opportunities and associations may turn out very differently: one a criminal, the other a law-abiding citizen? For Travis Hirschi (1969), all previously existing criminological theories fail to say enough about criminal (or non-criminal) motivation. Hirschi (1969) proposes that we all, at birth, possess the drive to act in selfish and aggressive ways that, if not controlled, will lead us to criminal behaviour. So, for Hirschi (1969), acting impulsively and aggressively is human nature. However, most of us "control" our natural urges while some of us do not.

For Hirschi (1969), this variation is explained by the bonds that people form and these important bonds come in four forms:

1. *Attachment*, which refers to the amount of psychological affection a person has for others. These attachments control our behaviour because

we do not want to disappoint the people we love—e.g., parents and friends—with bad behaviour.

2. *Commitment,* which refers to the way that law-abiding people avoid jeopardizing their important roles and relationships with deviant acts. For example, as adults, we generally avoid behaviours that will threaten a job or marriage. Having committed ourselves to a course of action, we do not want to upset it by breaking the rules and risking punishment.

3. *Involvement,* which addresses the ways people spend their time. People who spend all their time in **prosocial activity** will not have time to engage in anti-social or criminal activity. Youthful involvement in legitimate, law-abiding activities—clubs, team sports, band rehearsals, classroom learning, and otherwise—will also yield benefits like knowledge, cultural capital, and social contacts that make adult success in legitimate pursuits more likely.

4. *Belief* in and adherence to the values associated with law-abiding behaviours. For example, young people who believe in the value and legitimacy of hard work, sobriety, thrift, and obedience are more likely than other youth to succeed in a competitive, capitalist society.

The social bonds that Hirschi (1969) describes function from inside our heads, if we have been properly socialized; and we control ourselves because of our attachment, commitment, belief, and involvement in the social order. In turn, this means that, if you want to control people, you would do well to teach them self-control and conformity. Following up on the work of Hirschi and others in the 1970s and 1980s, Gottfredson and Hirschi (1990) developed a comprehensive theory of crime driven by the assumption that underlying all criminal (or delinquent) acts is a lack of self-control. In this theory, the ability to defer gratification is a good predictor of success in an educational and occupational career—also, in marriage. The inability to defer gratification—to seek immediate gratification—is more characteristic of people who commit crimes.

According to Gottfredson and Hirschi (1990), defective child-rearing practices produce these differences in self-control. Close and continued parental attention helps people develop "deferred gratification" as they grow up. Parental neglect of a child results in actions geared toward "immediate gratification." For Gottfredson and Hirschi (1990), then, low self-control is a result of insufficient nurturance and discipline in childhood. Often, parents who fail to instill self-control in their children have not been well socialized by their own parents.

Sometimes, schools can help to correct these problems of faulty socialization. For five to eight hours a day, the school can monitor children's behaviour closely, and teachers are in a position to recognize deviant and disruptive behaviour by their students. As a result, the school has a potentially positive socializing influence on children. After all, doing one's homework requires high self-control, as does sitting in a classroom and not disrupting the teacher when talking. Children who become delinquents typically report not having liked school because school requires self-control and restrains a person's behaviour. Thus, the school, like the family, is a social institution that helps to breed self-control, hence social control. We will have much more to say about this in chapters to come.

Strategies of Control

As mentioned earlier, all groups and institutions use social control to maintain their boundaries, regulate member activities, and perpetuate order. And they do so in two main ways: (1) by **social sanctioning** (i.e., by administering rewards and punishments) and (2) through **social management** (i.e., by *agents of social control* shaping the social settings and contexts in which people act, to channel behaviour in desired directions). The prison system (see Figure 1.2) is one of the more commonly known social institutions, but, as we will see, it is not entirely effective as a form of social control.

Social Sanctioning

Four techniques of face-to-face control, which chiefly rely on social sanctions, are persuasion, ridicule, gossip, and ostracism.

Persuasion
Persuasion tries to convince the listener to obey the stated rules. It is usually friendly in its tone and offers rewards. The effectiveness of persuasion will

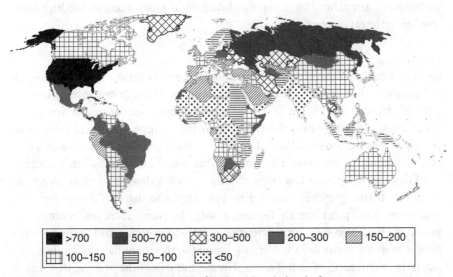

Figure 1.2 Incarceration Rate per 100,000 of National Population, by Country
Source: Adapted from data from the International Centre for Prison Studies. Retrieved 3 October 2012 from http://en.wikipedia.org/wiki/File:Prisoner_population_rate_world_2012_map.png

depend on the seeming credibility of the speaker (the persuader) and the evidence he or she uses to support an argument. Micro-sociologically, persuasion is a process like coaxing or seduction. Macro-sociologically, persuasion proceeds through *claims making,* a process by which groups create and promote claims they hope will be granted credibility or legitimacy by the mass public.

Shame

Shame, a second negative type of control that capitalizes on fear, is a painful sense of disgrace or embarrassment arising from the memory, or exposure, of disreputable acts. Shame is felt in the present and it often also lodges deep in a person's memory. Shame is rooted in **social norms** whose violation causes a sense of disgrace; in some communities, it may also translate into a loss of face, social ostracism, and ridicule. And often, feelings of shame are unwarranted. Many victims of sexual attack or abuse feel ashamed, for example, and are unwilling to speak out about the abuse or even report the abuse to the proper authorities.

Guilt

Guilt, a third type of negative control that capitalizes on fear, is the remorse a person feels for breaking a rule or committing a shameful act. Like shame, guilt often results when people break, or consider breaking, social rules. However, shame and guilt are different. Shame is associated with deviations from moral standards that significant others hold up to us, while guilt is associated with deviations from moral standards we hold up to *ourselves.* The two are also different in their consequences. Shame often results in social withdrawal, anger, and aggression, while guilt is more likely to produce positive behavioural change.

Gossip

Gossip, another powerful source of social control based on fear, spreads information that can mobilize shame, guilt, or ridicule by undermining a person's reputation. Gossip is also effective because, most of the time, people cannot easily separate the truth from the exaggeration and falsehood. Gossip works best in small social communities (including schools and workplaces) where people share a common value system and know one another.

Historically, gossip has been closely associated with women. Boys are taught to throw punches, while girls are taught to use less direct forms of aggression that prominently feature gossip. In some societies, women use gossip in ritual ways—as in a celebrity roast—to criticize and embarrass the people who normally are in charge—typically, the menfolk. Gossip is a particularly useful form of social control in the hands of otherwise vulnerable or powerless people precisely because anyone can do it and it draws power from widely accepted, traditional moral norms in the population. (See Box 1.2.)

Box 1.2

Gossip, Honour Killings, and Social Control

The practice of honour killings in some Middle Eastern countries is a poignant example of how gossip can serve as a form of social control. An honour killing is retributive violence by a male against a female relative for "dishonouring" their family. Middle Eastern societies are very patriarchal, and sexual purity is valued highly in women. If a woman is seen as having done something sexually impure, or even if she has had something impure forcibly done to her (e.g., rape), there is considerable pressure put on her family to "rectify" the situation through an honour killing.

Gossip plays a fundamental role in the practice of honour killings. A family's honour is largely rooted in its reputation. A family's honourable reputation can be ruined if the knowledge of even one infraction is spread around the community through gossip. If the knowledge of an individual's dishonour is spread through gossip, the situation is only rectified in the eyes of the community when the honour killing has been carried out. Gossip is used to keep a family's shame in the front of a community's consciousness and to pressure the family to commit the killing. An honour killing is only necessary if the dishonour has been brought to the attention of the community through the use of gossip. Thus, gossip becomes a tool of social control, reinforcing the patriarchal culture of blaming women for sexual impurity and carrying out violence against them.

Source: Based on Awwad, A.M. (2001). Gossip, scandal, shame and honor killing: A case for social constructionism and hegemonic discourse. *Social Thought & Research, 24*(1–2), 39–52.

Ostracism

Ostracism (also known as exclusion or shunning), another mechanism relying on fear, is the removal or expulsion of people from a social group. It may also accompany other forms of social control (for example, shame, ridicule, or gossip). The effectiveness of ostracism as a means of social control is largely due to its symbolic and emotional effect. People suffer emotionally when they are ostracized, even if they suffer no material deprivation. The painfulness of ostracism explains why ghettos commonly produce long-term anger, resentment, and self-segregation among the people they exclude and segregate.

Strategies that mobilize fear, on the other hand, identify and work on what people dread most: pain, discomfort, ridicule, loneliness, dire poverty, personal inadequacy, shame, and guilt. So, for example, consider an advertisement that says this: "Lose 20 kilos of ugly fat in the first three weeks of dieting by following these patented five simple rules." Threats, for their part, also capitalize on fear. A threat is a warning of imminent danger or harm. Often, unstated or implied threats work even better than stated or explicit threats. That said, threats are a comparatively weak form of social control; the people threatened may doubt that the threat will be acted on, for example.

Social Management

Agents of Control

As we will see in Part II of this book, social control is practised by all of the major institutions in our society, and we will now briefly consider them in turn. (See Table 1.1 for a summary.)

Families, Schools, Workplaces, Ideology, the State

We start with families. In families, parents use a variety of positive and negative methods to teach children the attitudes, values, and behaviour they consider appropriate. This process, which we will discuss in Chapter 4, is called socialization. The success of this socialization is measured in terms of not only monetary achievement but also whether the child "fits" into society.

Schools, for their part, indoctrinate their pupils in "correct"—that is, compliant—attitudes about work, authority, and patriotism. Textbooks, therefore, often contain the ideas and beliefs a society wants its children to know. For example, history books may be biased in the direction that authorities wish to perpetuate. This distortion of history is often a subject of great irritation to colonized, conquered, and other vulnerable people.

Workplaces exercise occupational and economic control over people's lives. Economic control is effective because it threatens people's livelihood or profit, in the event that employees fail to comply with company rules. Indeed, each occupational role in society carries with it a code of conduct that is hard to defy. Adhering to this code is essential to one's career as a doctor, lawyer, accountant, or otherwise.

Outside families, schools, and workplaces, **ideological control** is often more effective than other, more overt social control measures. Ideological control is provided by a variety of major institutions: by the mass media, the church, and the state and the legal system (and to some degree, by schools and families as well.) We will discuss each of these in Chapter 4 to 9. Through the socialization process, we all learn not only the rules or behavioural norms of our society but also the supporting ideology.

To the degree that this ideological process works, individuals do not have to be forced to conform: they actively want to conform because doing so makes them feel normal, admirable, and virtuous. A prime example here is control by religion. Religion tends to reinforce the status quo: as Marx said, it is the "opiate of the masses." Many religions make people feel virtuous and direct their attention away from worldly suffering to the dream of a blissful afterlife. They tell the poor to accept their situation because they will be rewarded in heaven. As well, religion tends to legitimize the rule of the upper classes and preaches submission to governmental authority.

Like religion, mass media reinforce the existing social system through ideological control, injecting a conservative social bias into their messages. Consider some of the messages portrayed or implied in the media: individual effort is preferable to collective action; free enterprise is the best economic system in the world; affluent professionals are more interesting than blue-collar or ordinary service workers; women, and ethnic minorities are not really as capable, effective, or interesting as white males; and the ills of society are caused by individual malefactors, not by anything wrong with the socio-economic system.

Like religion and the media, the state maintains its control partly through the manipulation of ideological ideas and symbols. Its supposed objective is to provide for the welfare of its citizens. However, every state, through the legal system, supports some social interests at the expense of others. Typically, it passes income tax laws that benefit the rich at the expense of poorer wage earners. Political and legal controls are the most powerful mechanisms of social control in modern life, relying as they do on the state's monopoly of force and violence, exercised by the police, the prisons, and the armed forces.

Table 1.1 Agents of Control

Agents	Methods
Families	• Socialization • Regulating self-image
Schools	• Framing historical narratives • Peer pressure
Workplace	• Economic control and sanctions • Codes of conduct
Ideology	• Internalization of morals and values • Mass media bias and religious doctrines
Government	• Legal systems and taxes • Violent coercion and penal systems

Surveillance and Governance: The Concept of Discipline

We now consider the role of surveillance and governance as agents of social control. The work of Michel Foucault, especially his work on the birth of the modern prison, is central to this perspective. Foucault (1977) draws our attention to the historic disappearance of violent and public displays of punishment that centered on the infliction of pain to the offender. What emerged in its place were techniques that rely on surveillance of the "soul." In his book *Discipline and Punish*, Foucault (1977) analyzes punishment in its social context and examines how the changing power relations in society affected the nature of punishment.

Before the eighteenth century, corporal punishment and public execution were common methods of punishment. Then, punishment served a ceremonial purpose and was directed at the offender's body. Details of various executions were often reported in the press, and the public actively participated. But in the mid–eighteenth century, a new type of punishment arose that Foucault (1977) calls **discipline**, a system of regulation designed to coerce and control an individual's actions and movements. Subsequently, the rise of discipline laid the groundwork for the development of imprisonment. Discipline was to operate by coercing and arranging an individual's movements. This was to be achieved through devices such as timetables and through military drills.

Central to this new strategy of control is *surveillance*. For Foucault (1977), disciplinary power requires hierarchical observation, normalizing judgment, and examination. Foucault (1977) notes that observation and "gaze" are especially key instruments of power, and Jeremy Bentham's Panopticon best exemplifies disciplinary power. The Panopticon is a tower-like structure located in the centre of a prison, from which guards can observe prisoners without the prisoners' knowing whether they are being watched. It illustrates how people can be controlled and supervised simultaneously.

Discipline, as conceptualized by Foucault (1977), does not prohibit certain forms of undesirable behaviour so much as it prescribes certain modes of desirable behaviour. From this perspective, disciplinary control is exercised in most social institutions in society, including schools, hospitals, and military barracks (many of them are total institutions in Goffman's [1961] terminology.) Discipline in modern society, Foucault (1977) proposes, is a "machine" that catches everyone. There is no dichotomy of dominators and dominated in a modern society—just people learning to act properly.

In *Discipline and Punish*, an emergent theme is the relationship between *power and knowledge*. For Foucault (1977), the modern "power to punish" relies on the supervision of "bodies" according to strict standards; thus, power and knowledge cannot exist without each other. The power and techniques used in punishment depend on knowledge, including knowledge that works to classify people. Similarly, knowledge derives its authority from relationships of power and domination.

For Foucault (1977), the same "strategies" of power and knowledge effectively operate in both the prison and society at large; and the techniques of discipline and surveillance that control the delinquent also control the law-abiding citizen. Thus, for Foucault, the prison is (only) one part of a larger "carceral network" that spreads through society and controls everyone's behaviour.

Note in closing that this chapter has considered a variety of mechanisms of social control, and some are more effective than others in controlling people. As we will see in the next two chapters, for example, fear of shame is often a much better way to control people than is legislation. Attempts to legislate behavioural change that are out of touch with people's values and attitudes will likely fail, since people will feel fear, shame, and guilt—even resentment—if they are obliged to do something they don't want to do.

Table 1.2 shows that there are various ways to define "effectiveness" and that, by these standards, some mechanisms of social control succeed, some do not, and some backfire—creating even worse behaviour than before. We will say more about effectiveness in subsequent chapters.

Table 1.2 Measures of Effectiveness of Social Control

Measure of Effectiveness	Outcome
Conformity to rules	• Engaged conformity: wilful acceptance of rules. • Disengaged conformity: begrudging acceptance of rules.
Overconformity	• Taking the rules too far can be undesirable. • Overzealous conformity is unpredictable.
Conformity promotion	• Adherents promote the enforcement of rules. • This shows commitment to rules, increases conformity.
Punishment of rule-breakers	• A community punishing rule breakers ritualizes and celebrates commitment to the rules.
Desistance from repeated offending	• Lack of repeat rule-breakers demonstrates effectiveness of punishment systems.
Guilt and shame	• Guilt resulting from rule breaking shows internalization.
Fear and anxiety	• Fear of punishment increases adherence.
Personal resistance to conformity	• Resistance to conformity by individuals demonstrates ineffectiveness of rules.
Membership in a rebellious community	• The larger the groups of non-conforming individuals, the less effective the rules.
Rebellious identities and cultures	• The prevalence of rebellious identities and cultures demonstrates low levels of control.

Conclusion

As we have seen, the concept of social control has a long history in sociology, and the topic leads us to discuss a wide variety of different, fascinating topics—many of which have direct and immediate relevance to our own, everyday lives.

That said, social control is often hard to understand and its effects, often hard to predict. Ask parents how well they succeed at controlling their children; ask teachers how well they succeed at controlling their pupils; ask employers how well they succeed at controlling their employees; or ask police officers how well they succeed at controlling ordinary citizens. In every instance, they are likely to smile and shake their heads in an admission of failure. Devising and applying an effective mechanism of social control that achieves the desired result is far from easy—in fact, almost impossible. The chapters that follow will help to explain why.

Questions for Critical Thought

1. Can you identify ways that social control is exerted on you in your home, workplace, school, and by this textbook?

2. In this chapter, we saw how one method of social control—the penal system—has changed over time. How have other methods of control changed, and what are the implications of these changes?

3. How do changes in technology affect the ability to exert and resist social control?

4. What methods of social control do you think are the most effective? Why?

5. What factors determine the success of rules and their internalization?

Recommended Readings

Curra, J. (2000). *The relativity of deviance.* Thousand Oaks, CA: Sage.
This book examines the intersubjectivity of what is considered to be deviant behaviour. It looks at how what is considered acceptable in society differs greatly in different time periods, cultures, and places.

Foucault, M. (1977). *Discipline and punish.* New York: Pantheon Books.
This book provides an exploration of power relations and control in society through an examination of the history of the prison system. Here, Foucault fleshes out his theories on discipline, deviance, and delinquency.

Goffman, E. (1967). *Interaction and ritual.* New York: Anchor Books.
Erving Goffman presents a discussion on rituals and norms that govern face-to-face interactions that occur every day. It is about the interaction between two individuals and small looks, gestures, and postures that define how we communicate.

Schissel, B., & Mahood, L. (1996). *Social control in Canada.* Toronto: Oxford University Press.
This book provides a study of social control in a Canadian context from a social constructivist perspective. It draws on a number of sources and discusses social control in a number of contexts, ranging from sexuality to education.

Recommended Websites

Florida State University Center for Criminology and Public Policy Research
http://criminology.fsu.edu/center-for-criminology-public-policy-research/
The Florida State University Center for Criminology and Public Policy Research offers a variety of journals and studies related to criminology, deviance, and social control.

Marx and Engels Internet Archives
www.marxists.org/archive/marx/index.htm
This website has an archive of the writings of Karl Marx and Friedrich Engels and is an excellent source for research into their central theories of social control.

Statistics Canada
www.statcan.gc.ca/
Statistics Canada has a plethora of data on Canadian society. Much of its figures, charts, and graphs can be useful in understanding the effects of social control in a Canadian context.

2

Micro-Strategies of Control: Appearance Norms

Learning Objectives

◎ To determine how people judge the appearance of others

◎ To understand how appearance norms affect men and women differently

◎ To define the concept "male gaze" and understand its implications

◎ To appreciate the power of the mass media in dictating appearance norms

◎ To see how beauty standards can impact other areas of a person's life

◎ To recognize how appearance norms differ in various social settings

---

Introduction

Every society has norms that dictate proper appearance and define beauty. People who obey these norms are respected, desired, and even imitated, while people who fail to obey these norms may be ridiculed and rejected. These social norms are rooted in a society's beliefs and values, and are imposed on every member of that society.

Appearance norms—that is, rules that reward appearances we admire and that punish appearances that fall short—exemplify informal social control in any society. No written laws are needed to get people to look a certain way. Rather, through socialization, people unconsciously internalize a society's appearance norms. Then, over time, they force themselves to live up to these norms and often judge their self-worth by how well they achieve the "right look."

Present-day Western societies put a high value on a youthful, slender, and symmetrical appearance, especially in women. For their part, men are expected to look muscular and rugged, if not classically handsome. These narrow definitions of "good looks" cause stout, disabled, or ordinary-looking people to be considered as "deviations" from these social norms. Often, deviant appearances—for example, uneven teeth or heavier-than-usual weight—are also attributed to a lack of self-control or a general disregard for society's norms. We hold people responsible for maintaining a "good" appearance and blame them for failing to do so.

However, sometimes, people overdo their efforts to meet society's appearance norms. As noted, in Western culture, we expect people to aspire to slender fitness. But some people, seeking to obey and exceed these norms, develop harmful eating disorders, such as anorexia nervosa or bulimia. Others, aspiring to finer features or larger breasts, undergo cosmetic surgery, while a great many others rely on costly cosmetics or clothing to make them appear more attractive or, at least, more "normal" (Freeburg & Workman, 2010). The social control exerted by appearance norms is especially harmful because it comes from inside the individual who has internalized society's appearance ideals.

Judging Appearance

When we judge other people's appearance, or even our own, we often look for points of likeness and familiarity that will make us feel comfortable. We also judge other people based on a comparison of them to the cultural ideal. So, when we observe someone who mirrors the cultural ideal—for example, someone who looks well off with a fit physique—we may admire and feel attracted to this person. Others who, by our judgment, deviate from this appearance norm receive less positive attention.

Freeburg and Workman (2010) studied two "advice columns," Ann Landers and Dear Abby, over a three-year period to identify social norms that people use to judge others. On matters of weight, they found that people expect others to be slim and to have a flat abdomen. Advice columns harshly criticized those who did not conform to the ideal body, describing overweight people as "addicted, lazy, indifferent, sick, slobs, stupid, and weak-willed" (Freeburg & Workman, 2010, p. 43). By contrast, thin women were described as intelligent, sexually desirable, strong, self-disciplined, and wealthy.

Height norms were also in evidence. Women who were tall also received harsh criticism because they violated the norm that a woman must not be taller than a man. On the other hand, men who were short found that women refused to dance with them; these men even had problems enlisting in armed services.

Even hair was subjected to scrutiny and evaluation: women with short hair and men with long hair reported being criticized and mistaken for a member of the opposite sex. People with grey hair were routinely assumed to be senior citizens, and women with body hair and facial hair were criticized as well.

Freeburg and Workman (2010) report that tattoos carried a heavy stigma. Writers of the advice column associated tattoos with nonconformity. Parents reported shame and humiliation if their child had recently gotten a tattoo, and there was even an instance of a husband who threatened to divorce his wife when she got a tattoo.

Norms surrounding hygiene were also discussed in advice columns. For example, people were expected to take a bath or shower daily and use antiperspirant. Office workers often complained about the body odour of colleagues who failed to do so.

Even dental norms were evident. People were expected to care for their teeth, to ensure that they were white. Many writers discussed how people with "deviant" teeth tried to hide their teeth when in public. And false teeth were a cause of shame and embarrassment. Finally, many people viewed bad breath—sometimes associated with wearing dentures—as offensive. People who admitted to having bad breath felt psychological distress and social rejection—and even marital problems—as a result.

Indeed, the importance of the "right look" expands beyond a person's appearance per se. According to Lorenzo et al. (2010), beautiful people are often viewed more positively by others; and often a person who is physically attractive is imagined to possess many other desirable qualities, such as friendliness, competence, and interestingness.

In an experiment, 56 women and 17 males were directed to have three-minute interactions with one another. The participants then rated one another on a variety of personality traits, on intelligence, and on physical attractiveness. These reports showed that people who were viewed as attractive by the others were viewed to have other positive and desirable traits. This is consistent with the physical-attractiveness stereotype of colluding good looks with a good personality as well. Overall, attractive people are seen more positively, as having better characteristics, and as being better understood. They also tended to view themselves in a positive light on all of these dimensions.

However, attractive appearance confers other advantages as well. For example, people who are seen as attractive are more likely to be helped by a stranger than are people not seen as attractive (Benson, Karabenick, & Lerner, 1976). Attractive people are also viewed as more socially competent (Desrumaux, De Bosscher, & Leoni, 2009) and as having greater academic potential, as rated by teachers (Kwan & Trautner, 2009). Finally, Andreoni and Petrie (2008) report that people viewed as more attractive earn higher incomes than co-workers who are considered unattractive.

Where do we learn these beauty standards and appearance norms? Perhaps the most powerful force transmitting these norms is the mass media.

Mass Media and Beauty Ideals

The mass media have several effects on appearance norms for both men and women. For example, the media connect slimness to desirable outcomes like happiness, love, success, and prestige (Saucier, 2004).

Effects on Women

Women's consequent desire to be thin (and thus beautiful) places intense pressure on women to control their appetite. In turn, this motivates women to buy diet products and undergo costly surgery, such as liposuction, so they can become slim and beautiful (Johnston & Taylor, 2008).

However, the media promote appearance norms that are impossible to reach, and beauty standards are becoming less attainable all the time. Consider the continued change in appearance norms illustrated by beauty contests. Spitzer et al. (1999) compared the body dimensions of living North Americans aged 18 to 24 with data on Playboy centrefold models, Miss America Pageant winners, and Playgirl models. The findings showed a stark and growing gap between reality and the cultural ideal, as Figure 2.1 illustrates. Since the 1950s, the body sizes of Playboy centrefold models have remained below normal body weight and those of Miss America Pageant winners have decreased continuously. In short, ideal women have remained or have become lighter and more slender than the average for "real people." Yet, over the same period, the body sizes of average young American women have increased considerably, mainly through an increase in body fat in the general population. Today, as you can see in Figure 2.2, there is a wide discrepancy between people's ideal and actual weight.

Figure 2.1 Different Standards for Female Body Size

Source: From Lassek, W., Gaulin, S., & Marano, H.E. (2012, 3 July). Eternal curves. *Psychology Today*. Retrieved from http://www.psychologytoday.com/articles/201206/eternal-curves

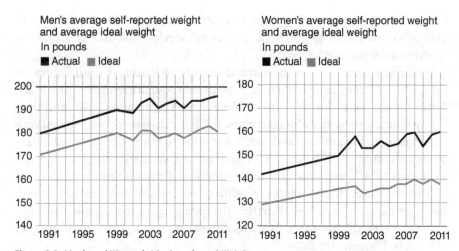

Men's average self-reported weight and average ideal weight. In pounds. Actual/Ideal.

Women's average self-reported weight and average ideal weight. In pounds. Actual/Ideal.

Figure 2.2 Men's and Women's Ideal vs. Actual Weight
Source: Figures from Mendez, E. (2011, 23 November). In US, self-reported weight up nearly 20 pounds since 1990. Based on Gallup's annual Health and Healthcare Survey, conducted 3–6 November 1990. Gallup. Retrieved from http://www.gallup.com/poll/150947/self-reported-weight-nearly-pounds-1990.aspx. Copyright © (2011) Gallup, Inc. All rights reserved. The content is used with permission; however, Gallup retains all rights of republication.

Major television networks also associate being thin with being beautiful; as a result, they over-represent women with below-average weight in their programs. For example, ultra-thin women, dominating the majority of TV programs, are often found to be more than 20 per cent underweight, a level that surpasses the underweight threshold of 15 per cent diagnosed for anorexia nervosa (Brown & Dittmar, 2005). Thus, television networks portray lighter-than-average women as the majority population in their shows, when in reality they make up a minority of the population. This over-representation of lighter-than-average women can suggest to viewers that being thin is the social norm.

Some men are among the other promoters of this social norm. They compare the women on television to the women they know and thus set unattainable beauty standards for their girlfriends, wives, and lovers. Women, wanting to achieve these new beauty standards, feel that they have to imitate the appearance of women on television to be considered beautiful. This causes a "thin-ideal internalization," which leads them to "engage in behaviors designed to produce an approximation of these ideals" (Thompson & Stice, 2001, p. 181; Thompson et al., 1999).

The appearance ideals portrayed in the media are unattainable by regular women, but, according to **cultivation theory,** they construct a vision of reality for people exposed to these media (Schooler, Ward, Merriwether, & Carruthers, 2004; Gerbner, Gross, Morgan, & Signorielli, 1994). This social construction causes normal women to compare themselves to these unattainable standards (Cattarin, Thompson, Thomas, & Williams, 2000), thus contributing to mental and physical health issues, such as depression, low self-esteem, and eating disorders. Particularly at risk are adolescent girls who are trying to conform to societal ideals (Schooler et al., 2004; Thompson & Stice, 2001, p. 181).

Likewise, interviews with cosmetic surgery patients reveal willingness to do the "work" they need to do to look younger and more feminine (Andrade, 2010; Leve, Rubin, & Pusic, 2011). Slevec and Tiggemann (2010) find that, for instance, among middle-aged women, "body dissatisfaction, appearance investment, aging anxiety, and media exposure to both television and magazines predicted some facet of attitudes toward cosmetic surgery" (p. 70). Edmonds (2007) remarks that the aesthetic defects that motivate cosmetic surgeries are "sociosomatic: produced by connections between mind, body, and society" (p. 368). Further, the data suggest that people who consume more media are more likely to accept and undergo cosmetic surgery (Slevec & Tiggemann, 2010).

Taken together, these findings suggest that throughout the economically developed world, cultural standards of beauty, the "beauty myth," and the normalization process encourage women to undergo often unnecessary cosmetic surgery.

The Anomalous Female Athlete

For their part, female athletes are often caught between two conflicting demands or social norms: on the one hand, the pressure to be muscular to succeed in their sport; on the other hand, the pressure to conform to feminine standards of beauty, which do not favour muscularity and strength. That is because muscularity is a masculine ideal; therefore, it cannot be a feminine ideal (Grogan et al., 2004).

That said, fitness and athleticism tend to satisfy other appearance norms. As a result, most athletes report a more positive body image than non-athletes (Galli & Reel, 2009). However, different sports carry different expectations for muscularity; in wrestling, for example, the athletes must remain within certain weight limits to compete in their chosen division. In diving, on the other hand, the aesthetic of one's body is as important as muscularity. And in distance running, a low body weight is considered a great advantage.

Still, when female athletes are judged by conventional beauty standards, they run into difficulties. Gruber (2007) studied athletes posing for the *Sports Illustrated* swimsuit edition, where "muscles are no longer automatically a threat to femininity" (p. 217). For athletes as well as others, the swimsuit edition portrayed women as sex objects, wearing skimpy bikinis in semi-nude poses. Thus, women still face pressure to maintain their femininity even if they choose to become muscular.

Here, too, the mass media impose societal norms on female athletes. When female athletes receive media attention, albeit much less commonly than males, their femininity receives more attention than their athletic ability (Crossman, Vincent, & Speed, 2007). For example, an analysis of the US National Collegiate Athletic Association (NCAA) Final Four Championship basketball tournament, held each year, revealed that women were more likely to be evaluated on their appearance, whereas men were more likely to be evaluated based on their athletic performance (Billings, Halone, & Denham, 2002). Moreover, the media's coverage of female athletes increases if the sport portrayed is deemed to be "gender appropriate" (e.g., figure skating or beach volleyball) (Pederson & Whisenant, 2003).

Overall, the message society sends to athletes is that muscles are needed for success in competition, but they can be a great hindrance off the field, in purely social interactions. This is especially true for female athletes who do not fit nicely into the cultural ideal of femininity or who fail to live up to the expectations of how a female must act in society.

Effects on Men

However, women are not alone in being subject to appearance norms in the mass media; men, too, feel pressure to conform to society's expectations. For instance, millions of men suffer from what Pope, Phillips, and Olivardia (2000) call the "Adonis complex," which is an obsession with meeting the culturally ascribed norms for beauty.

Indeed, men are beginning to develop as much body dissatisfaction as women (McCreary & Sasse, 2000). Men worry about unsightly physical features such as beer bellies, baldness, flabbiness, and a small penis (Davis, 2002). These obsessions lead to muscle dysmorphia, low self-esteem, an increase in eating disorders, the use of protein supplements, the use of steroids, and a pathological dissatisfaction with one's (visible) muscle mass (McCreary & Sasse, 2000).

Many male college students, for example, feel they have less muscle and more fat than both the ideal male and the average male (Olivardia, Pope, Borowiecki, & Cohane, 2004). Those with high levels of muscle dissatisfaction tend to have high levels of depression and low levels of self-esteem. They are also more likely to internalize beauty ideals set by society, leading to an increase in body-shape dissatisfaction and eating disorders. Along similar lines, Murray et al. (2013) found that men with muscle dysmorphia reported greater adherence to masculine norms. (So, for example, guys with anxiety about their baldness, shortness, or beer belly might be more aggressive in their behaviour toward women and even toward other men.)

As we can see in Table 2.1, men in our society are not supposed to be bald, flabby, lanky, or have a small penis, and, more than women are, are supposed to have short hair, big muscles, or small breasts.

Table 2.1 Gendered Appearance Norms

	Men	Women
Desirable traits	• Muscular	• Thin legs
	• Thin	• Firm buttocks and breasts
	• Tall	• Thin
	• Clear skin	• Clear skin
Undesirable traits	• Baldness	• Short hair
	• Flabbiness	• Muscular
	• Small penis size	• Small breasts
	• Lankiness	• Overweight

The mass media's influence on men, though profound, is different than its influence on women. In a study of 82 undergraduate men, Leit, Gray, and Pope (2002) concluded that muscular advertisements increase body dissatisfaction among men. Likewise, research on 96 homosexual and heterosexual men who consumed muscle/fitness magazines or pornography produced similar findings: that is, those men reported lower body satisfaction, with homosexual men having even lower body satisfaction than heterosexual men after viewing these magazines (Duggan & McCreary, 2004).

Though both men and women suffer from a need to obey our society's appearance norms, women are affected to a great degree because of the so-called "male gaze." (See Box 2.1.)

Racial Variation in Appearance Concerns

Although most women are eager to satisfy appearance norms, women from different groups attempt to satisfy somewhat different appearance norms. This is evident in a comparison of white and black girls by Melissa Milkie.

Milkie (1999) analyzed interviews with 60 girls in both urban and rural high schools, with a particular interest in uncovering the different effects of magazine images on black and white girls. She found that white girls read the magazines *Seventeen* or *Teen* and regularly discussed the content of the magazines during school hours and over the telephone. In fact, a significant amount of peer interaction revolved around these magazines. Black girls, however, read these magazines less often; they saw these magazines as being written mainly for white girls. Most of the black girls read *Ebony* or *Essence*, which are magazines aimed at black adults. They criticized the unreality of the images of white girls in *Seventeen* and *Teen* and deemed them irrelevant to their reference group. Indeed, they were less negatively affected than the white girls by a narrow body image of female beauty and defined themselves as being outside the dominant culture. Unlike the white girls, as a group the black girls were able to reject the dominant media images.

By ignoring the "white" media, black women develop fewer concerns about their weight and report higher satisfaction with their bodies, fewer

Box 2.1 The Male Gaze

The **male gaze** theory proposes that we all construct reality subjectively "according to stereotype cognitions which harmonize with the expectations of the male reader" (Brandt & Carstens, 2005, p. 235). According to male gaze theory, then, men have the privilege of being the "looker" while women are the "looked at" (Mulvey, 1975; Hartley, 2001). In accordance with this, most media, including television, movies, and magazines, try to attract male audiences by giving a heterosexual male point-of-view of the women they portray.

Mulvey's (1975) study of classical film in the 1930s and 1940s illustrates how the male gaze is implemented in media and entertainment. Mulvey notes that it is the male gaze that explains why female bodies are fragmented by camera shots that focus on the breasts and buttock areas, why women are punished at the end of films, or why they become sexual icons that rely upon the male-protagonist (as wives, girlfriends, or daughters) to have any meaning in the film (Mulvey, 1975; Warhol-Down & Herndl, 1997). These fragmented views of women reflect a patriarchic culture in which the male protagonist sees women as "objects" of desire that often need protection. In doing so, the male gaze oppresses women and upholds the gendered double standard.

In sum, the male gaze is essentially anything that portrays women from the perspective of a heterosexual male "consumer." And while the media have been changing to portray more egalitarian and equal perspectives, they still present the world mostly through the eyes of men. The male gaze in media creates a false reality; it presents only what heterosexual males want their society to look like. This may explain why women are more affected by media standards of appearance than men.

negative thoughts, and a weaker desire for thinness than do white women, holding constant the same amount of television viewing (Schooler et al., 2004). Additionally, black women who watch black media (with a mainly black cast) are inspired by more inclusionary black beauty ideals, while white women who watch white media are controlled and damaged by more exclusionary white beauty ideals (Schooler et al., 2004).

Early Socialization and Appearance Norms

Our first introduction to appearance norms comes from our families. From the earliest years, we are exposed to gendered appearance norms. We are dressed in pink or blue, in a superhero T-shirt or a Barbie outfit, and with running shoes or cute slippers, according to our sex. All of these appearance norms have future implications, but they are often taken for granted or seen as natural in the family home.

As children, we watch and imitate the appearance patterns of our parents and older siblings. Often, we also adopt the appearance anxieties of our families. For example, if your mom or older sister is constantly checking her weight in the mirror, saying negative things about her body and referring to the body standards often displayed in the media, you may come to think of these factors as important for self-worth and judge yourself by these standards as well.

This is evident from a study by Keery et al. (2005) that examined the effects of family teasing on body and appearance satisfaction and on the development of eating disorders. The researchers studied self-reports obtained from 372 middle-school (roughly 12-year-old) girls in Florida. Twenty-three per cent—nearly one-quarter of these girls—reported being teased about their appearance by their parents; of these, 12 per cent—roughly half—were teased because of their "heavy weight." As well, 29 per cent of the girls reported siblings teasing them about their appearance.

This teasing affected girls in different ways, depending on whether the teasing was by a father, a mother, or a sibling. Girls who had been teased by their father were most likely to display body dissatisfaction, thin-ideal internalization, bulimic behaviours, self-esteem issues, and depression, among others. Paternal teasing also resulted in a greater chance of sibling teasing, which produced many of the same appearance anxieties. Girls who had been teased by their mothers mainly displayed signs of depression. Finally, regardless of the source of teasing, more frequent teasing resulted in more negative consequences.

Even in the absence of teasing, children still develop biases against fatness and preferences for thinness at an early age, demonstrating the powerful effects of socialization and exposure to mass media. For example, in a study by Worobey and Worobey (2014), 40 preschool-aged girls (ages three to five) were shown three dolls ("thin," "average," and "fat"); they were read a list of adjectives (e.g., *stupid, strong*) and then asked to point to the doll that matched each word. Consistently, the drawing of a fat child was ascribed negative characteristics, while the thin or average doll was typically ascribed positive characteristics. Girls also described the thin doll as having a "best friend," likely to "help others," and "looking pretty." The fat doll was described as having no friends and looking tired. Finally, 70 per cent of the girls preferred to play with the thin doll, 20 per cent preferred the average doll, and only 10 per cent chose the fat doll.

Boys, like girls, are taught to idealize cultural standards of beauty from a young age. Even boys' action figures conform to cultural appearance norms, as is evident in research by Pope et al. (1998). These researchers measured the bodies of the most common action toys for boys that were manufactured over the past three decades (including GI Joe, Superman, Spiderman, Batman, and characters from *Star Wars* and *Star Trek*). They then scaled the measurements to the height of an average man. These measurements revealed that action figures have become much more muscular over the 30-year period, with many of the current figures exceeding the muscularity of serious bodybuilders.

Other evidence that the beauty socialization of children begins early is provided by child beauty pageants, as seen in shows like *Toddlers & Tiaras*. According to Tamer (2012), child beauty pageants portrayed in this show convert young girls to "sex puppets adorned with lipstick, mascara, false eyelashes, bleached hair, and high heels" (p. 85). The child beauty pageant industry earns its promoters $5 billion a year and draws thousands of participants, as well as many viewers. Tamer proposes that these pageants lead to early "sexualization" of children, which can later be psychologically harmful to them. Although promoters might imagine otherwise, sexualizing young girls—in the same way that the "male gaze" objectifies women—actually undermines the confidence of girls, leading to negative emotional outcomes, such as self-disgust, anxiety, and shame.

The American Psychological Association (APA) task force describes this sexualization as inherently dangerous because these girls are being "held to a standard that equates physical attractiveness with being sexy, or [led to think that] a person's value comes from her sexual appeal or behaviour to the exclusion of other characteristics" (Tamer, 2012, p. 88).

Workplace Appearance Norms

A meta-analysis of research studies by Hosada, Stone-Romero, and Coats (2003) shows that people in the workplace who are seen as attractive receive higher incomes, better work performance evaluations, and more promotions. Taken together, these findings suggest that in Western contemporary society, good looks are a valuable asset—especially in the workplace.

The workplace is particularly important because it is where people display the "reciprocal relationship including social ideas and relationships developed in domestic life and in gender, racial, and ethnic identities" (Steedman, 1997, p. 4). Translation: the workplace is a focus for all of our social learning, where we try out our various identities and seek acceptance for them. As a result, we adjust our social selves to responses we receive in the workplace.

So, if women, in particular, are subjected to appearance norms that control and determine their value in the workplace, then women will also be subjected to these norms and evaluations outside of the workplace. In workplaces, appearance norms create "oppressive gender-role expectations" (Bartlett, 1994, p. 2582). For women, these expectations include the need to wear provocative clothing in order to be valued or get attention. That is, in part, why men do not wear "work clothes"—e.g., suits, ties, or fancy shoes—at leisure, but many women wear provocative clothing during leisure time as well as work time.

Clothes present us to ourselves and to the world. We put them on to signify who we think we are and who we want to be. Today, we have a wider variety of clothing choice and, therefore, more opportunity than ever to use clothing for self-presentation and promotion. Through clothing, we link our personal identities to our shared social identities. Clothes redefine our place, role, and position in the social order. This expectation that women be involved with beauty and appearance is not a product of modern society, but it continues to be prominently associated with women.

People, especially women, are assumed to be making statements through their clothing choices. Consider, for example, the use of pockets. Historically, pockets on women's clothing have been smaller and fewer than pockets on men's clothing. For women, pockets have been decorative; for men, pockets are practical. A man who wears pants, or a suit, without any pockets is making a strong statement about his masculinity, as well as about his need to carry useful "equipment." That is because active, manly men are expected to have pockets full of useful stuff: wallet, comb, coins, cellphone, tickets, paperwork, and lists of things to remember, for example. They are not expected to carry this stuff in a purse. Sometimes these assumptions are challenged. Unisex styles of dress, for example, tend to blur gender lines; but typically they give women license to look more like men but not men to look more like women.

Just as clothes can be important markers of gender, they can also be important markers of social position. Consider uniforms: they are the ultimate means by which society and, especially, important organizations in society claim control over an individual. Only subordinate people wear uniforms. Powerful people—presidents, bank directors, and millionaires, for example—don't wear uniforms. This explains why rich people used to have their servants wear livery: to demonstrate the employer's importance and ability to regiment employees. Even today, many people still wear uniforms in the workplace, including soldiers, sailors, police, firefighters, priests, and nurses.

Uniform or no uniform, appearance is especially important in the retail industry, particularly in clothing stores. Many companies, such as Abercrombie & Fitch, Gap, L'Oréal, and W Hotels, try to hire the most attractive, available employees and seek those whom they consider to be handsome, pretty, and sexy (Greenhouse, 2003). Indeed, Abercrombie & Fitch, a clothing store popular among teens and young adults, admits to preferring to hire sales representatives who will represent the "brand," who "look great," and who will be "ambassadors" for the brand—according to conventional standards of beauty. This is problematic because a white, blonde, blue-eyed applicant will easily fit this description, while a black or Asian applicant will not.

So is there discrimination based on appearance in our society? "Lookism" is the term used to identify biases in the way people are treated based on their level of attractiveness. Physical attractiveness is a "prized possession," even in the workplace. As James (2008) proposes, "several positive qualities such as happiness and success are associated with attractiveness" (p. 637). He further notes that when two equally qualified people apply for a position in the workplace, "[y]ou will rather hire the applicant that you find more attractive because society taught you to associate beauty with other favorable characteristics" (James, 2008, p. 630).

Excess weight can be an important disqualification for people seeking a job. As the information in Box 2.2 shows, people are increasingly taking this problem seriously as a form of social inequality and discrimination.

By some accounts, this problem of discrimination has increased with globalization. Some employers believe that, to survive in a competitive global

Box 2.2   The First Canadian Summit on Weight Bias

"Stigmatizing people with excess weight is a popular sport in Canada and most other countries," says Dr Arya M. Sharma, scientific director of the Canadian Obesity Network (CON-RCO). "The bias against obese people feeds widespread discriminatory behaviours in health care settings, the workplace, schools, media and more. It's as serious as racism, and it is just as common."

Research in Canada and the United States has documented the widespread fallout from discrimination against this growing segment of society, including lower wages, fewer promotions, poorer health-care service delivery, compromised interpersonal relationships, and more. Canadians living with excess weight are also vulnerable to low self-esteem, depression, and other serious psychiatric disorders, as well as high blood pressure, stress, and a poor quality of life.

The First Canadian Summit on Weight Bias, co-hosted by the Canadian Obesity Network and PREVnet and supported by several sponsors, drew a crowd of 150 health professionals, students, policymakers, industry representatives, and educators, who heard from an expert panel of eight speakers from across Canada and the United States. Topics included weight bias, bullying, media literacy, mental health, professional education, human rights and complex systems approaches to research and intervention.

Source: Networks of Centres of Excellence of Canada. (2011, 7 June). First Canadian Summit on Weight Bias and Discrimination an eye opener. Government of Canada. Retrieved from http://www.nce-rce.gc.ca/ReportsPublications-RapportsPublications/ExcelleNCENewsletter-BulletinExcellence/v2_i1/CON-RCO_eng.asp

economy, they must place a premium on "good looks," preferring employees who are attractive and effectively discriminating against those thought to be unattractive (Cavico, Muffler, & Mujtaba, 2013).

Historically, appearance norms and judgments in the workplace have often been directed at women. Through interviews, Dellinger and Williams (1997) found that makeup use by women in the workplace is often connected to perceptions of health, heterosexuality, and credibility. Women who wear makeup are seen as embodying these three praiseworthy characteristics and are considered a "good fit" for the workplace.

In the workplace, women use makeup to seem credible and professional to both colleagues and clients, and to compete with other men and women. Indeed, both younger and older women make strategic use of makeup. According to Kwan and Trautner (2009), "young women can use makeup to try to look older (and thus more credible), older women can use makeup to appear younger (and thus more competent), and women of color can use makeup to signal that they 'fit in' with the norms of the dominant culture" (p. 58).

In academia, professors who are seen as physically attractive receive better evaluations from students. Riniolo, Johnson, Sherman, and Misso (2006), using data from a popular, publicly available website (www.ratemyprofessors .com), found that professors who were seen as attractive received higher evaluations from students when compared with a non-attractive control group, even after controlling for the academic department and the professor's gender.

Stigmatized Appearance

Physical attractiveness, like a role in a theatre production, relies on what we can and cannot see. Like actors, we bring social expectations to any situation, and these serve as scripts we feel obliged to follow. We are motivated to give believable performances. However, our performances and their credibility are put at risk by discrediting or discreditable features. A person who violates expectations may be excluded or ridiculed, hurting the performance. So, we make great efforts to ensure that our appearance is near flawless.

As Erving Goffman notes in his book *Stigma*, norm violators—including the violators of appearance norms—can be stigmatized. A stigma is a brand or a mark that brings disgrace. Such a mark reveals a gap between virtual and actual social reality and may cause the person to be rejected. People employ several strategies to deal with stigma. To appear normal, people try to hide their discreditable features with strategies of "passing" and "covering." Discredited people may try to compensate for their status-losing flaw by developing superior features in another area. Discreditable people try to hide their shame, pass for "normal," and worry about their secret getting out.

Wheelchair Use

However, there are many different kinds of stigmatized people and many kinds of stigmatizing treatments. Cahill and Eggleston (1995), for example, consider the various ways the general public treats people in wheelchairs. When in public, people in wheelchairs are commonly noticed by everyone and acknowledged by nobody. They are also subjects of "civil inattention," a glance followed by the immediate withdrawal of visual attention. Wheelchair users are often talked about as if they were absent. This most commonly happens when wheelchair users are in the company of walking companions. Sometimes, the wheelchair users are treated with kindly condescension. For example, wheelchair users may have people say to them, "You're much too pretty to be in a chair." Though perhaps intended as a compliment, the implication is that an attractive young woman does not belong in a wheelchair and that people in a wheelchair are unattractive. Wheelchair users are also treated as "open persons" who can be addressed at will. One wheelchair user noted that "they feel like they can stop me and ask me how much my lift or chair or whatever cost." Thus, in social terms, wheelchair users occupy a "twilight zone" of social identification, between health and sickness, competence and incompetence, normality and abnormality.

Eating Disorders and Obesity

As another example, consider people with eating disorders and their resulting body and appearance issues. "Eating disorder" has today come to mean anorexia (nervosa), bulimia, binge eating, and obesity. All of these disorders, except obesity, are more common among women than among men. Because of their greater concern about appearance, in fact, women are 10 times more likely than men to develop eating disorders in their lifetime (Statistics Canada, 2013).

People with anorexia or bulimia believe that attractiveness depends on being thin. Anorexia, one of the most common eating disorders, is characterized by a relentless pursuit of thinness and a refusal to preserve "normal" body weight, given the person's age and height. Women with bulimia nervosa, a related eating disorder, throw up after eating. Typically, bulimics binge—that is, they consume large amounts of food in a short time—then purge. Their binges often occur in secret, and involve high-calorie, high-carbohydrate foods they can eat quickly, such as ice cream, doughnuts, candy, and cookies.

Obesity, as noted, is also an eating disorder. A person is judged obese if his or her weight is at least 20 per cent above the statistical norm for that person's sex, age, height, and skeletal frame. The Body Mass Index (BMI) is a numerical tool (weight multiplied by height squared) that has become the standard statistical norm for determining obesity. Given women's preoccupation with thinness, it is no surprise that men are more likely than women to be deemed obese.

Obesity has underlying social as well as genetic causes. Over the past 30 years, middle-aged (45-year-old) Canadian men and women have become heavier and thicker, though also slightly taller. In over-nourished countries like Canada and the United States, prosperity is at the root of the problem. There are, however, class and regional variations in obesity. Children from low-income, ethnic minority families have experienced the greatest increase in child obesity over the past two decades. Fitness and leanness are much more common among higher-income people. There are also wide regional variations in rates of obesity among major cities of Canada. Likely, this reflects provincial variations in average income and education, eating practices, and exercise.

Obesity carries symbolic and moral meanings in our society, as many consider it a violation of appearance norms. In earlier time periods, people thought obesity revealed a hearty, healthy appetite, a lust for living, and a good sense of humour. Today, people are more likely to shun and/or criticize those who are obese or even those who are slightly overweight. They view obesity as signifying a lack of self-control. As a result, obese people, especially obese children, are often treated like deviants and are ridiculed and stigmatized. This may lead to heightened psychological stress and lower self-esteem. Therefore, obese people often develop a fear of interacting with peers, leading some to social isolation. They also often experience hardships related to employment, intimacy, and family relations.

Researchers have been highly critical of the media for perpetuating a cultural standard of beauty and thinness that is impossible to attain. A large study by Groesz, Levine, and Murnen (2002) found that women exposed to images of thin people in the media felt significantly more dissatisfied with their bodies than women who were exposed to other images. Along similar lines, another study found that women who thought they failed to conform to the thin ideal were more likely to show symptoms of disordered eating (Sanderson, Darley, & Messinger, 2002). Even girls as young as nine years old have expressed a desire to lose weight (Schur, Sanders, & Steiner, 2000). Clearly, young girls and women spend large amounts of time trying to achieve the "perfect" body. In the most extreme cases, the pursuit of the beautiful, thin body can lead to eating disorders, or even death.

A longitudinal study of 1,886 subjects averaging 63 years old suggests that obesity tends to cause depression. The authors propose that this is due to the deviant status associated with obesity, along with the "stigma toward and devaluation of the obese [which] may cause overweight people to suffer from lower self-esteem, have more negative self- images, think others dislike them, and have higher levels of depression" (Roberts, Deleger, Strawbridge, & Kaplan, 2003, p. 520).

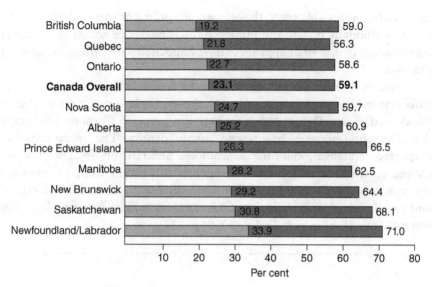

Figure 2.3 Obesity Levels in Canada
Note: Light grey represents overweight, dark grey represents obesity.
Source: Wikipedia (citing a Statistics Canada report). Retrieved from http://en.wikipedia.org/wiki/File:Obesity_rates_in_
Canada.svg

What's perhaps most interesting about this fact is that it coincides with an increasing number of obese, hence stigma-risking, people in our society. As the data in Figure 2.3 show, obesity levels are increasing in Canada, as they are elsewhere in the economically developed world.

Challenges to Appearance Norms

Of course, not all members of society conform equally to societal norms. Some people join communities of like-minded people to break appearance norms; while others challenge oppressive norms through activism. And still others, out of a desire to be different, refuse to internalize appearance norms.

Communities of like-minded people may initially be formed to challenge norms as part of a greater collective. These communities or subcultures celebrate attractiveness in unconventional ways that deviate from the mainstream. For example, some people rebel against appearance norms by dressing and grooming themselves in rebellious ways, to declare their independence of social norms. In time, lone rebels may band together to form a rebellious community. That's where appearance subcultures, such as goths or punks, come from. Collectively, these rebels reject appearance norms in the broader community but declare membership in and allegiance to an alternative lifestyle.

As these rebellious communities grow more secure and entrenched, they may even develop and promote rebellious countercultural values and identities. As they do so, conventional appearance norms are placed in jeopardy.

In small but noticeable ways, the appearance norms of these rebellious sub-cultures gradually invade and influence the appearance norms of the larger community. This is what appears to have happened with tattoos, as Box 2.3 discusses.

Some people have even organized to fight discrimination against norm violators: in this case, overweight and obese people. For example, Pretty, Porky, and Pissed Off (PPPO), a fat activism group in Toronto, challenges the connection between beauty and female identity. The group criticizes corporate capitalism, claiming it promotes unattainable images of women and unhealthy eating habits. The group also passes along its messages through street performances. PPPO discusses the "terrors, contradictions, and pain involved with living in a fat body" in a society surround by [thin] beauty ideals (Johnston & Taylor, 2008, p. 134).

 Box 2.3   Tattoos

Consider the spread of tattooing from a subculture to a fashion norm. In the past, tattoos were symbols of masculinity. Many tattoo wearers were likely to have spent much time in the presence of other men, such as in gangs or prisons, on ships or in military bases. For gang members and prisoners, the layers of tattoos recorded important personal events. Tattoos, in this way, told the story of their lives, ambitions, and group affiliations. They also symbolized the toughness or "manliness" required to undergo what was then a lengthy, painful tattooing procedure.

Today, tattoos are more widespread than in the past, even among women. However, they are still intended to communicate or record something: for example, sexual adventurousness. Koch, Roberts, Armstrong, & Owen (2007) collected data from a sample of 450 college students. Tattooed respondents were significantly more likely to be sexually active than non-tattooed college students. Additionally, tattooed men had become sexually active at a significantly earlier age than non-tattooed men.

Michael Atkinson (2004) proposes there has been a "tattoo renaissance" in North America, where tattooing has ascended to unprecedented levels. It is no longer solely a symbol of the male underclass. Atkinson conducted a three-year, participant-observation based study of tattoo enthusiasm in Canada, "hanging out" with tattoo artists and their clients in Toronto and Vancouver. From this, Atkinson concluded that the practice of tattooing is a learned cultural habit and a widespread practice of self-display. Tattoos also customize the body in the pursuit of individuality. One person told the researcher, "A tattoo is a piece of information about yourself that you put off for other people to download. It says, 'I want you to watch me.'"

Still, despite these acts of resistance, women remain concerned about being slender and beautiful because there is a "sexual division of labour that privileges the (masculine) act of looking over the (feminine) condition of being looked at" (Hartley, 2001, p. 20). As this section illustrates, efforts to resist appearance norms have experienced both successes and failures. Further research is clearly needed to "unpack" some of the effects of challenges to beauty ideals and cultural standards. Appearance norms hold a great deal of power in our society, so changing them will not happen overnight. Only through a concerted effort over time will we be better able to encourage the "resistance" of adherence to cultural norms surrounding appearance.

Conclusion

Appearance norms are very effective in controlling people's behaviour, although they are less so today than they were 50 or 100 years ago, when diversity was less celebrated. Appearance norms are continuously instilled in us over the course of our lives through the process of socialization; we observe others adhering to these norms and therefore seek to emulate them. Often, the people that others look up to will be role models, such as celebrities, which is indicative of how heavily the media influences what looks are deemed acceptable for society.

People enforce these rules on one another as well as on themselves. As parents, they teach their children how they are supposed to look. As peers and workmates, they exclude and ridicule people who fail to meet the expected standards. As employers, they discriminate against the overweight, the aged, and the plain-looking. As noted, most of us occasionally punish people who violate appearance norms; and we may not even be aware we are doing it. We unconsciously favour people who are handsome or beautiful, well-dressed, and well-groomed. We tend to reject people who are badly dressed, obese, and poorly groomed, assuming that they are lazy or socially ignorant.

As a result, we put great social pressure on people who ignore or violate appearance norms. People with above-average body weight are bombarded with messages, from media and other sources, telling them to be thin. These messages—which associate thinness with competence and self-discipline—can seriously affect a person's self-esteem and quality of life. More generally, people who don't conform to society's view of good looks are discriminated against and treated differently in many aspects of their lives, from dating and family life to the workplace.

As we have seen, appearance norms affect men and women differently, however, and society has distinct expectations on how each gender should appear. Some of the traits valued in men—for example, facial and body hair—are derided in women, and vice versa. Being uncomfortable with one's body image or appearance can lead to debilitating mental health problems, including eating disorders and depression. The high prevalence of these problems shows how powerful appearance norms can be as social control.

Questions for Critical Thought

1. Is anyone immune from appearance norms? Do people who reject mainstream norms (e.g., goths) in fact merely conform to another set of appearance norms?

2. Do you think it is possible to entirely separate a person's appearance from our evaluation of their skills and personality traits? Why or why not?

3. How can we account for the changing trends in appearance norms over time—for example, our growing preference for people who are slender and athletic looking?

4. This chapter focuses on many of the negative outcomes and consequences of prevalent appearance norms in our society. Can you think of any positive outcomes?

5. How are appearance norms different in Western countries than in other parts of the world, such as the Middle East or Africa? What impact do these differences have on the people who live there?

Recommended Readings

Black, P. (2004). *The beauty industry: Gender, culture, pleasure.* New York and London: Routledge.
Beauty salons are becoming the refuge of working mothers and female professionals, pampering them with facials and manicures. Interviews reported in this book— with beauty workers and their clients—help us rethink issues around the body, the maintenance of gender identity, and changing definitions of well-being.

Collins, J.L. (2003). *Threads: Gender, labor, and power in the global apparel industry.* Chicago: University of Chicago Press.
The author traces the links between First World and Third World producers and consumers, showing how the economics of the clothing industry allow firms to relocate their work anywhere in the world, making it harder for garment workers in North America to demand fair pay and good working conditions.

Lee, M. (2003). *Fashion victim: Our love–hate relationship with dressing, shopping, and the cost of style.* New York: Broadway Books.
This book, by the former editor of *Glamour* and *Mademoiselle*, offers an insider's account of how the fashion industry is able to manipulate people. It follows how trends are created in haute couture lines all the way to their demise once they hit the low-end shelves of Wal-Mart and K-Mart.

Wolf, N. (2002). *The beauty myth: How images of beauty are used against women.* New York: Perennial.
In this classic feminist work, Naomi Wolf discusses how an ideal version of the modern woman has been constructed through marketing and extensive advertising. She looks at how women deal with an unhealthy obsession toward becoming the "ideal."

Recommended Websites

Pew Research Center
www.pewresearch.org
> The Pew Research Center has a wide selection of opinion polls and statistics taken from the United States. It is an excellent source for information related to body image, self-esteem, and growing levels of obesity.

Status of Women Canada (SWC)
www.swc-cfc.gc.ca/
> A government website dedicated to women's issues and promoting gender equality in Canada. This website has information about how women are affected by appearance norms in a Canadian context.

The Organisation for Economic Co-operation and Development (OECD)
www.oecd.org
> The OECD website contains interesting figures comparing statistics for member countries, including Canada and the United States. Here you can find information about obesity and changing expectations about body images.

3 Macro-Strategies of Control: Laws against Substance Abuse

Learning Objectives

◎ To consider the social context of drug use

◎ To discuss the role of media representation in shaping drug use

◎ To understand how society controls certain substances

◎ To recognize why certain drugs are more acceptable than others

◎ To think critically about the medicalization of substance abuse

◎ To show how the strategy of control differs in different institutional settings

◎ To understand control theory

Introduction

In Chapter 2, we saw how both informal controls and mass media influence people's concern about their appearance and the efforts people make, as a result, to develop a more socially acceptable appearance. Most people feel some anxiety about their appearance, and for this reason they are easily influenced by media messages and efforts by others to change their behaviour—if only by buying clothes, cosmetics, and weight-reduction programs. As well, they are receptive to advice from experts about how to dress, how to eat, how to exercise, and how to present themselves in public: the media is full of such expert appearance-related advice every day.

At the same time, most people are inclined to occasionally, or even regularly, consume psychoactive chemicals—including alcohol, caffeine, nicotine, tetrahydrocannabinol (THC), and opiates, among others. In these cases, they are *less easily* influenced by media messages and efforts by others to influence their behaviour. In fact, as we will see in this chapter, they even resist government attempts to legislate and enforce controls on their drug-using behaviour.

That doesn't stop governments from trying, however. Every society has an interest in controlling the use of drugs and alcohol, since they are powerful substances. Yet oddly, as we will see, the use (and abuse) of *legal* drugs such as alcohol, tobacco, and prescription medicine is more common, and more dangerous, than the use (and abuse) of *illegal* drugs, such as heroin and cocaine. This raises some fascinating issues about social control and about the inability of governments to control (or even eliminate) behaviour that a majority of people are determined to continue. Indeed, the relationship between laws and attitudes is a long-standing topic of concern in the sociology of law. The question is: can you get people to change their behaviour by changing the law or by enacting harsher penalties for unwanted behaviour? So far, the evidence on this matter is mixed, but where drugs are concerned, the answer is largely "no."

This is a serious matter; not surprisingly, drug use sometimes results in serious health problems. The consequences of heroin use, for example, may include infections from injection (namely heart and vein infections, Hepatitis B and HIV/AIDS infections), and brain and lung abscesses. The effects of illegal drugs vary widely, depending on the type and strength of the drug and the frequency of use; for example, some people may suffer a long-term cognitive impairment from the effects of lysergic acid diethylamide (LSD); ecstasy; mescaline; psilocybin, or "magic" mushrooms; and various "designer" drugs.

However, official concern over the social and health consequences of drugs is *selective*. An estimated 15,000 people die annually from alcohol-related causes; and 35,000 from tobacco-related causes (see Figure 3.1).

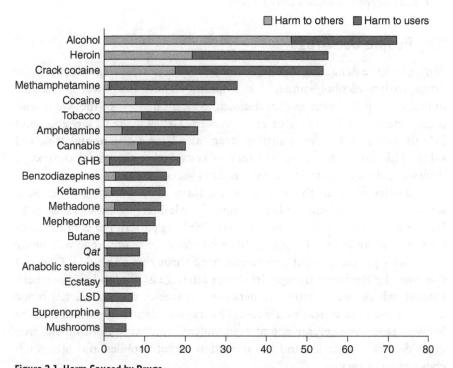

Figure 3.1 Harm Caused by Drugs
Source: From Nutt, D., King, L., & Phillips, L. (2010, 6 November). On behalf of the Independent Scientific Committee on Drugs. *The Lancet, 376*: 1558–65. Copyright (2010), with permission from Elsevier. Retrieved from http://www.sg.unimaas.nl/_OLD/oudelezingen/dddsd.pdf

In comparison, only a few hundred deaths each year are attributable to all the illicit drugs *combined*. In short, the drugs that carry the greatest health and safety risks are not, in fact, illegal. Social consequences associated with alcohol abuse range from personal family costs to indirect societal economic costs (for example, lost days of work). These consequences typically result from frequent, repeated episodes of excessive drinking, not from occasional drinking, which may have *some* positive effects on cardiovascular health (Walda et al., 2002; Lippi, Franchini, Favaloro, & Targher, 2010).

Alcohol abuse, too, has indirect economic consequences for society. Consider, for example, the loss of productivity in labourers who, because of alcohol abuse, can no longer work efficiently (Schmidt, Mäkelä, Rehm, & Room, 2010). In 2006, the estimated economic cost of excessive drinking in the United States was $223.5 billion (Bouchery et al., 2011; Center for Disease Control and Prevention, 2014).

The worst cost of alcohol abuse, however, is loss of life. Alcohol-related fatalities include deaths due to impaired driving, violence toward oneself and others, and various types of accidents. Statistics Canada (Perreault, 2011) reported 90,277 impaired driving incidents in 2011, of which 121 resulted in death. In addition, the risk of falling and drowning also increases with the degree of alcohol intoxication.

Why People Use Drugs

Why, given the danger, do people use drugs? To repeat, the answer is simple: drugs, such as alcohol, cannabis, and opium, all have the power to relax us, to reduce pain, to lower our inhibitions, to alter our view of the world, and (occasionally) even to cause us to see visions. Drugs make us feel good and help us have fun. In some cultures, drugs also have a ceremonial or sacred value. This points to the importance of considering the social context of drug use before considering mechanisms of social control.

Societies differ in the ways they use these drugs, making drug use a social as well as chemical phenomenon. In Mediterranean societies (e.g., Italy and southern France), the prevalent drinking pattern is a continued intake of small amounts of alcohol; this produces a sense of serene well-being and allows people to continue functioning throughout the day. Contrast this with the Northern Europe drinking pattern (e.g., Finland and northern Russia), where people alternate between abstinence and occasional binge drinking over the course of a week. This type of drinking pattern is more likely to result in aggressive, and even violent, outbursts, not to mention a great deal of danger around the operation of automobiles and other mechanical equipment.

Alcohol, tobacco, and prescription medicines are drugs that have been legalized and regulated in many countries, including Canada. The legality of these drugs permits them to be used more frequently, even though they can have harmful social effects. However, we choose to overlook these negative societal consequences because taxes on tobacco and alcohol yield revenue for the government and its public services. Even prescription medicines, which often "fall into" the hands of drug users without prescriptions, produce large revenues for the economy through taxes paid by pharmaceutical companies.

The Social Influence of Peer Groups

People form most of their attitudes through a two-step process, in which they evaluate information they receive about the world through communication and interaction with peers—that is, friends and acquaintances. So, for example, if people hear about a study that suggests that heavy marijuana use increases the risk of lung cancer or emphysema, they are likely to discuss this with friends before giving up marijuana use. In this respect, peer groups are key influences on drug use, especially among young people. As well, people tend to regulate their own use of a drug—whether tobacco, alcohol, marijuana or otherwise—according to what they see or imagine their peers are doing.

Unfortunately, most college and university students overestimate the degree of alcohol and marijuana use by their peers (on marijuana, see Wolfson 2000). This overestimation leads to more frequent use by young people, and occasionally, more harmful consequences (Kilmer et al., 2006). This excessive behaviour by students is motivated by a desire to gain the approval of one's peers (Neighbors, Geisner, & Lee, 2008). Where everyone is "following the leader," only the most self-assured people are confident enough to turn down drugs (Litt, Kadden, & Stephens, 2005). As a result, wherever drug use is common and people must use drugs to gain approval, people tend to use and abuse drugs (Walker, Neighbors, Rodriguez, Stephens, & Roffman, 2011).

Peer norms are also relevant in the case of alcohol. Drinking has long been a part of the college/university environment and a major part of social interaction outside classes. However, as Perkins, Meilman, Leichliter, Cashin, and Presley (1999) note, students often overestimate the extent of alcohol use on campus and imagine more permissive norms around alcohol use, for several reasons.

For one, students are more likely to remember alcohol abuse (manifested in a few students getting "trashed" or "wasted") than they are to remember an absence of drinking. In particular, they are likely to remember and exaggerate the drinking practices of popular, well-known students. Perkins et al. (1999) note that athletes and students who belong to fraternities and sororities may use more alcohol than the average student on campus, and may also have more visibility around campus.

Box 3.1   Religion and Drug Use

In the Western world, alcohol has been widely used by followers of what we may term *expressive religions* (e.g., the Roman Catholic Church). They use a variety of elaborate rituals and artefacts to celebrate religious observance. By contrast, *repressive religions*, such as the Protestant denominations of Calvinism and Quakerism, reject such rituals and artefacts, calling instead for simple modesty.

Drug and alcohol use for religious purposes are common because these substances increase social solidarity. In this way, drug and alcohol use within religions may contribute to the survival of the religious group and community. In *The Elementary Forms of Religious Life* (1995), Émile Durkheim discusses the use of religious rituals involving wines, spirits, or other substances in energizing group solidarity and reaffirming shared group beliefs. More recently, Doering-Silveira et al. (2005) discuss the ritualized use of ayahuasca, a hallucinogenic substance made of Amazonian plants. Ayahuasca is said to promote spiritual reawakening, enlightenment, and contact with higher spiritual dimensions.

Drug use has sacramental and spiritual value within many religious communities and rituals around the world. For example, Native Americans use peyote. Mescaline, the psychoactive and illegal ingredient in peyote, produces visions and allows deep introspection and insight into the spiritual nature of things, bringing the religious community together through shared experiences. Peyote use is legal in Canada, in recognition of its historic sacramental value (Controlled Drugs and Substances Act).

By contrast, the religious use of marijuana by Rastafarians is not legal. The Rastafari religion grew up in Jamaica as a reaction to capitalist exploitation in the 1930s. Many Jamaicans longed for a return to peasant life and freedom from white domination (Benard, 2007, p. 92). In this context, their dreadlocks, marijuana smoking, and communal living are symbolic reminders of a sacred, peasant past; and marijuana is considered a "holy herb" (Benard, 2007, p. 91). In this context, the Rastafari use of marijuana is religious and spiritual, not merely casual.

In addition to peers, culture, media, and religion all influence the ways we perceive and use drugs. Box 3.1 considers the effects of *religion* on the use of drugs.

Media Portrayal of Drugs and Alcohol

Just as the media influence our thinking about appearance issues, the media also influence how we view and use drugs. For example, studies have shown that exposure to alcohol advertising, whether through radio, billboards, or television, increases drinking habits in youth (Anderson et al., 2009). In general, film and TV depict drinking as a common, risk-free activity (Stern, 2005). Such depictions of alcohol use affect behaviour by influencing people's *perceptions of social norms*. The result of heavy media exposure to alcohol is earlier onset of drinking and increased consumption among existing drinkers (Anderson, DeBruijn, Angus, Gordon, & Hastings, 2009). This is partly because the media represent a culture in which alcohol consumption is normal and expected (Wallack, Grube, Madden & Breed, 1990).

The same is true for drug use, although drugs are displayed somewhat less frequently. Some television shows and films portray drug use as an activity associated with beautiful and successful people and no harmful consequences. Stern's (2005) study of films portraying teenagers found that little attention was paid to the long-term negative results of drug use. Instead, films highlighted short-term benefits, making substance use seem desirable to media viewers. In these films, 15 per cent of people are shown using drugs. Of the drug-using characters, only 35 per cent experience long-term negative consequences.

TV also tends to ignore the health and safety consequences of substance abuse. Consider a study of media coverage after four celebrity women were convicted of driving under the influence (DUI). Only 4 per cent of 166 stories presented DUI as an important societal issue or made any mention of the injury or potential injury. Rather, the coverage focused on the personal legal consequences the celebrity faced (Smith, Twum, & Gielen, 2009).

Additionally, popular songs often refer to substance use—whether to alcohol, drugs, or tobacco. A content analysis of music videos from two popular television networks, BET and MTV, found that 43 per cent of videos displayed or referred to substance use (Gruber, Thau, Hill, Fisher, & Grube, 2005). Typically, they highlighted the benefits of substance use—for example, popularity, success, and sexual attractiveness (Primack, Dalton, Carroll, Agarwal, & Fine, 2008). Such portrayals not only glorify these substances, they also create a popular demand for the substance portrayed (Diamond, Bermudez, & Schensul, 2006). For example, after hip-hop artists rapped about the expensive liquors Cristal and Hennessey, sales of these products increased dramatically (MacLean, 2004, as cited by Diamond et al., 2006).

Two theories address behaviour related to substance use. The **health behaviour theory** (Primack et al., 2008) proposes that when a behaviour is shown to have positive results, audiences are more likely to engage in the behaviour. Similarly, the **social learning theory** proposes that adolescents will mimic the substance use of celebrity hip-hop icons (Gruber et al., 2005). And a study of the most popular songs in 2005 according to *Billboard* magazine found that 77 per cent of rap songs portrayed some substance use, the most of any style of music (Primack et al., 2008). Research finds, moreover, that every hour spent watching music videos increases the likelihood that a person will take up drinking (Anderson et al., 2009).

Unlike the portrayal of substance use in the entertainment media (music, television, and film), the *news media* neither glorify drugs and alcohol nor promote their use. In fact, the news media try to decrease substance use by focusing on their negative legal, physical, and psychological effects (Taylor, 2008; Hughes, Lancaster, & Spicer, 2011). This negative portrayal reflects the fact that "news" is not intended to entertain but to inform.

However, even the news is not fully accurate in its portrayal of substance use. The news tends to link drug use disproportionately to lower-class citizens and "outsiders"—to criminal activity, rebellious people, gangs, and other threats to mainstream society (Taylor, 2008; Hughes et al., 2011). In reality, 33 per cent of heroin users have children, 17 per cent own their own homes, 74 per cent are employed, another 27 percent are in occupational classes I or II (which require a university degree or college certificate), 11 per cent are students in post-secondary institutions, and 64 per cent have completed or progressed beyond high school (Shewan & Dalgarno, 2005). In short, heroin users are often well-educated citizens with families and family responsibilities, contrary to their portrayal in the media.

The news also tends to focus on legal and moral issues connected to drug use, rather than on social issues. In one study of newspaper articles (Taylor, 2008), most articles focused on the criminal justice system's response to drugs. Fewer articles discussed health problems, social problems, or the cost to society. Many of the articles also simply moralized on the topic, asserting that drug use was not acceptable in any circumstance. Media reports, then, seem to characterize drug use as illegal and immoral, however common this use may be. The result may be prolonged moral panics about drug use, which we will discuss next.

Moral Panics Surrounding Drugs

Despite strongly positive attitudes toward drug use and strongly positive depictions of drugs in the media, "moral panics" erupt periodically that manipulate the way a society views drug use, often in a negative direction. These panics occur when "a condition, episode, person, or group of persons, emerges to become defined as a threat to societal values and interests" (Cohen, 1980, p. 9). Moral panics reveal and aggravate social tensions that are hard to resolve because open discussion of the underlying subject matter (for example, sexual behaviour or race relations) is taboo.

By definition, the following are five criteria that identify a moral panic:

1. *Concern* for an issue that is seen to be a threat
2. *Hostility* toward a certain group of people associated with the issue

3. A *consensus* that the threat is seen to be legitimate
4. A *disproportionate reaction* to the threat
5. *Volatile shifts* in the public mood concerning this matter (Goode & Ben-Yehuda, 1994)

Table 3.1 describes each of these criteria.

Table 3.1 Criteria for Moral Panic

Criteria	Description
Concern	• Significant public attention must be focused on the issue, expressing itself through press coverage and social activism.
Hostility	• The issue is defined as problematic to societal cohesion and as going against the values of society; it is, in effect, demonized.
Consensus	• A moral panic must affect a significant portion of the population for its effects to truly take hold.
Disproportionality	• A "panic" implies that the consensus response to the issue does not correspond with the threat level of the issue itself.
Volatility	• Moral panics can be set off at a moment's notice and can subside just as quickly.

Moral entrepreneurs, who are eager to preserve the status quo and reaffirm accepted moral boundaries, initiate moral panics, often through "deviance amplification," thereby drawing attention to deviant behaviour of smaller, less powerful social groups (Goode & Ben-Yehuda, 1994). These moral entrepreneurs may portray the members of these groups as "folk devils," which Cohen describes as "visual representations of what we should not be" (1980, p. 10). Such portrayals stigmatize drug users and create the notion of "us," the non-drug-using citizens, against "them," the drug users threatening our society (Taylor, 2008).

Consider the moral panic associated with Chinese opium use in Canada in the 1920s. Here, the moral entrepreneur of note was Judge Emily Murphy, whose book *The Black Candle* (1926) argued that drug use was a growing criminal and moral problem. She said she was concerned about the sexual exploitation of drugged white girls by Chinese men. In the resulting moral panic, Parliament passed the exclusionary Chinese Immigration Act of 1923—an act that stood for several decades until its repeal in 1947. Under the act, police were given unlimited search powers where these drugs were concerned—powers that persisted for over 50 years. Indeed, until 1985, a police officer could "at any time enter and search dwelling houses within Canada in which he reasonably thinks there is a narcotic and search any person found in such a place . . . break open any door, window lock, fastener, floor, wall, ceiling, compartment . . . or any thing" (Government of Canada, 2015). This single episode illustrates all of the main elements of a moral panic.

These panics, often sparked by political leaders and news media, mobilize support to remove the threats to society's norms and values by people such as drug users. Often, moral panics exaggerate the problem, distinguishing them from other social problems and highlighting their unique importance (Denham, 2008). For example, a moral panic may suggest that heroin use is an increasing problem, even though studies show that heroin use has remained consistent for the past 16 years.

Controls on Legal and Illegal Drugs

The state prohibits the use of marijuana and heroin—illegal drugs—but, as mentioned, it permits and regulates the use of tobacco and alcohol— legal drugs. Thus, the social control of legal and illegal drugs works differently. The agents of social control for *legal* drugs are health bureaucrats, physicians, and scientists. Agents of control for *illegal* drugs are the police, courts, customs officials, and prosecutors (Erickson, 1993). The criminal system focuses on preventing drug use by threatening punishment and setting normative standards of behaviour. However, people have become less afraid of illegal drugs and more likely to use them. The laws against drug use in Canada have lost the respect of many people and are less commonly enforced.

Given the abundance of other social control strategies—self-control, parental control, gossip, and ostracism, to give a few examples—it is odd that we have come to rely on the *law* to regulate drug consumption. However, according to Erickson (1996), options "closer to home" (i.e., reliance on family and communal authority) have become less available. Families and communities seem to lack the will or the authority to control the recreational use of drugs and alcohol.

Thus, drug use is criminalized and controlled by the police; but many people see this as overly restrictive. While people seem to agree, in general, on how we should punish "predatory" crimes, such as murder, kidnapping, rape, or arson, there is little agreement about the treatment of "non-predatory behaviour," such as drug use. Moreover, non-predatory offences are harder to detect and punish because people are less likely to report them.

Over time, the legal reaction to non-predatory crimes tends to pass through various cycles, including regulation, prohibition, and permissiveness. Permissive attitudes prevail when the effects of using a drug are not seen as inflicting serious harm. If large or influential groups in the population oppose prohibition, the efforts to prohibit use will likely be unsuccessful or short-lived. Then, the state may move to regulating, rather than prohibiting, these drugs. In Canada, for instance, alcohol use was prohibited for a period; after that, the country imposed restrictive laws that, gradually, became less restrictive. The focus changed, then, from prohibiting the use of alcohol to regulating it.

Unlike prohibition, regulation allows people to use legal alcohol drugs at a level deemed "acceptable" by officials or professionals. Here, think of the allowable level of blood alcohol in connection with driving after drinking. In regards to alcohol, tobacco, and prescription drugs, health bureaucrats (after consultation with scientists and enforcement personnel) are responsible for defining standards for product quality, conditions under which the drug may be sold (e.g., not to people under the age of 19), and medical conditions where the drug may be prescribed. Violation of these rules by vendors may be punished by revocations of licences and loss of revenue. Following these guidelines, the police, courts, and customs officials are empowered to detect and punish drug users and sellers alike. Such regulation not only controls the use of these substances, it also earns high revenues for the state. For example, taxes on legal sales of alcohol yielded $1.7 billion for the Ontario government in 2012–13 (Liquor Control Board of Ontario).

As far as informal social control goes, Black (2010, p. 105) notes that "wherever and whenever people hold each other to standards . . . [social control] divides individuals into people who are respectable and people who are not; it disgraces some, but protects the reputations of others." The extent of stigma the "disgraced" person experiences depends on whether a given drug is legal or illegal. That is because tobacco and alcohol users have a legal, respected place in our society. Marijuana users or heroin users, on the other hand, face moral stigma because they are seen as officially engaging in a deviant or criminal lifestyle. Howard Becker (1963) explains that this stigmatization of deviance results from society's current views of a particular action (in this case, marijuana or heroin use). In short, marijuana and heroin use are considered "bad" because we make laws that say they are bad—not the reverse. In time, many of the legal do's and don'ts become internalized as moral imperatives, leading people to stigmatize and judge people who fall outside of these lines.

Efforts to Control Illicit Drugs

Opiates have been subject to the most persistently demonizing mythology. However, in reality the most harmful effects of opiate use are severe constipation and reduced libido. Opiates are not otherwise significantly damaging to the minds and bodies of regular users. Problems arise only when opiate use is driven underground—when opiate addicts are forced to get their drugs from criminals, using money obtained through crime and prostitution, and cannot afford proper food or housing.

The unhealthy and degraded lives of "street" opiate addicts are attributable to a damaging, deprived, and marginal lifestyle generated largely by opiate prohibition itself. Other risks associated with illegal opiate use are due to the impurity of street drugs and the potential contamination of needles with hepatitis and HIV, through unsafe injection practices. Opiate use sometimes also involves engagement in criminal "black markets" (with their inherent violence) in order to obtain opiates. These so-called black markets provide narcotics that are produced and/or distributed illegally (Miron, 2003).

Let's now consider cannabis, the drug most often proposed for legalization in Canada and the US. There is an ongoing debate about legalizing cannabis because the laws aimed at preventing drug use have had no effect; drug use remains widespread, yet so, too, do some parental fears. Criminal sanctions do not appear to affect marijuana use and efforts to control its use through law enforcement strategies regularly fail. Governments wanting to address this problem of wasted money and effort can choose one of two options: decriminalization or legalization. **Decriminalization** means removing marijuana possession and use from the Criminal Code and eliminating many if not all current penalties. It still would be illegal to possess the drug for personal use. However, possession would be considered a non-criminal

Box 3.2   Social Control in the Workplace

The workplace is another institution that tries to control drug and alcohol use, largely through the practice of employee drug testing. This practice has become common in many private and public sector organizations in North America, increasing threefold since the 1980s (Brunet, 2002).

Drug testing is a way the state and its corporate enterprises exert control over workers (Gerber, Jensen, Schreck, & Babcock, 1990). Hanson for one, proposes that drug testing serves to reinforce "the automatic docility that people have" (1993, p. 172). Gilliom (1994) views drug testing as a means of surveillance, while other scholars view it as part of the disciplinary control system that emerged during the Industrial Revolution (Hecker & Kaplan, 1989).

Although employee drug testing fits the classic definition of social control, in that it is used to define, detect, and respond to deviance, in this case, the use of illicit drugs (Brunet, 2002), in several ways, differs from other forms of social control. First, private bureaucracies—not the state—are responsible for implementing drug testing programs and policies, including the penalties for a failed drug test (e.g., mandatory leave of absence or loss of job). Second, unlike the state, private corporate bodies cannot criminally sanction people. However, like state penalties, corporate measures are intrusive: drug tests measure drug use retrospectively, extending beyond the boundaries of the workplace and into employees' private lives.

Private organizations justify the use of drug testing in four ways (Brunet, 2002). The first is in terms of performance, health, and safety. Drug use is seen as making offence similar to a parking violation and punishable by a ticketed fine. Thus, marijuana use would remain a breach of the law, but the penalties would change. *Legalization,* by contrast, means regulating the sale of these substances, as well as removing penalties for possession and use. Regulating marijuana would allow the state to tax the sales of marijuana. It would also mean setting and enforcing quality standards, as the state does with other drugs and foods.

Both legalization and decriminalization are forms of harm reduction, but some research has found that legalization would be the better solution because it would destroy the criminal black market in drugs and ensure safe drugs for consumers. Many look to the Netherlands as a source of evidence about the likely effects of decriminalization or legalization. Since the de facto legalization of "soft" drug use there in 1976, neither "hard" nor "soft" drug use has increased in the Netherlands as a result of this policy.

Box 3.2 suggests yet another social context where the use of drugs is strictly prohibited.

---

a worker less productive, and threatening their safety. Employees using drugs regularly, by this reasoning, place a heavy cost on the company by being absent from work, using medical benefits associated with the job, acting in ways that endanger the public (and make the company legally liable), and hindering the performance of other workers. However, existing research on these matters is mixed. For instance, Thompson, Riccucci, and Ban (1991) found only a modest correlation between drug abuse and negative employee behaviours, including absenteeism, disciplinary actions, and injuries.

The second justification for companies using random, unannounced drug testing is to deter deviance—that is, to deter people from using drugs at any time. Especially in government jobs, drug testing has a "gatekeeper function," and all job applicants are tested. However, DeCew (1994) denies there is any justification for drug testing when there is no evidence the individual tested has a drug problem. For this reason, any potential gains from drug testing are insufficient to justify the harm being done to people who are tested.

Third, some organizations justify drug testing to identify employees who have a drug problem so that they can get them the help they need to continue working. Employees using drugs, according to this view, need help. However, treatment that is forced on employees may not produce outcomes as positive as those that result when an individual enters treatment willingly.

Fourth, and finally, drug testing is justified for symbolic purposes, to demonstrate managerial control and the organization's commitment to the values of mainstream society.

It remains unclear, however, whether such testing brings about the overall improvement in corporate productivity or personal rehabilitation that is intended.

Demand-Reduction vs. Supply-Reduction Strategies

The so-called war on drugs, or supply reduction, is an expensive approach to controlling drugs that, so far, has produced sub-par results. The Canadian government spends roughly $2 billion each year prosecuting drug-related crimes (Rehm et al., 2010). For decades in the United States, the "war on drugs" has targeted drug dealers, traffickers, and producers, rather than trying to reduce demand among users who demand the drugs; unfortunately, the demand has remained high. Consider the spending on these two approaches: the budget for supply reduction is $15.061 billion (roughly 60 per cent of the total), while the budget for demand reduction is $10.538 billion (roughly 40 per cent of the total) (United States Government, 2013). This spending pattern reflects the stronger initiative to capture drug dealers, traffickers, and producers, rather than users. It also reflects the intention to punish drug dealing, trafficking, and producing more harshly than simple possession (DEA, 2014a, 2014b).

However, studies have found that demand-reduction strategies are more effective in reducing consumption than supply-reduction strategies. For example, Caulkins et al. (1997) report that every $1 million invested in longer punishments for drug traffickers, a supply-reduction strategy, reduces cocaine consumption by 12.6 kg a year. By contrast, every $1 million invested in treatment programs—a demand-reduction strategy—decreases cocaine consumption by 103.6 kg a year (Caulkins et al., 1997, as cited by Donohue, Ewing, & Peloquin, 2011).

Another study shows that efforts to disrupt the methamphetamine supply in America produce only short-term results. A supply shock through tougher policing (which disrupts the sales of drugs) briefly triples the price of the drug, leading to a brief decline in drug use, drug arrests, drug-related hospital admissions, and drug-related hospital treatments (Dobkin & Nicosia, 2009). However, the price returns to normal within four months, and the drug-related behaviours return to pre-disruption levels within 18 months.

Significantly, despite a huge financial investment in tough drug policies, the US still reports rates of drug use that are higher than countries with more lenient policies (Donohue et al., 2011). According to one estimate, the "war on drugs" has cost American taxpayers about one trillion dollars since its introduction in 1971 (Branson, 2012), and this estimate may not even include the loss of worker productivity and breakdown of families caused by imprisonments related to drug policies.

Harm-Reduction Strategies

Some scholars have suggested reframing the "drug problem" as a public health issue that highlights the goals of prevention, treatment, and reduction of drug-related harm. This form of social control would also reduce the stigma attached to drug addiction, by considering drug use a medical rather than a moral issue. We can consider this type of harm reduction a subtype of the process sociologists call "medicalization."

Medicalization is the process of defining a problem in medical terms and then using a health intervention to respond to that problem (Conrad, 1992). This process allows drug-related issues to be viewed under a medical lens, for example using drug treatment courts (DTCs) to respond to drug-related issues both legally and medically. Along these lines, Canada established its first drug treatment court in 1998, and there are now six DTCs across the country. Drug treatment courts are good at responding to the needs of groups that are especially susceptible to drug dependency—groups such as youth or sex-workers—as they provide both counselling and medical attention.

Drug courts are consistent with Michel Foucault's proposals in *Discipline and Punishment* (1977), discussed in Chapter 1. Here, drug abusers undergo continued surveillance and supervision. Supervisors put pressure on drug abusers to conform to societal standards and abstain from drug use, or they will face criminal punishment. As well as rehabilitation, the drug courts also offer employment and housing opportunities (Hartley & Phillips, 2001). For participants who succeed in getting off drugs, the courts dismiss criminal charges. However, not everyone manages to get off drugs.

Hartley and Phillips (2001, p. 107), reviewing the case files of drug court participants, find that "employment status before and during the program, race, education, and referral time" are all important predictors of success. Specifically, having a job and having more education are positively correlated with rehabilitation, while cocaine use and minority racial status (typically associated with lower educational status) are negatively correlated with it. These findings are supported by past studies of drug courts (Schiff & Terry, 1997; Sechrest & Shicor, 2001—as cited in Hartley and Phillips, 2001).

Harm reduction programs also provide a more sympathetic, less controlling, response to drug and alcohol use. They focus on reducing the harms related to drug use, such as disease and overdose, by providing safe spaces for drug users. Wood et al. (2004) discuss one such space, Insite, which was developed in Vancouver in 2003 as a response to the frequent transmission of infectious diseases among injection drug users in Canadian cities. Insite provides a safe injecting facility, clean needles, and medical supervision and has successfully reduced the number of people harmed by unsafe injection methods that increase the risk of contracting the human immunodeficiency virus (HIV) and hepatitis C virus (HCV), among other diseases (Wood et al., 2004).

Mainly, however, government attempts to control drugs have had poor results. It is true that some government efforts have lowered drug activity, incarcerated criminals, prevented drug use introduction among youth, reduced drug-related violence, and decreased the availability and increased the price of illegal drugs (Miron, 2003; Strang et al., 2012). However, other efforts have caused new social problems: for example, an increase in criminal behaviour, criminal innovation, and criminal networking (Kerr, Small, & Wood, 2005). This has led many scholars to conclude that traditional police enforcement is an ineffective approach to drug control.

A Different Approach to Crime Control: Control Theory

Along these lines, Michael Gottfredson and Travis Hirschi (1995) propose a new *general approach to crime control*. *Control theory*, as presented by Gottfredson and Hirschi (1995), is a choice theory based on a few underlying assumptions. First, it assumes that people anticipate the consequences of their behaviour. As well, this theory assumes rational decision-making on the part of the actor: actors will seek anticipated rewards (such as the temporary break from "reality" offered by a drug or the satisfaction of a drug craving) and avoid anticipated punishments (such as criminal prosecution for using illicit substances). Table 3.2 provides a summary of some of the main features of control theory.

Table 3.2 Control Theory

Feature	Description
Situational	• Environmental factors that push people to commit crimes – Example: peer pressure to consume drugs
Personal	• Individual factors that influence a person's decisions – Example: drug addiction
Opportunity	• Having the means to commit a crime and a potential target – Example: having access to drug dealers

The point of view offered by control theory differs markedly from the view advocated by the formal criminal justice system. Currently, the criminal justice system tries to reduce drug use by making penalties harsher and consuming more public funds to do so (Millhorn et al., 2009). Formal controls, such as mandatory minimum sentences for drug use and possession, have not been found to effectively control or deter substance use (Mascharka, 2001; Weinstein, 2003).

The law places more and more control in the hands of a centralized government. Control theory, however, favours local responsibility for substance abuse prevention and assigns primary responsibility to the school and the family. In molding the character of potential citizens, it directs caregivers and teachers to recognize deviance when it occurs and punish the behaviour immediately.

Taking a cue from control theory, some social policies have emphasized the importance of early drug education programs. The most common method used is simple *information dissemination* (Botvin, Griffin, & Nichols, 2006). Information dissemination is the increased knowledge about drugs, consequences of use, and often includes anti-use attitudes to arouse fear (Botvin & Griffin 2006). However, this method can also provoke curiosity in students, leading to more and not less drug use. Siegel (2004) notes that the number of adolescents who abuse drugs has not been significantly reduced with the introduction of drug education programs in schools. To this end, Siegel proposes altering drug education programs to place a central emphasis on changing social norms surrounding drug use. Such programs would teach students to question where the use of drugs is necessary in order to "fit in." Future educational programs designed to reduce drug use, however, will have to carefully consider the best way to advocate messages to dissuade these habits from forming at a young age. The merits of control theory lie in its claim that the most effective social controls for substance use are not formal laws but, rather, may be well-thought-out drug education programs that elicit changes to social norms and peer groups. This may also allow the "drug problem" never to begin or to be ceased at an earlier age in youth, preventing addiction and a lifetime dependence on illicit substances.

Conclusion

As we have noted, the effort to control drugs and alcohol varies across societies. Most governments at least try to restrict the types of alcoholic drinks sold in stores; set a minimum legal buying age of alcohol; impose regulations regarding who can buy marijuana, where marijuana can be smoked, and the punishments for being in possession of marijuana and other substances (Manchikanti, 2007; Paschall, Grube, & Kypri, 2009, Chatwin, 2013).

The strategies different societies use to control drug use vary depending on how each society perceives the risk of the substance. If the substance is perceived as a low risk to society, minimal controls will be set (e.g., caffeine); a high-risk substance, on the other hand, will receive maximum control (e.g., cocaine). Most countries control substances with legal prohibition and police enforcement. Although such formal controls continue to increase, the crime rates associated with substance use have not decreased (Statistics Canada, 2014). Not all social control strategies are effective for all social groups, and some strategies are more effective in controlling substance use among a certain age or gender.

As we illustrated in the last section, research suggests that *formal* social controls of illegal drugs, such as criminal and regulatory laws, are not very effective at controlling substance use among younger populations. However, this does not mean that *informal* social controls are ineffective at controlling substance use among youth. Indeed, studies have shown that substance use among youth can be decreased and controlled through informal social controls that create anti-substance use norms and attitudes. These controls can be implemented through school-based prevention programs (Griffin, Botvin, Nichols, & Doyle, 2003; Sale, Sambrano, Springer, & Turner, 2003) and through community mentorship that changes youth's attitudes toward substance use (Hecht et al., 2003; Bahr, Hoffman, & Yang, 2005). Moreover, adolescents are much less likely to engage in excessive substance use if the student community they are a part of disapproves of its use (Kumar, O'Malley, Johnston, Schulenberg, & Bachman, 2002). In short, these informal social controls integrate young people into an anti-substance use community that can control their substance use better than the law (on this, see, for example, Vander Ven's (2011) interesting book on campus drinking patterns.)

As we have also seen in this chapter, most drug policies in effect in Europe and North America suffer from similar weaknesses. They all try to control drug use by reducing the supply of illicit drugs, rather than persuading people to avoid or moderate their drug use. Yet, in a qualitative study of European drug policies, Chatwin (2013) concludes that the focus of supply and demand reduction is not producing successful results, and should rather focus on harm reduction, a branch of drug policy that Canada has focused on (Collins, 2006).

The United States is known for its "war on drugs" and investment to deter drug distribution and use; yet drug use is still on the rise there. In the US, punishments for the possession and trafficking of illicit drugs are severe when compared to other societies, yet they are less effective. Despite stiffer sentences for drug dealers, a higher percentage of people use drugs in the US than in Canada.

Indeed, it is Canada—not the US—that has seen a decline in illicit drug use. Canada's illicit drug use is declining among people 15 years and older, falling from 11 per cent in 2010 to 9.4 per cent in 2011; and is expected to continue decreasing (Health Canada, 2014). This suggests that the US's severe punishments are not an effective way to control drugs. In Canada, despite periodic moral panics about drugs, the strategies of social control that law enforcers have employed have been relatively effective and un-dramatic.

Questions for Critical Thought

1.   Evaluate the view that "Since human beings are chemistry sets with an obvious desire to perform experiments on themselves, we spend far too much time and money trying to control a few of these experiments."

2.   Given the long, historic connection between drug use and sacred ritual, how do we account for the continued popularity of drug use in increasingly secular societies?

3.   Discuss why some drugs are legal and others are illegal. In connection with this, explain what factors play a role in defining some drug use as a "drug problem."

4.   Howard Becker explains that one must learn how to use marijuana. Is there any evidence that people also need to learn to use and enjoy other drugs—for example, alcohol, nicotine, ecstasy, or cocaine?

5.   Do you support the decriminalization of marijuana? Use sociological theories you have learned in this chapter to support your views on the issue.

Recommended Readings

Frey, J. (2003). *A million little pieces*. New York: Anchor Books.
This bestselling book—part memoir, part fiction—illustrates the process by which a drug user can overcome circumstances to become a non-user. Controversy surrounded the book and its author when it was revealed that Frey had embellished his story.

McAllister, P.A. (2005). *Xhosa beer drinking rituals: Power, practice and performance in the South African rural periphery*. Durham, NC: Carolina Academic Press.
Among the rural, Xhosa-speaking people of South Africa's Eastern Cape province, beer rituals became a crucial mechanism through which rural people maintained social and economic relations while affording an alternative to the disillusionment and suffering of black urban areas.

Valentine, D. (2004). *The strength of the wolf: The secret history of America's war on drugs*. New York: Verso.
Douglas outlines the war on drugs and the various federal agencies that have been put in charge of monitoring various controlled substances. Though a dense work, it is a detailed examination of the American war on drugs.

Vander Ven, T. (2011). *Getting wasted: Why college students drink too much and party so hard*. New York: New York University Press.
The book argues that college students continue to drink heavily, even after repeated bad experiences, because of the community and subculture of drinking they have established which supports them and helps them excuse embarrassing drunken behaviours.

Wilkins, J., & Hill, S. (2005). *Food in the ancient world*. Oxford: Blackwell.
This book describes eating and drinking from early Egypt (4000 BCE) to the end of the Roman Empire (fifth century CE). Throughout these millennia, people in power viewed bars, taverns, hotels, and other public eating places with suspicion because of the political discussions and competitive drinking that often occurred.

Recommended Websites

Centre for Addiction and Mental Health
www.camh.ca
The Centre for Addiction and Mental Health is Canada's leading organization for treating addiction and mental health issues. Its website contains many interesting studies as well as practical insights into the field of mental health.

Drug Policy Alliance
www.drugpolicy.org/
> The Drug Policy Alliance is an organization that works to improve drug laws in ways that are supported by scientific and social-scientific research. On this site you will find information about its policies and other issues.

Learn About Marijuana Washington, University of Washington
http://learnaboutmarijuanawa.org/
> In 2012, Washington State voted to legalize recreational marijuana, becoming one of the first states to do so. This website has information about the marijuana laws in Washington and other facts about the drug.

Part II

Sources of Control

4   Socialization and Culture

Learning Objectives

◎   To understand various processes of socialization

◎   To recognize the profoundly social nature of socialization

◎   To be familiar with socialization in different environments

◎   To identify agents of socialization and the strategies they use

◎   To understand negative socialization

Introduction

In Chapter 3, we discussed how societies try to regulate the use of illicit substances. This is a classic example of formal social control, which derives its power from the state and the law. However, we noted that these methods of formal control are not very effective at regulating illicit substance use. In this chapter, we consider a much more powerful and wide-reaching form of *informal* social control—socialization—that has its roots in social units much closer to an individual.

As we outlined in Chapter 1, informal control often originates in primary social groups composed of people with whom we have close, intimate, and direct ties. As you will learn in this chapter, the family is one of the most crucial agents of social control. Children learn about social life, for better or worse, in their immediate family environment. The family has a main responsibility to socialize the child into the norms, values, and traditions of social life.

Besides the family, the formal education system also exerts social control to teach self-control. Education is given the task of teaching discipline, co-operation, and obedience, as well as knowledge. Perhaps more importantly, schools also communicate ideas about equality and morality to students. Finally, workplaces also socialize people in ways that make them suited to performing certain occupational tasks. As you will see, socialization is a lifelong process of learning norms, behaviours, customs, and ways of thinking about aspects of the social world.

In his classic work *The New Utopians*, Robert Boguslaw (1965) notes that utopian visionaries have imagined building an ideal society in three different kinds of ways:

1. The first vision details desired goals or *outcomes* of ideal society: for example, in the ideal society, the means of production will be owned by the state and everyone will have roughly equal wealth and power.
2. The second vision details particular means or *heuristics*, on the assumption that desired outcomes will follow from these. So, for example, the ideal liberal democratic society assumes that certain organizational principles—free speech, the rule of law, and a market economy—will give rise to the best possible society, although the precise features of that ideal society are unknown.
3. Finally, a third vision imagines the creation of *ideal people*—the modern man, the good Christian, the Communist citizen, and so on. It does not necessarily imagine how that ideal person will behave or what kind of society such people will produce—only that the "right" kind of people will ultimately create the best kind of society in the best possible way.

Socialization as we commonly understand it draws on all three visions of social engineering in our own, less-than-ideal society. It teaches people what goals or outcomes they ought to desire: for example, what educational and occupational outcomes they should seek. Socialization also teaches people the norms of behaviour that are considered proper in different social situations and settings. And it teaches us what "normal" and "good" people look like, urging us to emulate them in thought and action. So, by combining these three types of control, socialization is perhaps the most powerful type of social control.

We should note, moreover, that ideas about socialization have been hotly debated for the last 100 or so years. The traditional sociological view is that both the society and the individual need socialization. Teaching people the norms and skills they need to function as adults in our society helps to integrate them into society. And integrating them into society, in turn, also helps society to develop social cohesion and to survive over time. Of course, this is the traditional "functionalist" view. The traditional Marxist or conflict view is that by teaching people the dominant ideology, socialization ensures they will be obedient and compliant workers. This helps the ruling class maintain its power in society, although such socialization is less beneficial to the rest of us.

The more current view, based on work by Michel Foucault, is that socialization is accomplished and reproduced by all the major institutions of society. It promotes certain notions of "normality" and uses the language of science to justify demands for compliance. Seeking to appear (and be) normal, people more or less willingly comply with the social norms they are taught. This Foucauldian way of viewing socialization is much closer to the theories of Freud than to those of Marx or Durkheim. In effect, this approach posits a society in which people are taught to repress their instincts and desires in the interests of "normality" and acceptance. From this standpoint, the outcome of socialization is not integration but regulation and even regimentation—or, as Foucault says, discipline and punishment.

Whichever interpretation of socialization we follow—and we can see elements of all these socialization processes operating in our daily lives—the outcome is the same: we all learn to value what we are supposed to value and behave in ways we are supposed to behave; and all of this is accomplished without laws, police officers, or guns. In effect, we are taught, through socialization, to police ourselves and to punish ourselves.

Varieties of Socialization

Socialization may be simply defined as the transmission and internalization of societal values and norms. Whether it occurs at home, in school, at work, or elsewhere, the process of socialization is "social" because it is through social interaction with others, and in response to social pressures, that people learn the culture and internalize the expectations of their community. The two major accomplishments of socialization are the **internalization** of social expectations—learning particular beliefs, norms, values, frames, and the like—and developing a **self-concept** (or identity).

The earliest socialization people receive is called "primary socialization." In the family, a young child learns many of the social skills needed to take part in our social institutions, including schools, offices, factories, and public spaces. This early socialization unintentionally also reproduces and perpetuates social inequality, by teaching people their "place" in society and convincing them that this social niche is indisputable.

Later in life, people begin to receive what is called "secondary socialization." This involves learning specific roles, norms, attitudes, or beliefs; sometimes, it involves self-imposed learning. Much of this type of socialization occurs in adulthood. We undergo secondary socialization whenever we change jobs, get married, or have children, for example. Secondary socialization differs from primary socialization in that it usually occurs outside the family, and is often based on already accumulated knowledge and previous socialization.

One aspect of "good" socialization is the inculcation of a desire for propriety and the approval of others—i.e., approval by the "generalized other." A well-socialized person doesn't want to attract the negative attention of the police and courts, for example, or of others in positions of authority (for example, teachers). This is another way in which socialization—especially, early socialization—teaches people to obey society's rules as a matter of course and without respect to the possibilities of punishment in a particular instance.

As we will see in this chapter, people learn all sorts of social skills in this way. They even learn what to think about gender through socialization, and through this socialization, they are controlled: women learn to behave in feminine ways; and men, in masculine ways. This gender socialization is the process of learning the attitudes, thoughts, and behaviour patterns that a culture considers appropriate for members of each sex. As tiny infants, gender and sex mean nothing. But by the age of three, little boys and girls are playing separately, at different kinds of games. Already, they have learned to want different toys, to enjoy different games, and to avoid fraternizing openly with the opposite sex.

Most of this gender socialization is unintentional, however. Parents may not mean to treat girls and boys differently, but they do so without realizing it. This gendered learning continues throughout life as secondary socialization and often becomes more—not less—important in the world of work. Consider the learning of emotion work as an example of this kind of social control.

Learning Emotional Expression

Human emotional expression is not an automatic display of internal feelings—it is a socially produced and socially controlled behaviour. In many lines of work—for example, service industries—controlled emotional expression is largely what is for sale. Customers are buying a pleasant experience, and they require certain emotional practices from the seller. As Arlie Hochschild points out in her book on this topic, *The Managed Heart: The Commercialization of Human Feeling* (1979), many businesses control not only their employees' behaviour but even their displays of emotion. Take the example of flight attendants, who (as we see in Box 4.1) receive detailed instructions about how they should appear to feel and communicate their (supposed) feelings to airplane customers.

Moral socialization—learning how to behave morally—has been studied for at least 80 years. Moral learning, like other learning, is a gradual process of social development. Children are not born with fully developed senses of morality and propriety; they have to learn them. Swiss researcher Jean Piaget notes that children progress from "heteronomous" morality—a respect for adult authority—to "autonomous" morality at particular ages.

What Piaget calls **autonomous morality** is found in older youth, who have already begun to think about proper rules of conduct. Like adults, they see rules as products of group agreement that promote co-operation within

Box 4.1   Flight Attendants

Airline flight attendants are in the business of selling smiles and putting people at ease, as much as they are in the business of bringing drinks and pillows. The making of a good flight attendant begins at the selection process, where applicants are expected to project a warm personality. The trainees are then chosen for their ability to take "stage directions" about how to do so without showing the effort involved, and they are schooled to improve in this area. Appearance is also very important in this occupation. In the past, flight attendants were taught to keep themselves within severe weight limits. Today, there is more flexibility on this matter, but appearance is still an important concern.

During training, recruits are constantly reminded that their own job security and the company's profit depend on a "smiling" face. The flight attendant has to treat the passenger "like a friend," although the passenger has no obligation to return the sentiment or even to be courteous. The passenger, in buying a ticket, buys the right to rudeness that the flight attendant cannot reciprocate.

In short, the attendant must learn to be unfailingly nice. He or she must learn to think of smiles as a commodity bought by the customer with his or her airplane ticket. Flight attendants must control their anger or impatience, and treat everyone with equal, unfailing courtesy. Of course, attendants vary somewhat in their manner. But they all need to de-personalize the criticism received from rude, tired, and frustrated travellers. And all flight attendants have to find ways to overcome feelings of phoniness.

This story about flight attendants illustrates several things about learned social control. First, becoming a flight attendant involves learning to sell oneself in a service occupation, which is a complicated process that takes time, effort, and self-discipline. Second, becoming a flight attendant involves *gendered* play-acting; many flight attendants are women. They know how women are supposed to behave, and they make sure they act that way. For women raised in a gender-equal or gender-neutral household, learning to do so will take considerable effort. Finally, becoming a flight attendant involves, to some degree, learning to be "phony." In that sense, flight attendants must learn to compromise their personal ethics to meet social and occupational expectations. And that reminds us that moral learning is also a type of socialization, and a type of social control.

the group. They understand why some behaviours are considered good and other behaviours are considered bad, and they are able to generalize about good and bad behaviour to apply these understandings in new situations. These older, more socialized children do not merely act to gain rewards or avoid punishment, the way younger children do. They act morally because they want to feel good about themselves by behaving in a "good," adult way.

In short, socialization controls people by channelling their behaviour in directions that the community considers right, proper, and moral. Gradually, people internalize their community's social norms, and obey them because they want to be approved members of the community. Doing so makes them feel good about themselves and gains them social support, but it also puts them under the control of the community. And people give themselves over to this because of their emotional ties to the people socializing them.

Agents of Socialization

As mentioned, a child's first emotional ties are usually to family members, who teach the child the language, norms, and values of the culture in a variety of ways. Much of what families teach children is unspoken. For example, children first learn the meaning of *woman*, *wife*, and *mother* by watching their own mother. They learn what is considered good and bad by witnessing how certain behaviours are rewarded or punished. Some parents are consistent in what they teach, in words and by example, while other parents are inconsistent. Obviously, inconsistent teaching is more likely to cause confusion and even distress. Schools are another agent of socialization, through both the stated and "hidden" curriculum. Peer groups are also agents of socialization, as are places of work.

Families and Parenting

Since path-breaking work by Diana Baumrind 40 years ago, sociologists have generally agreed that the best kind of parenting is "authoritative." Authoritative parenting, compared with other styles, is most likely to produce children who stay out of trouble with the law, do well at school, are happy and secure, and are mentally and physically healthy. These are all outcomes we can agree are desirable. *Authoritative parenting*—which is firm but loving—tends to reduce the likelihood of delinquency, school problems, interpersonal problems with friends, and a variety of health problems. In this parenting style, the parent controls the child, setting, and enforcing of rules, but is also warm and caring.

In contrast, *authoritarian parenting* is characterized by low acceptance and high control, which can hinder the development of expressiveness and independence in children. *Permissive parenting*, by contrast, is characterized by high acceptance and low control. Neither is as good as authoritative parenting, but both are better than neglectful parenting, which combines low acceptance and low control. Table 4.1 summarizes the types of parenting.

Table 4.1 Types of Parenting

Parenting Style	Characteristics	Possible Outcomes
Authoritative	• High acceptance, high control • Strict but encouraging	• Independent • Self-reliant
Authoritarian	• Low acceptance, high control • Tough yet unapproachable	• Hard-working • Self-doubting
Permissive	• High acceptance, low control • Indulgent and lenient	• Impulsive • Precocious
Neglectful	• Low acceptance, low control • Little involvement	• Truant • Taciturn

Research also suggests that the best way to teach or socialize a child is through *induction*, which is teaching by reasoning or explaining, doing, and modelling. *Inductive socialization* leads children to exercise *internalized moral control* over their behaviour. Inductive discipline, combined with parental affection, promotes deep moral learning and teaches a child how to communicate and reason with others. It also encourages the development of trust, a sharing of beliefs and ideas, and even intimacy. By creating emotional intimacy between parent and child, induction encourages the child to explore emotional equality and openness with others. It also trains children to look for their similarities with others, not their differences.

By contrast, *power assertion* and *love withdrawal*—hallmarks of authoritarian parenting—lead to superficial learning or no learning at all. This parenting style often leads the child to have prejudiced, violent reactions against others.

Of course, not all children are socialized in the same way, or taught the same values. In a classic book, Annette Lareau (2011) proposes that *societal inequalities* often determine which values children are taught, depending on their position in the class structure. Lareau (2011), in her book *Unequal Childhoods: Class, Race, and Family Life,* focuses on parenting style and how it varies from one class to another. The book presents several case studies of children from three different backgrounds: middle-class, working-class, and poor.

According to Lareau's research, middle-class parents use a strategy called *concerted cultivation.* As part of this, they involve their children in activities such as team sports and music lessons to cultivate their children. They also speak to their children more frequently and encourage them to debate, to build up a strong vocabulary. In these and other ways, the children of the middle class learn how to navigate through institutions, and develop a sense of entitlement, which will serve them well in their advancement into middle-class careers.

Poor and working-class families, on the other hand, often engage in very different strategies, using what Lareau (2011) terms *natural growth* strategies, where the children are left to control their own schedules. These parents do *not* sign up their children for soccer or hockey because team sports can be expensive; moreover, they may demand a lot of time, which parents with rigid job schedules may find hard to manage. Instead, they let their children pursue their interests on their own, leaving structure and organization mainly to the public school system.

Unlike middle-class parents, poor and working-class parents are also more deferential to teachers and medical professionals, and are less likely to question these professionals. Additionally, working-class and poor parents, by reacting passively to authority, implicitly teach their children to do the same. The working-class style often results in better-behaved and more creative children. As well, working-class children in the more natural, less structured system are less often bored and learn to be more creative. They are also more energetic than middle-class children.

One outcome is not better than the other, but the outcomes are different. Middle-class children learn to negotiate institutions better and pick up a better vocabulary and a sense of entitlement that help them get ahead in the job market. Through concerted cultivation, middle-class parents teach their children to be confident, assertive, and persistent. By teaching them to aim for the top, these parents prepare their children to climb the ladder of success. By teaching their children a sense of entitlement—as well as time management, organization, discipline, and multi-tasking—middle-class parents set their children up for academic success in adolescence and adulthood. For their part, working-class children mature more rapidly than middle-class children because they have been forced to "grow up."

Schools and Schooling

Schools, as we have indicated, are also important agents of socialization. Unlike family homes, schools are populated by strangers. Some of these strangers—the teachers—hold positions of great authority, in the child's eyes. Teachers expect obedience and punish deviation; and, unlike parents, teachers exert control without delivering affection. In this way, school is a child's first exposure to the "rule of law"—that is, to the impartial application of universalistic rules.

School also exposes children to *inequality* for the first time. The classroom is a structure of unequal power, over which the teacher presides. Children may also see economic and status inequality for the first time at school, for their fellow students are likely to come from a variety of different social and economic backgrounds. That said, children have little control over a school's rules and practices, which provide a basis for cohesion. As well, their powerlessness at school gives them real-life training for the adult workplace, where obedience will be amply rewarded.

A large part of what children learn at school is part of what is called the "hidden curriculum." This hidden curriculum includes learning how to identify who holds power, knowing which behaviours are rewarded, faking interest and ability, showing deference and accepting humiliation, and coping with boredom and repetition. This hidden curriculum encourages in students a passive acceptance of authority, a belief in external rewards, and a high valuing of conformity and competition. As such, it prepares young people for real adult life: for a class division based on "credentials" and evaluation standards devised by those at the top.

Aside from the stated curriculum and the hidden curriculum, even the use of space produces order and control, preparing students for submission and co-operation (Johnson, 1982). Consider how classroom furniture arrangement varies by grade level. The dimensions of a preschool classroom are $11.5 \times 9 \times 3.1$ metres—a space that is intended to contain roughly 15 students. Such a large classroom, containing so few students, encourages movement by students.

As well, round tables encourage the students to interact as equals. Round tables are used for group activities, such as arts and crafts (cutting and pasting, drawing), and playing board games that involve both co-operation and sharing. Likewise, a rug in the classroom is used for "story time" and it, too, encourages social interaction. Children may sit on the rug together to sing a song or hear the teacher read them a story, for example. By contrast, rectangular tables reinforce distance and discourage interaction.

Kindergarten classrooms are typically smaller—$9 \times 8.5 \times 3.1$ metres—and contain more furniture than the preschool room, so the space available for free movement decreases. Students are required to spend more time seated at their desks; so rectangular tables are pushed together to facilitate interaction and sharing. In the middle of the classroom, two circular tables provide space where the teacher or teacher's aide can spend time with small groups of students—for example, with small reading "ability" groups. The rug is still present, but children spend less time on it together and more time working at their desks.

Now, let's jump ahead a few years. In Grade 5 and 6 classrooms, the desks are organized into rows, an arrangement that discourages mobility and student collaboration even more. Here, a distance of at least one metre is maintained between desks. Students may be punished for sharing, talking, and interacting with each other while working. They are graded on universal criteria and compete for the scarce resource of "grades." In these and higher grades, students may move from class to class for different subjects, but all of the classrooms are configured identically, suggesting the students themselves are identical and replaceable. Because regimentation is an intended part of the socialization process, larger class sizes are acceptable at the higher grades, as we see in Figure 4.1.

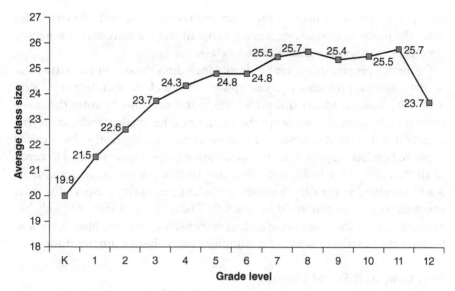

Figure 4.1 Average Class Size in Alberta across Grades
Source: From Government of Alberta. (2004, 7 January). Average class size remains relatively steady. Retrieved from http://
education.alberta.ca/department/newsroom/news/archive/2004/january/20040107.aspx

Most important for control, the standard arrangement of the classroom—students in even rows facing the front—focuses all attention toward the teacher. Students are thus socialized to focus on their own tasks: to mind their own business and minimize interaction with peers during class. The focus is clearly on doing one's own work and following the teacher's instructions.

Though school organization may seem to be gender neutral, in fact it benefits girls and penalizes boys. Schools typically demand what Levine and Ornstein (1981) call "female norms," which consist of obedience, cleanliness, and politeness. Schools also punish students for using vulgar language and fighting, which may be considered historically as traits of "maleness." This cannot be unrelated to the fact that girls earn higher grades than boys throughout elementary school and that more boys fail, are disciplinary cases, and drop out of school. In the classroom, everyone is supposed to behave "like girls." The classroom setting forces students to remain focused on only one task at a time and to stay seated at their desks for long periods of time. As well, many of the tasks are linguistic in nature.

Classroom etiquette is a concern even in colleges and universities. According to Robert Emerick (1994), even at the post-secondary level a lack of classroom etiquette poses problems. Emerick, an experienced sociology professor, devotes a whole page of his university syllabus to his expectations of student behaviour in the classroom. For example, one rule concerns tardiness. He tells students that coming late is better than not coming at all, but he expects latecomers to enter the room and take a seat quietly. Emerick also notes the problem of students leaving early. In fact, he considers this a more serious infraction than coming late to class.

Emerick reports that once he started including classroom etiquette rules on his syllabus, problems and disruptions in the classroom decreased dramatically. Some students still arrive late, but those who do enter the classroom quietly, so as not to disrupt the lecture or other students who are trying to hear it. Emerick also reports that some students—especially those raised in polite families—appreciate the clarification of his expectations. However, of all the rules of academic behaviour that instructors try to inculcate, none is as important as the rules regarding academic integrity—especially, rules about cheating—as discussed in Box 4.2. These are important not only because they go to the heart of individual responsibility for schoolwork but also because they further a sense of community and cohesion among students.

Sex, God, and Social Control

The public educational system, to which parents entrust their impressionable children, is often used to promote important (though contentious) points of view. Consider two such areas of the formal school curriculum

Box 4.2   Cheating and Academic Integrity

Moiseyenko (2005) notes that schools also promote social cohesion by enforcing academic integrity and fostering a sense of community through a common commitment to honest scholarship. At the centre of good student behaviour is a commitment to a shared code of ethics. An "honour code"—or shared "code of conduct"—outlines the rules around plagiarism, cheating, misrepresentation, and stealing, for example. McCabe and Trevino (2002) report that honour codes serve important social functions on university campuses and also reduce cheating.

Of course, as Daniel and Cheryl Albas (1993) note, where there are rules, there will be temptations to break them. That is why teachers institute supervision and sanctions to achieve control. Students, knowing that teachers expect some of them to cheat, take great pains to avoid looking like cheaters. With this in mind, many students engage in what Erving Goffman calls "impression management" at tests, using what the authors call *disclaimers*.

An understood rule in the exam room is that there should be no looking at other people's papers or exchanging glances with others that might be interpreted as unfair communication. In short, students are expected not to have "roving eyes." But students need to relax from time to time and to move their eyes from the paper in that socialize people in especially profound ways: sex education and religious education.

"Sex education," according to Thorogood (1992), is far from neutral; it constructs notions of normalcy and deviance, which then regulate and control people's behaviour. Through sex education, the "body" becomes the site of regulation and monitoring. What we come to *know* as **sexuality** in a society is the product of many social influences and cultural assumptions. Sexual beliefs, as well as actions, are therefore important sites of social control: points at which society regulates our individual bodies. Sex education, it follows, is the formal expression of how our bodies are to be trained.

Teenagers inhabit what Thorogood (1992) calls "dangerous moral territory" because they are in the midst of learning to negotiate the passage from childhood to adulthood. Indeed, it is in the teenage years that people are most likely to engage in deviant and socially destructive behaviour, in the context of sex and otherwise. So, sex education is important, but it is also laden with problems. Some see sex education as essential to promoting the "right" values and behaviours. Others view sex education in a more liberal manner, believing that it will help students to achieve a more fulfilling life.

front of them, to gather their thoughts. At such times, they take great care in selecting where to look when looking away from their own paper. Many students keep their eyes fixed on the invigilators. Others stare at the ceiling, while others stare at the back of the head of the person right in front of them.

Some students even sit directly in front of the invigilator, so that they can be seen as innocent. Others avoid sitting near the "high achievers" so they will not be suspected of trying to copy from them. Students also avoid sitting next to known cheaters, to escape any possible guilt by association. A favoured position is the aisle seat, where students can angle their body away from the person sitting in the next seat, and where it is impossible to see the paper of the person across the aisle. Any pause or lack of activity is damning, so students do things to avoid seeming devious. For example, if stumped by a question for a long period of time, they may put on a show of diligence by moving their lips exaggeratedly as they read the question, or underline or circle words on the question paper, while others turn to diligent doodling.

In general, and despite what students fear, instructors and invigilators are reluctant to find cheaters. Some will avoid looking for cheaters, to increase the likelihood of a high course rating from the students. Others avoid looking for cheaters because of the scene it would create if they were to find any, or out of sympathy for the students, whose careers could be harmed by such stigmatization. Others still want to avoid the work they would have to do to document and prosecute an act of cheating.

Consider two sexual education models, which illustrate the contentious nature of deciding how to educate teens about sex.

One model, which Thorogood calls the *restricted information model,* or "traditional model," is the most widespread practice. It is "normative" in approach, teaches respect for the sanctity of married life, and condemns deviant sex, such as extramarital affairs. Traditional sex education promotes heterosexual monogamy and ignores all other forms of sex. It also tends to focus on the reproductive function of sexuality. Indeed, "sex" seems to be universally linked to "reproduction" in sex education classes, where students are taught about the means of birth control available, as well as family planning. In this model of sex education, to be "normal" is to be heterosexual.

An alternative model, which Thorogood calls the *empowerment model,* promotes participation in learning about sex and individual responsibility for learning. Here, sex education promotes discussion of various lifestyles, while making reference to the social institutions that prescribe these sexual roles. This kind of education does not portray heterosexuality or child bearing as normative—merely as options. Such education also counteracts some of the sexual stereotypes associated with particular races and sexual orientations.

However, the empowerment model is also risky. For example, the discussion of sexual desires and preferences in class makes visible the private aspects of students' lives that were previously invisible, and gives others a chance to scrutinize them. For better or worse, our peers have the ability to regulate, or at least criticize, our sexual behaviours. Since sex education includes the transmission of social values, it always has the potential to act as a strong means of social control.

A second contentious area of the school curriculum surrounds the inclusion of *religious* education. While we will discuss religious social control in much greater detail in Chapter 5, Paul Vermeer (2010) proposes that religious education is an important means of socializing people into the larger society. By his reckoning, religious education helps students develop both a personal and a social identity. For Vermeer, religious education should introduce students to personal narratives underlying religious beliefs. As he notes, education always involves the transmission of values, so it is difficult for a denominational school not to pass on some of its religious culture to students. However, even *these* schools should present their students with an opportunity to understand other religions in a fair, unbiased way, and to develop critical skills for examining their own religion.

The most important, though least discussed, job of schools, however, is to train students in patient obedience—the essential qualification for most non-professional work in our society. As well, the school promotes a meritocratic ethic, teaching students to hold themselves responsible for success and failure—an ideologically suitable message in a capitalist society.

Peer Groups

The **peer group** is another important agent of socialization. This is a group of interacting companions who usually share similar social characteristics (age, gender, social class, and religion, among others), interests, tastes, and values. Like parents and teachers, peers are also part of a child's **reference group**—people to whom the child mentally refers when evaluating his or her own thoughts and behaviour. A reference group provides the standards against which people and behaviour are evaluated.

Peers can have a good or bad influence on children, just like parents and teachers. Peers who misbehave will often influence their friends to misbehave. The likelihood of associating with delinquent peers, however, is influenced by the quality of family life and school life. Children with bad home and/ or school situations are more likely to hang out with trouble-making peers. Children from strong, cohesive families, with parents who exercise careful supervision over them, are less likely to associate with drug-using or otherwise delinquent peers.

University and the Workplace

Socialization in schools continues even in colleges and universities. Consider, for example, the socialization that prepares people to be professional sociologists. Such "professional socialization" occurs in graduate school, where students are gradually transformed into professional "academics."

Shulman and Silver (2003), in studying this process, focus on the "informal culture" associated with becoming a professional sociologist. Becoming a "professional sociologist" means fulfilling all of the formal requirements, including coursework, examinations, and dissertation research; but that is only part of the socialization that takes place. Students also have to learn professional, sometimes unspoken norms. To succeed, students need to become *strategic* in figuring out how they are going to produce social research, and not simply consume it. This means learning how to get their research ideas out to the broader community—through conferences, books, or journal articles. It also means learning how professors network, how scholars view the prestige of various sociological journals, and how colleagues can help to navigate the peer review process for publishing.

Producing publishable research, even while in graduate school, will help to ensure employment after graduation. Graduate school also teaches a student that research excellence is far more important than teaching excellence in decisions about hiring, tenure, and promotion. So, graduate students are advised to focus on research from the very beginning: to recognize, for example, that writing a dissertation, not teaching, is the key to earning a Ph.D., and earning the Ph.D. is key to future employment.

Once graduate students go on to the job market, **social networks** play a huge role in getting a job. Getting an interview at a top research institution is rare. In part, this depends on the student's publication record: whether he or she has already published papers in respected academic journals. Equally important are recommendations—both written and word-of-mouth—from respected faculty members in their home department. For this reason, students need to learn how to align themselves with faculty members who have the time to advise, and who can help them gain employment.

Often, students collaborate with faculty on research projects, but must learn how to develop research projects of their own. Hiring institutions typically look for this kind of research self-sufficiency when evaluating candidates for jobs. Besides faculty members, other graduate students are important sources of information and support. Grad students must learn to work well with a few of these peers, who will eventually become professional peers.

Now, consider the socialization practices associated with a career in occupational therapy. Occupational therapists, like other professionals, are socialized to uphold the values of their profession. A study by Aguilar, Stupans, Scutter, and King (2012) identified the professional values of occupational therapists and sorted them into categories. First, students of occupational therapy learn that they have a responsibility to keep up-to-date on the knowledge of the field with the latest interventions and research findings. A therapist who keeps up to date on this is considered a "good" therapist.

Another important aspect of professional practice lies in knowing how to develop the client–therapist partnership. Therapists learn the importance of working with the client to find a treatment that is going to work for them. They learn to empower the client to take the lead in treatment sessions and to seek a better understanding of the individual client, including his or her circumstances, needs, strengths, and social supports.

Finally, therapists are expected to display qualities such as warmth, empathy, honesty, kindness, fairness, caring, and thoughtfulness toward the client. As part of this, they are expected to acknowledge that they do not have the answer to every question or the solution to every problem. However, they learn to respect their clients' emotions, beliefs, values, and priorities. Finally, they learn the importance of respecting colleagues, who can be valuable sources of information and professional knowledge.

As we can see in these two instances, professional socialization extends beyond gaining the required "technical" knowledge needed to succeed in one's field. In both cases, professional socialization means learning the professional norms governing the field, how to effectively interact with colleagues, and how to go about gaining employment. But note that occupational therapy is very client-centred, while professional sociology is very publication centred; and because professions differ in their goals, they teach students to behave in different ways.

Negative Socialization: Learning to Behave Badly

You might imagine that deviant or anti-social behaviour is a sign that socialization has failed, but that is not always the case. Often, people who behave badly do so because they have never been taught to do otherwise or because they have been taught to behave badly.

That's because cultures (and subcultures) differ in the values they promote. For example, some cultures promote individualism and self-expression, while others promote obedience and conformity. Obviously, cultures that promote individualism and self-expression will produce more behaviour that is disobedient, non-conforming, and even criminal. In these respects, then, consider the differences between American adolescents and Danish adolescents.

Not surprisingly, American adolescents are more likely to engage in risky and delinquent behaviour. For example, according to a study by Arnett and Jensen (1994), American adolescents are more likely than Danish adolescents to drive an automobile while intoxicated and are also more likely to drive a car at a high speed. In fact, at the time of the study in 1994, only 34 per cent of Danish adolescents had driven a car at all in the preceding year, versus 100 per cent of the American adolescents. However, American adolescents are more likely to believe they need to drive a car. Because the crime rate is lower in Denmark than in the US, Danish adolescents feel safer taking public transportation at night.

Danish adolescents are more sexually active than American adolescents but they are also more likely than American adolescents to use contraception. The failure of American adolescents to use contraception as often may be due to poorer sex education, less access to contraceptives, or higher religiosity in American society. As a result, adolescent pregnancy is higher in the United States than in Denmark. Indeed, as we see in Figure 4.2, there are wide cross-cultural differences in the acceptance and use of contraceptives: these differences are not only evident in a comparison on Denmark and the US.

Conceivably, some of this cross-national difference in risk-taking is due to differences in inequality, although the research also reveals gender differences in risk-taking in the two countries. In Denmark, parents teach more or less the same behaviour expectations to both boys and girls so behaviour is much less gendered. In US culture, on the other hand, boys (but not girls) are allowed to express more aggressive behaviour in risky ways, without the fear of strong condemnation or punishment. In short, American adolescents are taught to be less mature and responsible than Danish adolescents.

Let us now consider another example of **negative socialization**, or learning to behave badly: that is, learning coercive sexuality on college campuses. Research finds that American fraternities are common staging grounds for rape and other coercive (i.e., unwanted) sexuality. According

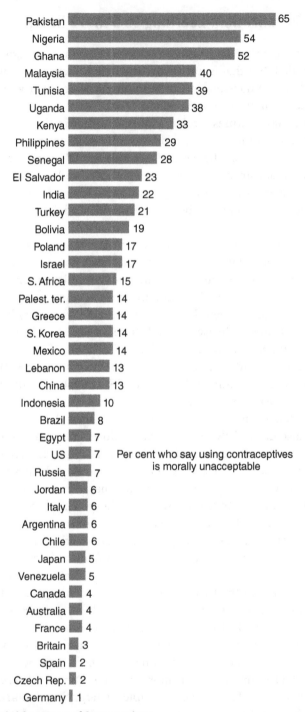

Figure 4.2 Global Acceptance of Contraceptives
Source: Poushter, J. (2014, 15 April). What's morally acceptable? It depends on where in the world you live. Pew Research Center, Fact Tank—Our Lives in Numbers. Retrieved from http://www.pewresearch.org/fact-tank/2014/04/15/whats-morally-acceptable-it-depends-on-where-in-the-world-you-live/

to Martin and Hummer (1989), fraternities provide a physical and socio-cultural context that encourages the sexual coercion of women. This is wrapped up in the gender socialization of American males. More than anything else, American fraternities are concerned with masculinity. They try hard to stamp out any signs of "wimpishness," effeminacy, or homosexuality.

Instead, fraternities promote a conception of "masculinity" that stresses athleticism, dominance, winning, wealth, willingness to drink alcohol, and sexual prowess vis-à-vis women. They seek members who are "athletic, "big guys," "who can talk college sports," "willing to drink alcohol," or "who can hold their liquor." They try to avoid "geeks," nerds, and men who will give the fraternity a "wimpy" or "gay" reputation (Martin & Hummer, 1989).

After all, fraternities are male organizations, run by and for men. Fraternity "brothers" have a quasi-familial relationship with each other. Practices of brotherhood that contribute to the sexual coercion of women include preoccupation with loyalty, group protection, and secrecy; use of alcohol as a weapon; involvement in violence and physical force; and an emphasis on competition and superiority. Members are continually reminded to be loyal to the fraternity and to their members. They are warned to avoid getting the fraternity in trouble and to bring all problems "to the chapter" (local branch of national fraternity), rather than to outsiders. Protection of the fraternity often takes precedence over what is procedurally, ethically, or legally correct. Secrecy is a priority where outsiders are concerned.

Alcohol use in the fraternity is normal and normative. In fact, alcohol is used on weekdays to relax after class, and on weekends to "get drunk," "get crazy," and "get laid." Fraternity men also have a history of violence: e.g., hazing, property destruction, and rape. University officials report that fraternities are the third riskiest property to insure, behind waste dumps and amusement parks. Fraternities are increasingly defendants in actions brought by pledges, in cases that involve hazing and women being raped.

Access to women for sexual gratification is a presumed benefit of fraternity membership. Strategies aimed at obtaining sexual gratification include individual strategies, such as getting a woman drunk and spending a great deal of money on her. They also include collective strategies: for example, parties are organized to result in sex. At these parties, men and women arrive wearing little or nothing. There are pornographic pinups on the walls and porno movies playing on the TV.

Fraternity norms are learned and then taught to new generations of recruits. Such norms emphasize the value of maleness and masculinity—values that undermine the status of women as people who deserve consideration and care. Fraternity norms and practices socialize members to view the sexual coercion of women, which is a felony crime, as a sport, a contest, or a game. This sport is played between men and men, with women as prizes and prey in the middle.

Conclusion

In all these respects, socialization can be seen to be a powerful means of social control. It is a way of controlling society by controlling the minds and hearts of people who make up society, and it starts in childhood (although, as we have seen, it doesn't end then). Socialization occurs in all social settings where there are expectations of how one ought to behave. It provides an excellent platform for certain values and behavioural norms to be internalized and accepted as natural by the individual. Even before preschool, socialization determines our identities through behaviour taught to us by our parents, both explicitly and through mimicry.

Socialization can also have very negative outcomes, when harmful behaviour is normalized and seen as acceptable because it is so commonplace in a group. Nazi ideology is an excellent example of what can happen when socialization toward an authoritarian identity goes unchallenged. The only time when socialization is particularly unsuccessful is when it encounters systematic social barriers: what Merton, in his famous theory of deviance and conformity, called "anomie." Then, people faced with obstacles to their learned values and behaviours must decide whether to persist in those values and behaviours, despite a lack of payoff.

Questions for Critical Thought

1. Is it likely that some aspects of socialization are the same across all cultures and societies, or are they all culturally variable, as we saw with Danish and US adolescents?

2. Can you identify processes of socialization in your own community, school, or workplace?

3. How effective is socialization as a form of social control? Is socialization mainly a conscious or an unconscious process?

4. Is primary socialization more important or foundational than later socialization, or merely earlier?

5. What implications can negative socialization have on your life? On a society?

Recommended Readings

Albanese, P. (2015). *Children in Canada today* (2nd ed.). Toronto: Oxford University Press.

This book is part of a series of works on important sociological topics with specific emphasis on Canadian issues. Albanese explores themes of childhood socialization, such as socializing agents and their impact, changes in social policy, and the relation of socialization to family and social problems.

Becker, H.S., Geer, B., Hughes, E.C., & Strauss, A.L. (1961). *Boys in white: Student culture in medical school.* Chicago: University of Chicago Press.
This is a classic sociological work on professional socialization. It not only explores how medical students learn about medical terms, health care, disease, prevention, and so on, but also focuses on how medical school socializes students into the social role of doctor.

Handel, G. (Ed.). (2006). *Childhood socialization* (2nd ed.). New Brunswick, NJ: Aldine Transaction.
This book examines agents of socialization that have an impact on social learning by children. It gives an interesting account of how socialization differs in different societies and cultures.

Tapscott, D. (1998). *Growing up digital: The rise of the Net generation.* New York: McGraw-Hill.
In this book, Tapscott argues that the children of baby boomers are part of what he calls the "Net generation," meaning that they are growing up surrounded by high-tech toys and tools from birth. This preoccupation with technology may have a significant impact on the future of these children, changing the nature of education, commerce, recreation, the workplace, government, and the family.

Recommended Websites

Childcare Canada, Childcare Resource and Research Unit
www.childcarecanada.org
This website has a large selection of resources related to child care and early childhood education. It contains interdisciplinary research related to the impact of child care, a major aspect of socialization.

DonTapscott.com
www.dontapscott.com
This website contains some of the work done by Don Tapscott in regards to how digital media impacts socialization. It includes discussions on a range of topics about how technology is changing the way we think through socialization.

Health Canada
www.healthcanada.com
Here, you will find links to important information and resources regarding health and well-being in Canada, such as reports and statistics. They relate to Canadians of all ages and backgrounds.

5 Religious Beliefs, Religious Institutions, and Sources of Social Control

Learning Objectives

◎ To understand religion as a form of socialization

◎ To recognize religious sources of social control

◎ To understand how religious beliefs and practices relate to social behaviour

◎ To determine how religion is related to education, health, and socio-economic status

◎ To distinguish spirituality from organized religion and to understand their impacts

◎ To understand secularization theory

Introduction

In Chapter 4, we saw how socialization through the family, school system, and other social institutions influences child development and social behaviour over the life course. We are all born into families and will attend educational institutions from a very early age. By contrast, we will not all attend religious institutions. Religion, the focus of this chapter, is not mandatory in our lives. Many Canadians lead secular lives and do not visit a religious institution—except for weddings and funerals—more than once a year, if at all. Yet, as we will see, for people who hold religious beliefs, religion can be a powerful form of social control. All religions provide guidelines for how to live a righteous life; in this context, they act as authorities on proper behaviour. Largely through the promise of rewards and punishments in the afterlife, most religions encourage good behaviour and discourage bad behaviour.

In today's secular society, it may be hard to believe that a century ago, even in Canada, most people took religion and religion-based morality very seriously. Most people attended religious services once a week, read and discussed religious sermons, and took pains to lead their lives according to the precepts of good behaviour enunciated in their church, temple, or synagogue. Already, though, Canada at that time was much more secular than it had been a century earlier. By then, all Western societies had been gradually secularized, first by the anti-Catholic Protestant Reformation of the sixteenth century, then by the anti-religious Enlightenment debates of the eighteenth century, and finally by the separation of Church and State accomplished by

Napoleon's nineteenth-century conquest of Europe. However, throughout the nineteenth century, many Europeans and North Americans continued to take religion seriously, and to hotly dispute the opposing claims of religion and science—a dispute that continues in many parts of the world today. In fact, it wasn't until 1960 that the Catholic Church lost its hold on Quebec schools and political life. And even today, religious zealots continue to exercise political and social influence in the United States, the Middle East, and other parts of the world.

In short, religious institutions continue to exercise a significant degree of social control in many parts of the world today, and do so even in important immigrant, rapidly growing communities in Canada. Religious institutions, like other major institutions discussed by Foucault, control through "technologies of the body." For example, they often exercise control over people's thinking about virginity, sexuality, modesty, purity, and the like.

Generally, religions with the strongest views on these matters tend to be the most traditional, patriarchal, and sexist religions; they tend to favour traditional families and high fertility for women, for example. Women who have sex outside of marriage or use contraception are especially criticized; and women, generally, have little voice in the hierarchy of these religious institutions. To a large degree, religious control operates in just the way Foucault describes: from the inside out, by implanting notions of shame and guilt and promoting fears about the afterlife. In religious institutions, moral "expertise" is wielded by highly trained clergy with a presumed direct connection to the supernatural.

Churches have tended, throughout time, to be "greedy" institutions, demanding the loyalty and conformity of followers in both thought and action. Often, religious institutions have asked their members to stigmatize, discriminate against, and even punish minority groups (or "non-believers") for their failure to hold the correct views. And, for centuries, religious institutions have encouraged people to express prejudice and discrimination against religious minorities, culminating in events like the Holocaust—the biggest religion- and race-based massacre in human history.

"Religion" is a complicated idea. Accordingly, sociologists have found it necessary to develop both substantive and functional definitions of religion—that is, to define (*substantively*) what a religion is—i.e., its formal qualities—and what it does to and for society (*functionally*). Sociologists also distinguish between organized religion and spirituality. **Organized religion** refers to a set of social institutions, groups, buildings, and resources, while **spirituality** refers to a set of beliefs that, though shared, may not be enacted in the presence of other people. Many people today claim to be "spiritual but not religious." Sociologists do not locate the effects of religion within the individual but, rather, within the *human group*, which Émile Durkheim was among the first to point out.

Durkheim noted that we lead most of our lives in a **profane** world of routine social objects, such as everyday clothes, food, ways of speaking and behaving, and so on. However, on special occasions, we try to shift to a sacred plane marked by special (and even other-worldly) objects, such as "holy water," ceremonial clothing, symbolic foods, and unusual ways of speaking and behaving. Indeed, we associate specific locations (such as churches and temples) with **sacred**, special activities, and deem only certain behaviours as acceptable for these locations. For example, you dress up to go to church, although not to go to a movie, a sociology class, or a slumber party.

In this context of ceremonial objects, Durkheim was fascinated by the practice of **totemism**, the widespread use of natural objects and animals to symbolize spirituality. These emblematic objects—particular plants, birds, fish, animals, or even imaginary creatures—evoke a sense of collective loyalty. Around these totemic objects, special rituals and ceremonies are enacted. These totemic objects reinforce group solidarity and shared beliefs in the community as a whole. They connect people and give them an opportunity to escape "profane," everyday life into a higher, sacred plane of experience.

Most important, these totemic objects do not have a meaning in themselves. Their meaning and significance lies only in the social cohesion they promote, maintain, and celebrate. Often associated with these rituals are strange sounds, smells, and images, as well as strange prayers, dances, songs, and even occasionally, drugs, alcohol, and sexual abandon. For Durkheim, then, religion expresses a **collective consciousness**: a shared sentiment and a shared way of understanding the world. And this collective consciousness controls people's behaviour.

So, religion performs both integrative and regulative functions in society; and Durkheim was the first to notice this. As a *regulative function*, Durkheim notes that many religions give rules that believers are expected to follow, not only in religious and spiritual matters but also in other areas of life, such as eating and sexual intimacy (McCullough & Smith, 2003). Durkheim also notes that religion serves an *integrative function*, providing people with strong and meaningful social connections that give them a sense of belonging and a feeling that they are cared for (McCullough & Smith, 2003). It does both of these, in part, through religious socialization.

Religious Socialization

Religious education itself can be considered an important form of socialization and, thus, of social control. Through religious education, the parent's faith or religion becomes extremely important to the child. When it comes to religion, children often have no choice but to adopt the faith of their parents (Okon, 2012).

Religion, at first glance, may seem to be a personal activity, but there is also a strong communal dimension to it. Young people are often initiated into religion by rites of passage that involve atonement for wrongdoings. Religious socialization can be especially effective if children become trained in the "languages" of their religions and ideas of what is "sacred" during their formative years. Through this process, children learn not only the physical nature of our world but also the "invisible" sacred domain (Okon, 2012).

Berger and Berger (1976) also note that children commonly follow the religion they were born into because parents exert power over the child. Occasionally, children resist a particular religious belief or resist attending a religious service or event; but as Erikson (1977) says, "it is [the parents] who control most of the rewards that he craves and most of the sanctions that he fears . . . the simple fact that most children are eventually socialized affords proof of this proposition" (p. 63). Likewise, Berger and Berger (1976) point out that the child is not exposed to any alternatives. It is only later in life that children become aware of other religions and of the possibility of doing without religion in their life.

Family and religious institutions can work together to exert social control by enforcing religious norms in the home, which can, sometimes, have social benefits. For example, Rodney Stark (1996) notes that religious involvement is more likely to deter delinquent behaviour, especially when the youth is involved in a broader religious community, where norms and values are constantly reinforced. In part, that is because, as Mahoney, Pargament, Murray-Swank, and Murray-Swank (2003) note, parents who are religious put more emphasis on family relationships than parents who are nonreligious. And parents who are religious often have supportive community members to help them monitor their children and reinforce the religious values taught in the family home (Smith, 2003).

Religion does not always lead to lower levels of delinquency, however. Stark's (1996) **moral community hypothesis** says that religion is most likely to deter people from delinquent behaviour when the individual has the same beliefs as the surrounding religious community. And, while religion can often bring children and parents together, it can also push them apart if parents and children hold differing religious beliefs. In fact, when there is a discord where parents value religion more than their children do, adolescents report worse relationships with their parents (Stokes & Regnerus, 2008). Youth have little choice but to follow their parents' wishes early in their lives, but as they grow older, they often stop doing so.

All of this behaviour is gendered: females are more likely than males to be religious (Spilka, Hood, Hunsberger, & Gorsuch, 2003). When compared to boys and men, girls and women attend religious services and events more often, pray more often, and are involved in more social activities related to religion (Coles, 1990). This means that religion will exercise more control over women than over men. Hyde (1990) notes that girls are also more likely to discuss religion than boys.

This is a somewhat confusing finding because in many of the world's religions, including orthodox Christianity, Judaism, and Islam, the structure, symbolism, and language of the churches are profoundly anti-woman, as noted earlier. Churches promote the concept of hierarchy, with "God" at the apex, followed by men (in some churches, various levels of male priests, then laymen), women, and children. Even Protestant churches, which do not necessarily promote a hierarchy of clergy, have traditionally viewed men as closer to "God." This hierarchy is strengthened and promoted by an overwhelming number of male images. Most often, "God" is still presented as male; images of Jesus abound in many churches; figures of the (male) apostles appear everywhere, from church windows to children's books.

In Christianity, and especially Catholicism, often, the only apparent female image is that of Mary, viewed as mother and described in ways that (as many feminist theologians and sociologists point out) make plain that she is set apart from "ordinary" women and so cannot be truly emulated. Besides, she is spoken of as merely an "intercessor." Even as mother of "God," she does not form part of the male Trinity. When, in 1987, the world's first female Catholic theology professor, Uta Ranke-Heinemann, challenged the concept of the Virgin Mary as asexual, untainted, and pure—an impossible model for women—the Church revoked her authority to teach theology.

Until recently, women were considered by mainstream churches to be incapable of acting as priests or ministers: and although in many Protestant churches women can now be ministers, this change was not achieved without a struggle. And, as many religious historians have now pointed out, not only is this exclusion of women from the clergy—indeed, from any important role in the religion—unfair and patriarchal, it is also in conflict with many of the earliest documents of the religion: for example, the Gnostic Gospels in Christianity.

Socializing through Rewards and Sanctions

Understanding that religious behaviour is no different from other behaviours, as Sherkat (2003) points out, will help us make sense of why people (including women) turn to religion and religious practices. In all realms of behaviour, *social rewards and sanctions* push people to perform in particular ways, and especially to shun "bad" behaviours (e.g., smoking, drinking, and pursuing criminal careers). The rewards for religious involvement do not only arrive in the afterlife; even in this life, religion gives people access to social networks, friendship groups, business contacts, potential mates, and even social status in the community. Belonging to a religious institution, as Sherkat (2003) notes, can also keep people from feeling lonely and socially isolated.

According to Okon (2012), religion is an integrative force that "shapes collective belief into collective identity." It is through the enactment of religious rituals, such as weddings, baptisms, burials, and celebrations of birthdays, that group solidarity and cohesion are fostered in a diverse, largely individualistic society, and this imposes control on individuals. At the same time, religion fosters exclusion and feelings of rejection among people who are "outside" the group of members. Andersen (1977) notes that, "in the extreme, groups who deviate from religious proscriptions may be tortured, executed, or excommunicated; in more subtle ways, religious deviants may be ridiculed, shunned, or ostracized" (p. 226).

Some would say that religions also "brainwash" people into believing that there is only one truth and that truth is knowable only through religious doctrine and religious practice. Most religious institutions also have rules they try to impose on followers. These rules provide useful information about the religion's beliefs, values, and organization. Often, they highlight the religion's "founding myths." For example, a founding myth of Judaism is that God gave Moses tablets of stone with the Ten Commandments written on them, and told Moses to enforce these rules among the Jews, who were God's "chosen people." Most religions make reference to these myths in their sacred texts, calendars, rituals, symbols, and even holidays (Beckford & Richardson, 2007).

In turn, religious rules are codified and refined through the kind of religious scholarship that goes on at monasteries, universities, seminaries, and theological colleges. Out of these institutions come elaborately detailed ways to think about the religion. These religious educational institutions develop and disseminate "correct" religious beliefs, through the preparation and interpretation of texts. They also train religious ministers and teachers, preachers, evangelists, and other religious figures (Beckford & Richardson, 2007).

Religions also have *regulatory rules* to monitor the behaviour, thoughts, and feelings of religious adherents. The Roman Catholic Church, for instance, has a college of "cardinals" (priests who have made their way up the hierarchy) centred in the Vatican, who regulate the Church's teachings. By contrast, Judaism, Islam, Hinduism, and Buddhism do not have a single authoritative structure; in these religions, local or national organizations regulate activity in the religion. Also, religions vary widely in the degree of formality with which they regulate members and respond to rule-breaking. Christians, for example, have central agencies that deal with breaches such as misconduct by a clergyman. Other religions are less formal and rely more on local judgments by key members of the congregation (Beckford & Richardson, 2007). Nevertheless, all religions are concerned with preserving the integrity of their values and preventing rule violations that may undermine it.

As in the secular world, in the religious world sanctions are used to punish and deter rule-breaking. Religious authorities can no longer (for the most part) impose the death penalty for a rule breach. Such extreme punishment is limited to countries in the Middle East, North Africa, and South Asia, where Islam is the dominant religion (Beckford & Richardson, 2007). It is far more common today for religious authorities to punish rule breakers by censuring them, expelling them, or removing their authority to preach, teach, or attend ceremonies.

A religion regulates social life through many different processes and institutions. In more traditional or pre-modern societies, religious views intrude into education, the law, and sometimes government. And even in modern, secular societies, we find religious broadcasters, publishers, and lobbyists. Religions also support certain kinds of voluntary associations and try, in this way, to influence political decision-making. Such religious groups have, historically, campaigned against the public sale of alcohol, capital punishment, abortion, euthanasia, experimenting with human embryos, organ transplantation, and surrogate motherhood (Beckford & Richardson, 2007).

Religion also teaches an *"internal"* or subjective source of social control. As a result, people who are "spiritual but not religious" are also subject to social control by religion. Some religions encourage people to share their feelings with others, in order to become more aware of their true selves. Healing rituals also fall into this category since they often force people to become "different" people by making themselves available to healing processes. This form of "subjective" religion frees people from the more formal constraints of organized religion, but the subjective freedom is only available to people who think their self needs to "grow" (Beckford & Richardson, 2007).

How Education Undermines Religious Socialization

Formal education, however, tends to undermine the influence of religion on individuals and families. Generally, the more education people receive, the more likely they are to rely on evidence and reason in their decision-making, and the less likely they are to rely on faith, sometimes even eliminating religion altogether (Sherkat, 2003). Indeed, **secularization theory,** to be discussed later in this chapter, holds that formal education is key to the historic replacement of religious faith with scientific reasoning based on evidence. Nonetheless, religion has not disappeared from our secular society.

As students ascend the educational system, they are more likely to encounter people who hold contrary religious views, and even people who reject religion altogether. Research has repeatedly found that college professors, especially in the humanities and social sciences, have a greater-than-average sympathy for **atheism** and **agnosticism** (Stark & Finke, 2000). Secular philosophies found in the humanities and social sciences often express hostility or contempt toward religion; prime examples include Marxism and Freudian theory.

Western societies typically forbid religion from interfering in the economic and political realms and also prevent the state from forcing religious beliefs on people, leaving them to choose and express their own beliefs. Religious groups, in turn, are treated neutrally in the competition for public funds and other public privileges. Nonetheless, religious believers, as we have pointed out, are subject to external and internal regulation by their religious communities.

How Religious Beliefs and Practices Relate to Social Behaviour

Given the historic role of secularization and the rise of science, we are surprised to find that religious institutions continue to exist and, indeed, continue to play a more important role in the lives of Canadians than many have suggested. Roughly one-third of adult Canadians attend church at least once a month, but more than half conduct their own private religious activities, such as praying, meditating, worshipping, or reading sacred texts, for example. This means that church attendance, on its own, is not an accurate measure of religiosity in Canada.

A more useful indicator devised by Statistics Canada is the "religiosity index," which includes four dimensions of religious adherence: (1) affiliation, (2) attendance, (3) personal practices, and (4) stated importance of religion. According to this measure, 40 per cent of Canadians have a low degree of religiosity; 31 per cent, a moderate degree; and 29 per cent, a high degree. Measured religiosity is highest among older people, women, and people from religious families, especially families in which both parents had the same or a similar religious background (for example, where both parents were raised as Catholics).

Still, fewer Canadians are highly religious today than they were in the past (see Figure 5.1). This decline in religiosity has been most marked in Quebec. Since 1960, church participation in Quebec has declined dramatically, due to a view of the dominant Roman Catholic Church as anti-modern, oppressive, and pro-establishment. In the past 50 years, Quebec has been consistently less religious than the rest of Canada. For example, Quebeckers have turned their back on Church teachings about birth control, abortion, and marriage. In these and other ways, Quebec has rejected a great deal of their religious inheritance.

Embeddedness as a Form of Social Control

Nonetheless, religious sentiment remains strong in most modern Western societies. To explain why religion has remained an important institution in society, Durkheim drew upon the idea of *social immersion*—a concept that remains useful today in understanding religiosity. Stroope (2012) notes that immersion in a group or network pushes individuals to bring their beliefs into conformity with those of other members of the group. **Embeddedness**

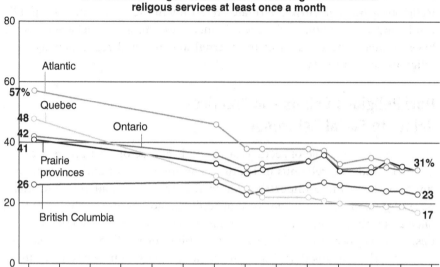

% of Canadians ages 15 and older in each region who attend religous services at least once a month

Figure 5.1 Changing Religiosity across Canada
Source: Pew Research Centre. (2013, 27 June). Canada's changing religious landscape. Retrieved from http://www.pewforum
.org/2013/06/27/canadas-changing-religious-landscape/

or immersion in a religious social network increases the likelihood that an individual's behaviour will be monitored by other members of the network who are seen on a frequent basis. This monitoring serves to remind members of their commitment to the beliefs and values that the group holds.

James Coleman (1990) uses the term "closure" to capture this phenomenon. Networks with a high degree of closure—in which people all tend to know one another or, at least, the friends and family of one another—are especially likely to monitor and sanction people. Equally, people whose social ties are located in one particular network are subject to especially intense pressure to conform (Blau & Schwartz, 1984; Granovetter, 1992). For example, Cornwall (1989) finds that a high proportion of friendships in a religious congregation results in a stronger average religious commitment.

Similarly, social embeddedness in a religious congregation is associated with higher levels of church participation among older adults (McIntosh, Sykes, & Kubena, 2002), even when other factors are statistically controlled for (Stroope, 2012). In fact, Cavendish, Welch, and Leege (1998) find that embeddedness in a Catholic parish is the strongest predictor of participation in such religious activities as Mass attendance, Bible study, and religious conversation. This kind of external religiosity can flourish even when the salience of religion in one's life is low (Ellison & Sherkat, 1995). That is because religious social networks put pressure on people to conform to religious norms, even if they do not fully and wholeheartedly believe in them. Embeddedness serves to maintain religious belief by giving individuals the feeling that they are not alone in their quest to better understand God or strive for religion's promised rewards.

People participate in religions, at least externally, because they want *social approval*—that is, they want to be regarded as an "exemplary" person by others in their network. Where the rewards and punishments associated with conformity are weaker—for example, among people embedded in a "liberal" congregation—the outward expression of religious behaviour is less consistent. By contrast, evangelical churches tend to discourage their members from involvement in secular activities. They also expect a stronger degree of commitment and religious participation from their members, delivering both positive and negative sanctions to ensure conformity (Ammerman, 2005).

Being embedded in a religious network increases engagement in religious activities, even when other factors are statistically controlled for (Stroope, 2012). Embeddedness also leads people to perform their religious duties faithfully, even if this performance is more enthusiastic than their inner devotion.

Divine Control

As we have seen, people experience social control when they participate actively in a religious congregation, network, or community; but some people also report experiencing "divine control." Schieman and Pudrovska (2003) define the sense of divine control as "the belief that God personally exerts a commanding authority over the life course and direction of one's life" (p. 2). People who report a strong sense of divine control typically believe that God controls all outcomes in their life, both good and bad, and that their fate is in God's hands (Schieman, Pudrovska, & Milkie, 2005). This belief in divine control is, for Schieman and Bierman (2007), a core facet of religious life.

Also, many religions—including Christianity—promote the idea that God intercedes in the lives of people, and has the capability to form a personal relationship with every human being (Ellison, Boardman, Williams, & Jackson, 2001). For example, *praying more often* increases a sense of personal relationship with God (Ellison, 1993). Prayer is believed to facilitate the entry of divine power into social spaces (Schieman & Bierman, 2007). By praying, people anticipate that God will enter into their life to influence their affairs (Williams, 2010). This notion is supported by present-day evidence that African-Americans are more likely to engage in religious activities, such as prayer, attendance at church services, and Bible study than other more advantaged demographic groups (Sherkat, 2002; Krause, 2003).

In short, people continue to embrace religion because doing so gives their lives meaning and supplies them with fellowship and social capital. The benefits of meaning and social capital, in turn, are reflected in measures of good health. For many people, religious faith contributes to their health and their ability to deal with sickness, which we will discuss next.

The Relationship between Religion and Health

Particular world views may be especially helpful when people enter *stressful circumstances or significant transitions* in their lives, such as illness, the loss of someone close, the loss of a job, or transition to long-term or nursing home care. At such times, religion may help to relieve suffering by offering a helpful interpretation of *physical or religious suffering* through a religious lens. In this way, religion can provide consolation in times of stress, and this support will have a positive effect on health.

McCullough and Smith (2003), reviewing scientific evidence of the relationship between religion and health, note that many studies have found that people who are devout report less worry, higher levels of well-being and life satisfaction, higher levels of marital satisfaction, more family cohesion, and a better ability to cope with stress; not surprisingly, they are also less likely to report symptoms of depression. The scientific evidence regarding this relationship is inconclusive, but much of the evidence points in this direction.

In short, religion helps people cope with stress, especially health-related stress. For example, Siegel, Anderman, and Schrimshaw (2001) found that religious beliefs and activities give people feelings of hope, acceptance, comfort, and strength, and these effects are especially strong among people with serious diseases, such as cancer, arthritis, and HIV/AIDS. In situations where people are unable to control the outcome of treatment, religion may offer them hope of divine intervention (Siegel et al., 2001). And because religious texts give many instances of the sick being healed, religion may help ill patients sustain hope for their own recovery (Ellison, 1994).

Religion also gives people a way to interpret and make sense of their illness. For instance, some cancer patients consider their illness to be a challenge from God, sent to strengthen their faith in Him (Taylor, 1983). Religious faith can also lower a person's fear of death by promising eternal rewards in another world to the person who lived a good life on earth. Also, people who think that God will never give them more than they can handle are likely to see an illness as a challenge they can overcome. People who use religion to cope with stressful life events feel connected to God's love, and find meaning and purpose in life (Graham, Furr, Flowers, & Burke, 2001).

Disadvantaged people are especially likely to turn to religion for these reasons, as Marx was the first to point out. Mary Abrums, in a piece appropriately entitled, "Jesus Will Fix It after Awhile" (2000), examines how oppressed people use religion to give their lives meaning and value (see Table 5.1). She used qualitative and ethnographic research methods to study a group of black women, their families, and their church leaders at Morning Sun Church in Seattle, Washington.

The women Abrums talked to were quick to express their love of God and distrust of health professionals and to highlight the difference between education and intelligence. Some of the women noted, "It is easier for the simple people to accept Jesus. If a mind is analytical, it's a little hard to get through to."

Regardless of what happened in their lives, members of the Morning Sun Church encouraged one another to count their blessings. The pastor helped his congregation cope with illness by ascribing meaning to it. He believed the best action an ill person could take was to pray: "When you got problems . . . what you need to do is Operation Pray." He added, "We'll try everything else and then we'll try Jesus last" (Abrums, 2000, p. 99). As well, church members agreed that they had to "acknowledge that their experience and power was limited, and they needed to turn their lives over to God." The goal of the church, according to the pastor, was to "be a hospital to all kinda people, a place where someone in distress can come and it rescues us from the forces that hurt us" (Abrums, 2000, p. 99).

These are women who believe in prayer and the power of the Holy Spirit. They had all, at one time or another, experienced major medical problems and suffered through poor medical care. Their experiences in the health-care system led to feelings of fear and distrust, which is often why they looked to their church for support. In these respects, their experiences were characteristic of people who live in poverty and are subjected to high levels of stress on an everyday basis. Their fears were based on actual experiences with life and death in the context of a mainly white, middle-class health-care system. Often, the health-care system treated them in a racist manner. Encounters with the health-care system and health professionals were often frustrating, a waste of time, and sometimes, even humiliating.

Some of the women in Abrums's study felt that they were being judged when they were in the health-care system. In particular, they felt that health

Table 5.1 Themes of Christianity in Low-Income Communities

Theme	Manifestation
Women's wisdom	• Education does not equal intelligence. • Experience is the most reliable knowledge.
God's relation to the body	• The body is a gift from God and is made in His image. • God controls the body and health.
Experiences with the health-care system	• These are overwhelmingly frightening and negative. • Experiences are associated with pain, death, and grief.
Race and the health-care system	• The health-care system is viewed as a threatening, white institution.
Taking power in the face of racism	• Their religious choices allow them to retake control of their bodies and health through God.

research had rarely been used to their benefit. Even those who had benefited from health research felt that African-Americans were the "guinea pigs" and looked worse on paper than they were in reality. They felt that statistics that "blamed the victims" hide the "essential" racism of American society that perpetuates systems of poverty and inequality.

Abrums's study showed how poor, disadvantaged women use religious meaning systems to interpret their own experiences and counter the dominant ideology. Doing so enables them to take control of *their own* healing, subject only to God's wishes. In short, religion allowed the women of Morning Sun to feel as though they had control over their own bodies and their own health, despite harsh social disadvantage and what to them was an unfeeling health-care system.

Religion, Socio-economic Status (SES), and Social Control

The women of Morning Sun Church may have felt empowered by religion, but Karl Marx viewed religion as a disempowering ideology—and, therefore, as a form of social control. He theorized that all religions support the *dominant ideology* of society—i.e., that set of values that benefits the most powerful members of society.

Recent research has continued to support Marxian claims about religion. For example, Schieman (2010) notes that people in disadvantaged socio-economic positions are more likely to try to "construct a bond" with God or a divine force to compensate for their low position. They also try to attain rewards in the afterlife, since they may be limited in attaining rewards in their earthly life. The available evidence shows that, accordingly, people of low socio-economic status (SES) are more likely to pray, report higher levels of interaction with the divine, engage more in religious coping, and believe in divine control—just as we saw with the women in the Morning Sun Church.

This notion is supported by present-day evidence that African-Americans—and other disadvantaged people—are more likely to engage in religious activities, such as prayer, attendance at church services, and Bible study than other more advantaged demographic groups (Sherkat, 2002; Krause, 2003). Relying on God to satisfy unmet needs and desires may help disadvantaged people to bear up under the adversity and hardships they face in everyday life. Because of their historic disadvantage, African-Americans have higher and more stable baseline levels of divine control than white Americans. However, it is disadvantage, not race, that accounts for this black–white difference. Equally disadvantaged white people are just as likely to believe in divine control, and disadvantaged people who participate in little religious activities also believe in divine control. Nowhere is this more evident than in the domain of health, as we have pointed out.

Of course, there are caveats to consider. Disadvantage is not the only pathway to faith; and people who are surrounded by religious ideas are likely to become more religious, regardless of their social position. Also, educated, less-disadvantaged people often play an important leadership role in religious communities. For example, they may give spiritual guidance by reading and interpreting religious texts, and by leading religious study sessions. As well, doctors may give other church members medical advice, lawyers may offer them legal advice, and accountants may offer them accounting advice. Finally, highly educated people also have larger social networks, hence more contact with other professionals, than other people, and they may use this to the benefit of their religious community.

So we can say with confidence that social advantage does not automatically decrease religiosity, nor does disadvantage automatically produce religiosity. But the tendencies are there, as Marx predicted. However, there are also national differences in the importance of religion and the effects of religion on social behaviour. Next, we will consider the differences in religiosity between Canada and the United States, and the different effects of religious institutions in each society.

Cross-Cultural Differences in Views of Religion

According to social analyst Michael Adams (1998), Canada lacks a historical ideology that has had a lasting influence like the "American Dream." This has resulted in socio-cultural differences between Canadians and Americans, especially with respect to the fundamental institutions of religion, the state, the marketplace, and the family. Canadians, at one time much more religious than Americans, are now much less religious than Americans. Adams (1998) notes, for example, that in the 1950s, 60 per cent

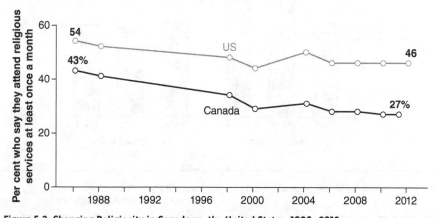

Figure 5.2 Changing Religiosity in Canada vs. the United States, 1986–2012
Source: Pew Research Center. (2013, 27 June). Canada's changing religious landscape. Retrieved from http://www.pewforum.org/2013/06/27/canadas-changing-religious-landscape/

of Canadians attended church regularly each Sunday; today, that number has dropped to 30 per cent, while in the United States, attendance continues to hover at around 40 per cent, little changed from the 1930s and 1940s.

In Canada, the Catholic and Anglican churches have played a huge role in society. They did so with explicit government approval, through constitutional provisions that protected Catholic and Protestant denominational schools in order to protect the two founding cultures. Ironically, by contrast, the American constitution demanded a separation of church and state. Today, however, most Judeo-Christian denominations are losing their hold on both societies. Many of the values traditionally associated with religious institutions have come under critical scrutiny, if they have survived at all. These traditional values include honour, duty, deference to state authority, patriarchal notions of family, and fear of divine retribution.

In Canada, religion has not so much disappeared as fragmented, with the majority of Canadians holding on to bits and pieces of traditional faith. Bibby (2002) notes that, in Canada, we now see a wide variety of beliefs. As Figure 5.3 illustrates, immigrants are more likely than the Canadian-born population to engage in both private and public religious practices (Statistics Canada, 2006). Yet immigrants are a widely diverse lot: Canadians with the highest levels of religiosity come from South Asia (e.g., Pakistan), while those with the lowest levels come from East Asia (e.g., China) and western and northern Europe.

Also, religious diversity is fostered by Canada's state policy of multiculturalism. The growing presence of non-Christian religions in North America

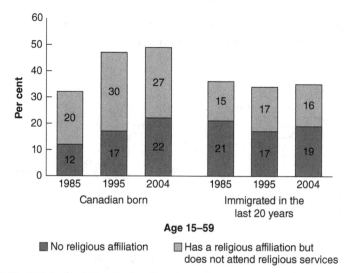

Figure 5.3 The Religiosity of Canadian Immigrants
Source: Statistics Canada. (n.d.). *General Social Survey*. Retrieved from http://www.statcan.gc.ca/pub/11-008-x/2006001/c-g/4097586-eng.htm

has increased people's cultural and religious consciousness; and eventually, it may even slow or reverse the trend toward secularization. Canada is doing everything it can to protect religious diversity. Consider the example of Gurbaj Multani, who brought to school a kirpan—a ceremonial dagger that symbolizes the Sikh faith. In March of 2006, the Supreme Court of Canada ruled unanimously that an existing ban on the kirpan in schools violated the Canadian Charter of Rights and Freedoms by infringing on the Charter's guarantees of religious freedom.

Immigrants aside, in Canada and Europe religion is losing some of its importance, thus curtailing its role in social control. But is present-day society becoming less religious, and is religion compatible with what we call "secularization"?

Secularization Theory

The seeds of *religious secularization* were sown during the Enlightenment, a period in which more and more people came to oppose arbitrary power and religious superstition, and the hierarchies they supported (such as the aristocracy and clergy of revolutionary France). Enlightenment thinkers, between 1650 and 1800, favoured free inquiry, the study of nature, individual autonomy, private property, equality under law, and, above all, liberty. They looked for natural (or universal) laws of justice and equality, and supported the scientific method as a means of finding the truth. Everywhere, the Enlightenment challenged religious orthodoxy and the blind faith that religious institutions demanded. The result was a centuries-long contest between science and religion.

Religions, on the whole, are committed to creating and preserving order, while sciences are not. But secularization is not primarily about the triumph of science. It is about the steadily dwindling influence of religion in public life, due to the continued differentiation and specialization of social institutions. *Secularization theory* seeks to explain why many religious institutions have lost their control over society. Of course, public institutions in our society and others still close during Christmas, Easter, and other Christian holidays, although not during the holidays of other religions. So organized religion—especially Christianity—remains embedded in our society. On the other hand, many people find religion irrelevant to their day-to-day lives.

Three features are commonly associated with secularization (see Table 5.2), and we see them throughout the modern, industrial world:

1. *Social differentiation*: This is the process by which a society becomes increasingly complex and diverse. In the past, churches—besides being centres for worship—also taught children basic skills, supported people in need, cared for the sick, served as meeting places, and organized social events. In modern societies, these social functions are split among

Table 5.2 Features of Secularization

Feature	Description	Effect
Social differentiation	• Increasingly diverse and complex societal institutions have more impact in people's lives.	• Social functions become run by many institutions, not just by the church.
Societalization	• People connect with an abstract society rather than a concrete community.	• People relate to and interact with society at large rather than with a small religious community.
Rationalization	• This is the tendency to explain the world through use of the scientific method and empirical evidence.	• People are less willing to accept things on faith alone and grow skeptical of religious doctrine.

many separate institutions: schools, hospitals, government agencies, and social clubs, for example.

2. *Societalization*: This refers to the way people increasingly connect to an abstract "society" and not to a concrete community in which every person knows everyone else. In North America and Europe today, most people look to "society"—a large, shapeless unit made up of organizations run on bureaucratic principles—to provide for their needs. Interaction with this impersonal and bureaucratic type of society leaves little room for religion, which people increasingly view as marginal to their lives and, at best, a lifestyle choice.

3. *Rationalization*: This represents an effort to explain the world through the systematic or scientific interpretation of empirical evidence. This emphasis on rationality has largely replaced the traditional reliance on religious texts and beliefs with a reliance on empirical evidence, scientific thinking, and non-religious "rule of law." As Max Weber pointed out, rationalization is a key feature of all modern social organizations, found in every social institution.

We are far from seeing the establishment of large and powerful communities of atheists and agnostics as alternative communities for people who were formerly religious. That said, certain religions (like Unitarianism) might serve that purpose for people who have rejected an earlier, stricter religious code. Far more commonly, people simply leave their church (or temple or synagogue) and work out their own pattern of religious observance, if any. To the extent that people seek and receive support in their new religious activities, they may do so through religious out-marriage; and patterns of religious out-marriage are steadily increasing in North American society.

Religion may be less apparent in today's world, but it is not completely absent, and it continues to show up in different aspects of people's lives. The power of religion to exert its influence on people may be decreasing overall, but it does continue to play a role in many people's lives (see Box 5.1).

**Box
5.1**   Religious Fundamentalism

What we have discussed so far sounds pleasant and benign, and we mustn't forget that we are discussing the regulatory as well as integrative aspects of social control. Nowhere is religion more controlling than among fundamentalists. *Fundamentalism* is the belief that religious adherents—whether Christian, Muslim, Jewish, or otherwise—should strictly follow the theological doctrines that are claimed to be the oldest, most traditional, and most basic.

Christian fundamentalism first arose in the United States in the late nineteenth century. By the early decades of the twentieth century, it had spread to conservatives among the Baptists and other strict Protestants. Christian fundamentalists think that whatever is written in sacred religious texts is literally true in fact. They emphasize a strict belief in such tenets of Christianity as the virgin birth of Christ and the historical reality of the miracles attributed to Christ. Today, American fundamentalists are noted for their opposition to abortion and their support for a traditional, male-dominated family.

Fundamentalist thinkers and leaders have been criticized for their unyielding approach to political issues. They have most often been criticized for hanging on to beliefs and making claims—such as creationism—that are irrational, resistant to empirical evidence, and devoid of scientific support. Most religious fundamentalists are also opposed to homosexuality. In these ways, fundamentalism opposes modern values of tolerance and liberality in the political arena. Most fundamentalist groups are non-violent, but the rate of violence by religious fundamentalists is increasing, especially around issues like abortion.

Conclusion

Religion has far from outlived its usefulness, nor lost all its power, in Canadian society. As we have seen, there are still many Canadians who are open to religion, if religion appeals to them in the right way. However, because a multiplicity of religions coexist in North America today, religious groups will have to work together if they want to see organized religion continue in Canada's future.

In many ways, we can see that religion remains an important kind of social control even in modern, industrial societies, although its role is far weaker today than it was in traditional rural communities of the past. And while people—even modern, urban people—continue to seek meaning and guidance from religion, they are less willing than in the past to accept control by religious bodies. That said, we see a great variation in this respect among immigrants in Canada, depending on the religion, country of origin, and length of time since arrival. Generally, immigrants assimilate and secularize, just like native-born Canadians.

In this chapter, we have considered how religion controls people's behaviour, and how modernizing societies in the West struggled to control religion. We have also considered how people's interactions with others are shaped by their socialization and integration into religious communities. We have also addressed how adherence to various religious beliefs tends to vary across social statuses like race and class, reflecting, as Karl Marx pointed out, social disadvantage.

Finally, we have discussed the extent to which secularization operates in a modern society, and we have considered a powerful, anti-modern source of religious control: religious fundamentalism. Altogether, this chapter has shown that religion continues to operate as a source of socialization and control.

Questions for Critical Thought

1. Do you think secularization theory is correct? Why or why not?
2. How has the social control exerted by religion affected your life? Has your life been affected by a religion other than your own?
3. What factors, in addition to income and education, might affect religiosity? How so?
4. Should the state ever make laws concerning religion? Why or why not?
5. How do various religions exert social control differently? Can you think of any examples?

Recommended Readings

Beaman, L.G., & Beyer, P. (Eds.). (2008). *Religion and diversity in Canada*. Leiden; Boston: Brill.
The essays that make up this book explore the many diversities of religion in Canada today, including the different ways people have adopted a variety of religious practices into their everyday lives.

Dawson, L.L. (2006). *Comprehending cults: The sociology of new religious movements* (2nd ed.). Don Mills, ON; New York: Oxford University Press.
The author summarizes major theories of cult formation, examines the type of people that are most likely to join cults, and discusses various issues surrounding cults, such as social stigma.

Habermas, J., & Ratzinger, J. (2006). *The dialectics of secularization: On reason and religion*. San Francisco: Ignatius Press.
This book by two contemporary thinkers—Joseph Ratzinger (Pope Benedict XVI) and Jurgen Habermas (a sociologist and neo-Marxist social critic)—provides a balanced and provocative discussion about secularization.

Reitman, J. (2011). *Inside Scientology: The story of America's most secretive religion*. New York: Houghton Mifflin Harcourt Publishing Company.
This book is a comprehensive journalistic history of the Scientology movement, using confidential documents and interviews with ex-members and officials.

Thomas, R.M. (2006). *Religion in schools: Controversies around the world.* Praeger
    Publishers.
    The author, using case studies from 12 countries and all regions of the world, as well as
        all major religions, analyzes the conflict of religion in schools and addresses the
        causes of the conflict and its consequences.

Recommended Websites

Beliefnet
www.beliefnet.com/
    Beliefnet is an online compendium of information about world religions. It provides
        tools for exploring faith and spirituality from a multi-faith perspective. It has news
        reports, entertainment, discussions, book reviews, and so on from many different
        religious perspectives.

Pew Forum: Religion and Public Life
www.pewforum.org/
    Pew Research's Religion and Public Life Project offers many different statistics
        and poll results concerning religion. Pew has information regarding many differ-
        ent countries on an extremely diverse range of topics.

Statistics Canada Religion Page
www.statcan.gc.ca/search-recherche/bb/info/3000017-eng.htm
    Statistics Canada offers a wide variety of information about demographics in
        Canada. This page contains entries related to religion, comparing them with other
        categories.

6 Media and Mass Communication as Social Control

Learning Objectives

◎ To understand how the media acts as a form of social control

◎ To define and apply the idea of *conceptual entrapment*

◎ To think critically about how the advent of the Internet has affected and continues to affect our relationship to the media

◎ To understand the different forces that affect media bias

◎ To think critically about how different demographics are treated in the media

◎ To understand how the media affect violent behaviour

Introduction

The mass media have assumed an ever more important role in modern life over the past century. As the media have multiplied—from books to newspapers, radio, movies, television, and the Internet—our ways of seeing the world have been transformed forever. People today do not merely receive more information than any humans that ever lived; our ways of viewing reality have been transformed by the infinite reproduction of facts, ideas, and images, and by their seemingly authentic distortion.

To say the least, this has led to profound doubt about the nature of reality. Social critic John Berger, influenced by an earlier cultural critic, Walter Benjamin, remarks in his classic work *Ways of Seeing* that the modern means of cultural production have destroyed the authority of art by destroying its uniqueness and authenticity. He writes, "For the first time ever, images of art have become ephemeral, ubiquitous, insubstantial, available, valueless, free" (p. 32).

French cultural critic Jean Baudrillard goes even farther along these lines, claiming that the mass media have created a new culture in which we all learn—even prefer—to live in a state that author Umberto Eco has called "hyperreality," which is the simulation or representation of something that does not in fact exist. In effect, it is a dream of reality, not reality itself. It results when the line between the representation of a thing and the "real-life" thing being copied becomes blurred. According to the *Oxford Dictionary of Critical Theory*, Eco devised the term

> [. . .] to account for the particular attraction to Americans of waxwork museums, Ripley's "Believe it or Not!," and the seemingly relentless replication of icons of European culture, such as Las Vegas's mini Eiffel Tower. [. . .] Eco regards the logic behind such exhibitions as compensatory. For the lack of an authentic culture of its own, he argues, America creates pastiches of European culture. But because their inauthenticity cannot really be disguised, they strive to be more real than the original [. . .]. (pp. 238–9)

"Reality television" is one of many examples of hyperreality we find in mass media: with its contrived scenarios and scripted behaviours, it portrays a version of reality that does not and could not exist. Movies that evoke the past with props, sets, and costumes made of modern materials not available during the historical time the filmmakers are attempting to dramatize are another example. Paris Hilton, the Kardashians, and other supposed but insubstantial celebrities are hyperreal in the sense that they have become media representations of themselves; and the members of *Duck Dynasty*, likewise, dress up like hillbillies to simulate their imagined lack of wit and culture.

This process of producing artificiality and selling it as reality, according to Baudrillard and other cultural commentators, continually (and intentionally) blurs the line between fact and fiction. It confuses us under the guise of informing us. At the very least, we can agree that from a sociological perspective, the mass media control us by shaping us into a particular kind of people: innocent consumers.

We need to begin this chapter with a general warning: there will be somewhat more American content in this chapter than in other chapters of this book, for the simple reason that media influences are most extreme in the United States. Effects of the media in Canada—through American programming and pale imitations of American programming—are far less dramatic. So, if our goal is to understand how the media can create a hyperreality that controls us, we need to go to the source: the US media. Or, to say the same thing in Foucauldian terms, we need to look at American media as the source of "technologies of self" that control all media consumers in North America.

Media messages, through advertising and other content, teach us all *how* to be consumers; and in so doing, they integrate us in an international system of consumption. They also lead us to think about public issues in particular ways: for example, to vote in particular ways, just as they teach us to buy in particular ways. In political matters, the media set the public agenda. They identify which news stories will receive attention, decide how each story will be pitched, maintain stereotypes of powerless people (e.g., welfare mothers, black men, criminals), and even influence our behaviour (e.g., make us more violent).

Media are also complicit in creating and enforcing our notions of appearance and sexuality, as suggested in Chapter 2. Consider, for example, the sexualization of children in the media. We usually think of models as being young and sexy, but a recent wave of celebrity children in magazine photo shoots has raised awareness of just how young—and sexualized—some child models are. A notable case occurred in 2011, when then 13-year-old Elle Fanning—little sister of child actor Dakota Fanning—appeared, looking much older than her age, seductively clad in short dresses and full makeup in a spread for the arts and culture magazine *BlackBook*.

Girls' fashion has already begun to reflect the impact of the media's sexualization of children, with clothing retailers rushing to offer sexy styles to prepubescent girls. In recent years, Abercrombie Kids has sold padded bikinis and lacy camisoles to its young clientele, while La Senza Girl carries its own lines of lingerie marketed expressly to kids. The sexualization of young girls creates enormous problems for society.

According to Brigham Young University professor Heather Johnson, fashion designers and the media "set our girls up for horrible situations like eating disorders, low self-esteem, depression issues" by placing them in adult roles before they know how to handle them (as cited in HuffPost Living, Canada, 2011). The issue has arisen in part because many girls see fashion models as people whose lives they would like to emulate. A 2008 British survey of 13- to 18-year-old girls found that their top career choice was modelling. Among the respondents, 32 per cent aspired to be models, while 29 per cent dreamt of becoming actresses; only 14 per cent said they wanted to be scientists (Gould, 2008).

Experts say that the desire to model for pay originates from the misconception that models lead lives of glamour and ease. In fact, many accounts of modelling depict a highly stressful lifestyle, with low pay, long hours, and job scarcity. Unaware of these harsh realities, little girls like the idea of being paid to be attractive—a sign that they are already used to their bodies being seen, and valued, as objects. Influenced by advertising and other media representations, girls may abandon comfortable play clothes in favour of fashions that make them look more grown up. As Queen's University professor Jane Tolmie states, the fashion industry, through the media, "is using young girls to send a message to adults everywhere, male and female, about what is desirable" (as quoted in SexyTypewriter, 2011).

Media and Social Control: Creating Hyperreality

Formally defined, the **mass media** are large organizations that use technology to communicate with large numbers of people. They have two important sociological characteristics: first, using mass media, a very few people are able to communicate to a great number; and, second, the audience for this communication has no effective way of answering back. Sociologists ask, how do these media messages control us, and who controls these powerful media?

According to Gamson, Croteau, Hoynes, and Sasson (1992), media-generated images of the world interpret the social world around us, from the perspective of the political and economic elites who control its content and dissemination. For this reason, understanding the *control of knowledge* is central to our understanding of how powerful elites maintain their power and control over our behaviour (Donahue, Tichenor, and Olien, 1973). For Donahue and colleagues, the mass media is an institution that serves to reinforce the social system. In that sense, the mass media provide a type of *social control* over everyone.

As we will see, the media have a sorting or filtering function in public affairs. They serve as "gatekeepers" by choosing to put an issue on the public agenda, or not. Bringing the issue to public awareness is a way of influencing public opinion.

Shaw and Martin (1992, pp. 902–3) say that the media perform this function by "providing a limited and rotating set of public issues around which the political and social system can engage in dialogue." Lens (2002) also sees the media as a "channel of communication" through which elected officials send messages. Zaller (1992), for instance, sees the media as a "mouthpiece" for the political elite, which provides a selective and stereotyped view of reality that conforms to the dominant group's ideology.

Of course, people are not just passive recipients of mainstream communication. They evaluate information they receive from the media; and they receive and evaluate information from other sources, too (such as their friends). The "two-step flow of communications" (Katz and Lazarsfeld, 1955) concept posits a movement of information and ideas from the media to "opinion leaders," and from them to other people in their social network.

So, messages from the mass media are not the only influences. Personal and informal sources also have a great impact. However, informal opinion leaders have a limited influence compared to the massive effects of the media. Except in the rarest of circumstances, when social movements form to resist their impact, mass media messages shape people's knowledge, attitudes, and behaviours—despite networks of interpersonal communication. As a result, consumers tend to accept media definitions of reality. But how, precisely, do the media "make news?"

To answer this question, Herbert Gans explored how the media set their agenda. In his classic study *Deciding What's News* (1979), Gans examined how real world events become the news that we see on television or read in the newspaper. Gans (1979) studied four major news organizations: the CBS and NBC news network, and *Time* and *Newsweek* news journals. To gain information for his study, he carried out extensive participant observation at the four companies, interviewing personnel at all levels. Additionally, he performed a content analysis on 3500 news stories that spanned a period of eight years.

Gans found that news reporting is concerned with gaining and keeping the attention of a mass audience. As such, it includes stories that appeal to a mass audience, such as stories about famous people, sex and scandal, and violence. Second, he found that national news reporting works in the interests of people in high social positions and avoids embarrassing the network owners or their friends. Third, despite the particular self-interest of media organizations, Gans found a strong consensus among news organizations on key values such as individualism, a belief in responsible capitalism, and a desire for social order and strong national leadership. Gans also noted "efficiency and source power are parts of the same equation, since it is efficient for journalists to respect the power of official sources" (Gamson et al., 1992, p. 375).

To understand the role of economic power, Bagdikian (1990) focused on media ownership. He concluded that concentrated ownership of media narrows the range of information that is disseminated: "Contrary to the diversity that comes with a large number of small, diverse, media competitors under true free enterprise, dominant giant firms that command the nature of the business produce an increasingly similar output" (Gamson et al., 1992, p. 376). When the number of corporate owners is reduced, so, too, is the range of interests and political views.

Whatever the number of owners, the pressure for media corporations to turn a profit and to protect the images of corporations influences journalists to err on the "politically safe" side. For Schiller (1989), the media speak with "'corporate voice' . . . across the entire range of cultural expression" (Gamson et al., 1992, p. 380). Barthes (1973) goes even further, suggesting that the media serves to legitimate the entire bourgeois culture, making it appear both normal and universal.

A few large multinational corporations have now become global media "empires" that own large numbers of newspapers, TV stations, magazines, publishing houses, and movie studios. This concentration becomes problematic when corporations own both the production houses and the media distributors because this guarantees that a captive audience will hear the same message. While the potential exists for more diverse interests to be heard in the global age, this is unlikely to come to fruition because "when new technologies conducive to increasingly diverse and smaller scale mass communication emerge, commercial market forces and deeply ingrained media habits pull back hard in the other direction" (Neuman, 1991 as cited in Gamson 1992, p.379). The result of global media ownership, then, has been an increase in the volume of media produced but not an increase in diversity.

Even if more competition is introduced through the presence of a larger number of media organizations, all of the organizations will have to maximize profit to survive, inevitably leading to the same reporting as other organizations. Similarly, Entman (1989) argues that media competition does *not* result in better quality news. But Gamson et al. (1992) propose that Entman fails to consider other issues related to the media, such as advertising and the integration of new global media sources.

Advertisers are concerned with maximizing the size and "quality" of their audiences (i.e., attracting people who have the most purchasing power and the most potential interest in buying their products). Accordingly, advertisers influence programmers and editors to display content that puts viewers in a "buying mood." Herman and Chomsky (1988) note that corporate advertisers will have little interest in sponsoring media content that targets audiences who are unlikely to buy their products or that displays images that are critical of corporations. Additionally, advertisers will likely not sponsor "disturbing" material since this will not facilitate "buying moods" in viewers. Dull and predictable news stories and programs, on the other hand, make ads seem more interesting to viewers because they are more likely to be seen as "fresh" or innovative.

Given their goal—to attract viewers and turn them into buyers—the media play a role in setting the public agenda. As Herbert Gans noted, news reporting is concerned with gaining and keeping a mass audience so it includes (and even features) stories that appeal to a mass audience: stories about famous people, violence and bloodshed, sex and scandal. Even the national news attracts viewers and furthers the interests of people in high positions.

From this standpoint, we can view the mass media as a mechanism promoting unreality—that is, an imagined or socially constructed picture of reality that suits the interests of the powerful. In this endless struggle, disadvantaged groups—e.g., the working poor, women, racial and ethnic minorities, and gays and lesbians—tend to be both *under*-represented and *mis*represented in mainstream media.

Imagining Disadvantaged Groups: Welfare Mothers

According to Lens (2002), public policy is largely built around public images and image-making. To repeat, we will examine this mainly in the American context because the media effects are most dramatic there. In recent times, public assistance programs have become unpopular with members of society. Indeed, poverty has come to be equated with dependency, and, as a result, policies tend to focus on reforming welfare recipients rather than on reforming the social system (e.g., labour markets) that keep them in poverty.

Media representations of the social world tend to distort objective reality. Consider one such distortion: the imaginary welfare recipient and, especially, the imaginary "welfare mother." The media typically depict these less advantaged and vulnerable groups in a negative light, if they portray them at all.

Consider how the media depict poor African-American mothers receiving public assistance. Maura Kelly (2010) found that television news was critical of the behaviour of such welfare mothers, particularly African-Americans. The "welfare mother" image is often used in reference to women of various races and ethnicities (including European-Americans). But mainly, the image is used in reference to African-American women, and 58 per cent of public assistance recipients profiled in the news stories are African-American. Blacks, overall, are over-represented in media depictions of welfare recipients compared to their actual use of welfare programs (Somers & Block, 2005). Indeed, news coverage over-represents African-Americans in images of public assistance recipients, uses racialized language, and deploys racist stereotypes associated with the welfare mother image. The stories featuring African-Americans (58 per cent) significantly over-represent the percentage of African-American welfare recipients (39 per cent), which is consistent with research that has shown that Americans believe that more blacks are on welfare than actual statistics suggest (Gilens, 1999). By contrast, European-Americans are under-represented in news stories about welfare. And Canada isn't immune to the negative portrayals of welfare recipients who belong to racial minorities. As Harell and Soroka (2010) found, Canadians had less support for social assistance programs when recipients were Aboriginals than when the recipients were white or members of a different racial minority group.

In typical stories, media used racially coded language to inflame the audience. This language stressed "dependency" and "culture of poverty" in connection with welfare. In these stories, women on public assistance were explicitly stereotyped as childlike, hyper-fertile, lazy, and bad mothers. Even employed women are not immune to negative portrayals in the media. For instance, Gazso (2004) found that women's unequal experience in workplaces when compared to men was depicted to be a result of their "inability" to fit in because of their difficulties in achieving work–family balance. Putting these pieces together, the stereotypical "welfare mother" was portrayed as trapped on welfare due to her unintelligence or childlike nature; the stereotypical "welfare queen" was also portrayed as abusing the system for personal gain. In this way, hyperreality is created and sold to us as "the truth." As we can see from the data in Figure 6.1, there is a considerable distance between the real demographics of social insurance and the media representation of black welfare mothers and welfare queens.

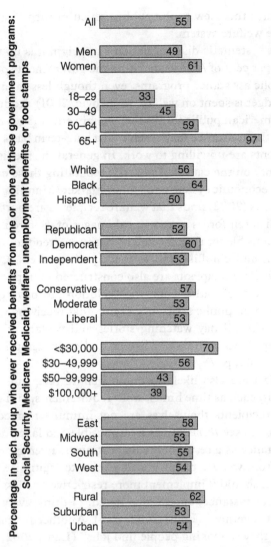

Figure 6.1 The Demographics of Social Insurance (percentage in each group who ever received benefits from one or more government programs)
Source: From Morin, R., Taylor, P., and Patten, E. (2012, 18 December). A bipartisan nation of beneficiaries. Pew Research Center. Retrieved from http://www.pewsocialtrends.org/2012/12/18/a-bipartisan-nation-of-beneficiaries/

Shaping Public Perception of the Welfare System

The media, then, have tended to portray welfare recipients and poor people more generally in a negative way. Like welfare mothers, the "undeserving poor" are more likely to be portrayed as black than as white. Additionally, welfare recipients, often portrayed as African-American mothers and teen mothers, are conceptualized as the "other." De Goede (1996) concludes that the media are not an objective provider of information but, rather, an institution that draws on the dominant, conservative explanations for poverty and disseminates this view to the public, which in turn shapes public perceptions of the welfare system.

Given this systematic disinformation campaign, it is no wonder that in polls, over 50 per cent of Americans think the government spends too much money on public assistance programs, even though less than 10 per cent of the overall budget is spent on welfare (Sotirovic, 2001). Additionally, a majority of the American public thinks that welfare encourages recipients to be dependent on the assistance they receive on a long-term basis and that many welfare recipients are unwilling to work. In general the media put an "individualistic slant" on the causes of poverty, separating these causes from the realities of the economic system and labour market (Manning-Miller, 1994).

Overall, Lens (2002) finds that welfare recipients are portrayed in a negative light, which reinforces stereotypical images of welfare recipients as individually responsible for their fates. The narratives tend to frame recipients as incompetent and childlike and as inadequate workers. Quotes in news sources from welfare recipients are also constructed to implicate the welfare system as the "cause" rather than the "solution" to poverty. One source quoted a woman on public assistance saying that receiving welfare allowed her to "lay in bed all day watching stories and welfare will pay the rent and food stamps," which became "like an addiction, tempting you to sit at home" (Lens, 2002, p. 7).

The media were also likely to quote welfare recipients agreeing with welfare reforms, such as time limits, work requirements, and the family cap. Even welfare recipients themselves are not immune to media portrayals. They may come to see *themselves* as irresponsible and lazy and undeserving of public assistance as a result of media portrayals. Even more importantly, these quotes from welfare recipients also serve to legitimize the actions of the government should it implement more restrictive and less generous welfare policies. For instance, one woman noted, "I think five years is enough to get your act together" (Lens, 2002, p. 8). Another recipient stated, "It was good that they're making people find jobs" (Lens, 2002, p. 8). Welfare recipients were also quoted in the media for expressing gratitude for being placed into a work program, as it "kind of put a light on things. It was time to get off public aid, raise my kids, maybe send them off to college and meet my destiny" (Lens, 2002, p. 8).

Perpetuating Racial Stereotypes Surrounding Crime

A similar problem besets media discussions of crime. Here, the problem is the media's tendency to portray criminality by black men as inevitable, uncontrollable, and inexplicable. In large part, the problem comes down to racially biased news reporting.

In a study of racial bias in crime reporting, Dennis Rome (2004) notes that the *positive* image of violent *white* Americans as social bandits was carried well into the post-WWII era. During the early to mid-twentieth century, "almost every boy in America wanted to be Jesse James, the strong, fearless bandit who came to symbolize the individuality of the American West," he says. This image effectively "white-washed" the seriousness of *white* violence in the American consciousness through a process of turning attention away from the horror of white predatory crime and refocusing it on fabricated, overly romanticized biographies.

By contrast, *black* violence was seen as dark and threatening. In painting black criminals as socially undesirable, white-dominated American media use their social status to vilify less powerful people. To do so, they make use of an official preoccupation with "street crime," using information from the racially biased Uniform Crime Reports (UCR)—established in 1930.

The evidence shows that minority communities are policed more intensively than other communities, leading to more arrests. In fact, only

Box 6.1   Uniform Crime Reports and Race

The Uniform Crime Reports (UCR) are divided into two parts: *Index* (or Part 1) *Crimes* include major felonies that are believed to be serious and have a high likelihood of being reported by the police. These felonies include murder, rape, robbery, burglary, and motor theft. Part 2 Crimes include offences that are more common and less dangerous to life and limb, such as embezzlement, forgery, counterfeiting, and running away. That is to say, it largely excludes white-collar and probably most middle-class related crimes. (White-collar crime includes such crimes as stock market fraud, price-fixing, product misrepresentation, corporate tax evasion, industrial pollution, maintenance of unsafe working conditions, and illegal intervention in the political process.)

African-Americans are typically underrepresented; and whites, overrepresented in white-collar crimes. The opposite is true of street crimes, including Index Crimes. Therefore, the selection of crimes called "Index Crimes" is skewed away from criminal activities in which whites are over-represented—thus, biased away from middle-class and elite-white "suite" crimes (i.e., white-collar crimes), exaggerating the relative amount of criminality by poor, black perpetrators.

And it is not only the conventional UCR Crime Index that is biased toward blacks and blue-collar offenders. Police exercise wide latitude in their decision-making authority when dealing with minor offences and, at these times, police discretion is strongly influenced by the perpetrator's race and class. Indeed, police are most likely to arrest people they perceive as "troublemakers," and are less likely to arrest middle-class, white, and prominent citizens.

25 per cent of arrested white youths go to adult prison versus 60 per cent of arrested black youths. Other things being equal, black and Latino youths with no prior record of crime are treated far more severely than whites in the juvenile-crime system. To summarize, minority youths are more likely than white youths to be arrested, held in jail, sent to juvenile or adult court for trial, convicted, and given lengthy prison terms.

These racial disparities result mainly from the stereotypes decision makers apply at each point in the juvenile justice system. Being black; wearing low-hung, baggy pants; and sporting dreadlocks: these are all appearance features likely to put a person into prison, other things being equal. Part of the problem here also lies with the mass media, which often, depict African-Americans as criminals (or "gangstas"). The media imply that African-Americans are disproportionately likely to be involved in crime and that they are responsible for most of the crime in America today.

Television news programs, for example, present crime in a way that misrepresents or distorts the propensity of African-Americans toward crime. Indeed, Dixon and Linz (2000a) found that African-Americans are twice as likely as whites to be portrayed as perpetrators of crime on local television news. In addition, African-Americans are more likely to appear as perpetrators of crime than as enforcers or officers of crime; the opposite is true for whites. As well, African-Americans are over-represented in the media as perpetrators when compared to the numbers listed in official crime reports. Similarly, Entman (1992) discovered that African-Americans are more likely than whites to have their mug shots displayed and to be handcuffed on television news and local programs.

On the other hand, whites tend to be portrayed in either positive or "benign" roles on local television news programs (Dixon and Linz, 2000b). For instance, whites are over-represented as homicide victims, compared to the reality. They are also more likely to be portrayed as victims than as perpetrators of crimes. Moreover, whites are over-represented as police officers on television news programs and in reality-based television programming, compared to official employment records.

These negative stereotypes also play an important part in supporting harsh treatment of blacks by the police. Such treatment is a continuation of the treatment of black people during and after slavery in the US. Consider the "myth of the black rapist:" during the 1850s, the "myth of the black rapist" was used to legitimize lynching. Today, a similar image is used to perpetuate white society's fear and subjugation of African-Americans—especially, black men.

Southern whites, believing that all black men wanted sex with white women, were in part justifying their own secret access to black slave women that they had long enjoyed. To justify their continued sexual subjugation of black women, white men had come to view black women as highly sexed animals who encouraged, even welcomed, their own violation. By contrast, they viewed Southern white women as "exquisite, fine, beautiful; creatures of peach blossoms and snow, languid, delicate, saucy; now imperious, now melting, always bewitching" (Page, 1905, p. 162).

These beliefs about the over-sexualization of both black men and black women are the result of racial hoaxes: false beliefs that, like moral panics, serve to justify oppressive and violent behaviour by the dominant social group. In other societies, we find hoaxes about other religious groups, ethnic groups, or social classes. In every instance, they are used to justify discrimination, vigilantism, and violence. In many instances, they justify biased treatment by agents of the law.

The importance of historic stereotypes reminds us that laws are made and enforced by the most powerful social group. In every society, the criminal justice system works to secure and protect the needs of the powerful. When people develop behaviour patterns that conflict with those needs, agents of the powerful (i.e., the justice system) define them as criminals (Quinney, 1974). As a result, in a socially stratified society, people have different probabilities of being defined as criminal, depending on their position in the social hierarchy. In turn, this means that poor people and black people—and especially, poor black males—are going to be imprisoned or killed. And as we see from the data in Figure 6.2, many of these killings will result from the operation of white-friendly Stand Your Ground laws in the US.

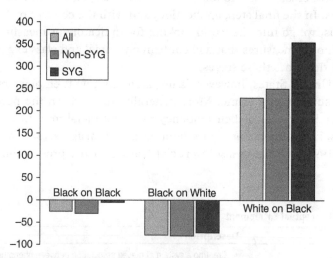

Figure 6.2 Stand Your Ground Killings Perceived as Self-Defence by Race
*SYG refers to Stand Your Ground laws.
Note: Stand Your Ground (SYG) laws in the United States permit killing in self-defence.
Source: From Childress, S. (2012, 31 July). Is there racial bias in "Stand Your Ground" laws? PBS *Frontline*. Retrieved from http://www.pbs.org/wgbh/pages/frontline/criminal-justice/is-there-racial-bias-in-stand-your-ground-laws/

Conceptual Entrapment

Most directly relevant to our current discussion of the mass media, conceptions of crime are constructed and diffused by various means of communication. That is to say, the "social reality of crime" is constructed through the formulation and application of criminal definitions to different social groups. Thus, for Quinney, "social reality" is the world that powerful people create in their own interest. And the social world of crime and punishment is just as imaginary (and biased) as every other social world.

However, things believed to be real are real in their consequences, as sociologist W.I. Thomas once pointed out. Once people perceive ideas and stereotypes to be real, they go out and look for examples of these concepts. In doing so, they become trapped by their concepts about crime, leading Rome (2004) to suggest that a process of **conceptual entrapment** occurs when people are exposed to media imagery that contains bias. Media portrayal is, for Rome, the first step in conceptual entrapment.

Public actions support this media portrayal. For example, law enforcement is concentrated in lower-income and minority areas. People who are "well-off" do a better job of hiding their crimes from public exposure. And although white-collar and elite crimes "cost" society more than "street crimes," they often go unreported in the media.

Under conditions of *conceptual entrapment*, our actions make our fantasies come true. The first step of conceptual entrapment involves creating a self-perpetuating system of racial and class bias in the justice system, and the second step involves giving it a name: "crime." Then, we reify the system we have created. We no longer see "crime" as just a summary of media depictions. In the final step, application, and with the concept of "crime" in our minds, we go into the world looking for indicators or measures of this phenomenon—measures that will confirm our racial and class expectations. Table 6.1 describes these stages.

The United States, however, is not alone in how it employs racial stereotypes surrounding crime. More generally, research on the news media in Canada has revealed their tendency to depict racial minorities as social problems, including being high school dropouts, drug users, and homeless (Fleras, 1994). Crime is also a crucial feature in the production of news

Table 6.1 Conceptual Entrapment

Stage	Description
Construction	• Creating a system of biased association between phenomena
Conceptualization	• Understanding the system as a heuristic tool
Reification	• Internalizing and accepting the system
Application	• Looking for examples that confirm the system

in the Canadian context (Dowler, 2004). Similar research performed in Canada has also documented the racialization of crime.

In one study, a survey was given to Canadian participants that demonstrated a widespread belief that blacks were more prone to committing crimes. In fact, almost half of the participants believed that race directly affected criminality, whereby blacks commit more crimes than any other social group (Henry, Hastings, and Freer, 1996). Similarly, Dowler, Fleming, and Muzzatti (2006) found that victims of crimes who are racial minorities received much less attention in mainstream news coverage.

While our focus in this chapter has been overwhelmingly on the US, these findings suggest that the Canadian media, much like their American counterparts, are not fair or objective in their presentation of racial minorities, particularly surrounding crime. This is problematic since the news media wield a considerable amount of power in choosing which images of racial minorities to present to the general public.

In sum, then, news media constructions of groups of people provide a "heuristic" or "mental shortcut" that significantly influences policy decisions (Dixon, Azocar, & Casas, 2003). Negative stereotypes of African-Americans, then, lead the public to believe that the subordinate group is deserving of harsh treatment (Rome, 2004). In this perspective, crime is a social text or narrative whose writers are human agents. We can only combat this process by "deconstructing crime" and forcing the media to stop dramatizing it.

However, our desires to do this are stymied by monopoly media ownership in the hands of the few. As we see in Box 6.2, this problem may diminish with the continued rise of the Internet as a source of news and opinion that is outside the control of any powerful interest groups.

Social Media: Giving Voice to the "Ordinary" Person

Twitter and Facebook are prominent social media websites that are deserving of attention in contemporary society. You need only look around at the laptop screens in a university lecture hall to see the effect they have had on students! Social media can be thought of as a forum for "everyday" people (as opposed to professional journalists) to create "user-generated news," defined very broadly.

In fact, the "social" aspect of social media derives in opposition to traditional forms of media. Facebook and Twitter (particularly Twitter) allow for interaction with people that one does not know personally, such as celebrities or authors. This is contrasted with social network sites such as LinkedIn, where users create public or semi-public profiles of relevant credentials, skills, contact information, and current occupational position, which only allow for interactions with people that are immediately known or recognized as someone one would like to be in direct contact with for occupational reason.

Box 6.2

How the Internet Affects Our Relationship with the Media

We noted earlier that privately owned media tend to distort the reporting of news events. If you are wondering whether media ownership poses problems for political life, just consider a 2014 event in Canadian politics. After a week of editorials during the lead-up to the provincial election in Ontario, the nation's leading newspaper, *The Globe and Mail*, finally endorsed Tim Hudak's Conservative Party. On Election Day (12 June 2014), the blog Canadaland leaked information from insiders at *The Globe and Mail* making clear that the paper's editorial board had voted to support Kathleen Wynne's Liberal Party, but that this decision had been overturned at the last minute by *The Globe's* managing editor, David Walmsley. On this, Canadaland reports, "It is widely felt that Walmsley was carrying water for publisher Philip Crawley, who in turn was carrying out the orders of the Globe-controlling Thomson family, whose interests would be best served by a Conservative government" (Gavin, 2014).

In short, the media serve the interests of the owners of the media and act on behalf of those interests. And that leads us to wonder: can we avoid the problems of bias and distortion associated with privately owned media by producing our own content? If yes, this will happen through the Internet.

Today, the Internet is the first place we go to for information. The Internet has also made it possible to communicate simultaneously with multiple receivers and senders. For example, bloggers are able to present their independent thoughts with no overhead costs. Many Internet users are both information consumers and information producers. The Internet turns information into something to be shared and exchanged, rather than a commodity to be owned. As well, the Internet spreads information through non-mainstream media, circumventing the powerful owners of mass media.

But this does not eliminate fraudulent information. In computer-mediated relationships (CMRS), people come to think they know each other intimately much more quickly than they do in face-to-face relationships. This leads them to fantasize about their cyber-love objects, and such fantasies sometimes have real consequences in the real world. For example, such cyber-romances may reveal (for some) defects in a marital relationship that they had not previously noticed or that they had preferred to ignore. At the same time, partners may come to feel betrayed by such Internet intimacy, thinking that all intimacy —whether real or virtual, emotional or sexual—must remain within the boundaries of the marital relationship.

Web-based media sources such as Twitter are becoming much more interactive. For instance, people with Twitter accounts can subscribe to CBC's Twitter feed and comment on news articles that have been "tweeted." People can also "retweet" events or news stories from Twitter feeds they have subscribed to. In essence, tweets may be considered a public version of "status updates" on Facebook (Murthy, 2012).

Beyond the more obvious observation that tweets are another area of social life that is centred on "self-presentation," Murthy (2012) argues that Twitter represents a refreshing way for "ordinary" people to break their own news stories, comment on current stories, and voice their views through a public forum. Given that Twitter is organized around "events" that occur, it allows for the views of people to be expressed alongside those of traditional media outlets. One source people look to for opportunities to share their views is through "trending topics" on Twitter, which is a list of the most popular daily and weekly subjects, including new popular songs that people are listening to, celebrity gossip, and breaking news, such as election results, fatal shootings, or catastrophic weather.

This process operates in a different fashion than traditional media outlets because on Twitter, many trending topics can be traced back to one single tweet or a group of tweets from members of society who are not employed by traditional media outlets. In some instances, tweets may refer other subscribers to full-length news articles written on the particular subject.

In this way, rather than just accepting social media outlets like Facebook and Twitter as inevitabilities of our time, Murthy (2012) instead suggests that social media can help democratize the controlling practices of the media that we have documented thus far. Twitter may provide the media consumer with greater individual choice on what to follow—a choice that is not set by the agenda of elite dominated media outlets. As Murthy (2012) notes, "Twitter users are individual consumers who make reflective decisions on what information they want coming up on their Twitter feeds" (p.1070), thus potentially reducing some of the effect of the media in shaping news agendas in every instance. That said, much more work is necessary to examine the processes of news-making on social media outlets before we can make a more compelling case for the decline in significance of more traditional news outlets.

How the Media Control Our Views on Violent Behaviour

As we have seen, media depictions of race, poverty, crime, and punishment are merely backdrops to a public interest in danger and violence. The media make money from pandering to this interest in danger and violence. As the old newspaper dictum says, "If it bleeds, it leads." So, it is appropriate for us to ask the question, "Do the media really create and increase violent behaviour, or merely reflect it?" Finding an answer to this question is critical because, as we see in Figure 6.3, North Americans consume a huge amount of television—including television programming about violence—every week.

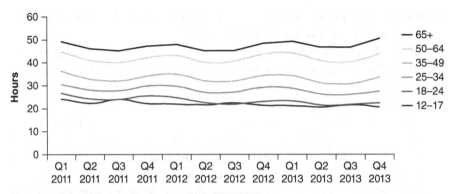

Figure 6.3 Television Consumption per Week, 2011–2013
Source: MarketingCharts. Are young people watching less TV? *MarketingCharts.com*. Retrieved from http://www.marketingcharts
.com/television/are-young-people-watching-less-tv-24817/

According to Gerbner (1995), the heavy consumption of television programming creates a population that is unnecessarily fearful. Television largely focuses on "happy violence," which is swift, painless, "cool," and even thrilling. It leads, typically, to a "happy ending" because its purpose is to entertain, not to upset. Most important, television exposes us to plenty of violence.

In these ways, television cultivates biased conceptions about life. To confirm this, Gerbner undertook a *"cultivation analysis"* of television content. His results suggest that, consistent with "mean world syndrome," heavy TV viewing promotes a stronger sense of fear and apprehension than one finds among light TV viewers. As a result, viewers who watch a great deal of television are more likely to overestimate their likelihood of being involved in violence, to think the neighbourhood they live in is unsafe, to admit that fear of crime is a serious personal problem, and to assume that crime rates are rising, whatever the facts may tell us. These viewers also come to be more accepting of an increase in the number of jails, of capital punishment, and of harsher sentences as a result of this fear.

Early studies claimed that media violence "triggers" physical aggression and creates a climate in which criminal and anti-social behaviours are more likely to occur. However, that assessment may be too simple. Barrie Gunter (2008) asks us to rephrase the question, in light of a subtler, current understanding of media effects. Today, we understand that other social factors also influence and shape the effects of media on our behaviour.

Exposure to media violence is neither a necessary nor sufficient condition for violent behaviour. For instance, extremely violent people may have the same exposure to media violence as normal, non-violent people (Hagell & Newburn, 1994). Likewise, many people who are heavy television viewers never display seriously aggressive or anti-social behaviour

(Ferguson, 2007). Moreover, historically, there have been periods of time when levels of violent crime were higher than or equal to contemporary levels (Gunter, 2008). In fact, in a major work of historical scholarship, Stephen Pinker (2011) argues that violence levels have been gradually and steadily declining over the past hundreds of years, with industrialization and "modernization," despite the spread of mass media.

Gunter (2008) notes that a limitation of cross-sectional surveys is that they collect data on only one occasion. For this reason, they cannot track changes that may occur over time, as children develop with respect to media exposure and patterns of social behaviour. Since exposure to media violence is hypothesized to be a cumulative "build-up" over time, retrospective surveys are one way of addressing this problem. Data are still collected at one period of time, but respondents are asked to provide accounts of their media-viewing habits in the past.

Some researchers, Gunter (2008) notes, have been less accepting of these research findings. Canadian psychologist Jonathan Freedman, for instance, questioned the conclusions of a generation of research on this topic. Of course there is a body of both experimental and non-experimental evidence that points to the conclusion that media violence increases the risk of viewer violence. Yet, hard-to-explain exceptions remain.

Freedman (2002) notes, for example, that Japanese television and comic books contain some of the most violent images in the world, especially when compared to Disney productions that are commonly shown to children in North America. Yet Japan has a much lower murder rate than either Canada or the United States. This finding reminds us that whatever the effects of media violence on our arousal and aggression, the cultures we live in teach us different ways of dealing with or expressing our arousal.

Personal experiences with violence may also moderate people's willingness to use violence as a way of settling disputes. For example, Boxer, Huesmann, Bushman, O'Brien, and Moceri (2009) discovered that viewing violent media was found to increase the general likelihood that a person would behave aggressively. However, the decision to behave violently was also influenced by previous experiences with violence, in the family home and elsewhere.

Conclusion

North Americans spend many hours each week consuming media. There seems to be a never-ending supply of new ways to communicate with technology. From television, to movies, to advertisements, the Internet, and social media, people are almost always exposed to the media in one form or another. The mass media are an important aspect of socialization and have a major impact in defining the framework with which we view the world.

In all their programs, the media present morality tales: who is rewarded and for what reasons, versus who is punished and for what reasons. This is as true for fictional stories pitched at children and young adults as it is for nonfictional presentations of the news and current events. In the stories presented, certain kinds of people are presented as rule-breakers, and after difficulties and delays, they finally receive their due punishment. In this way, the media teach morality and social expectations about punishment.

The media are, to a large degree, morally ambivalent about good and evil. In support of consumption and consumerism, they are mainly concerned with free markets and free choice. There is no guilt and shame in this moral universe, unless it is the guilt and shame associated with dressing badly or failing to take advantage of bargain items that are on offer. Thus, people may feel bad—even ashamed—about their inability to look, dress, and act like people on television or in the movies; but, the media offer absolution: if you change your behaviour and consume in a different way, you will gain acceptance.

Due to the profit-oriented economic system in which they are embedded, the media have certain values and ideals that they project onto their content. The biases of the individuals who control the major media conglomerates filter through to their programs and have a profound effect on our own world view.

Not only do the mass media succeed in influencing or controlling our values, attitudes, aspirations, and behaviours here at home, but increasingly, they are exporting these same values, attitudes, aspirations, and behaviours abroad to far more numerous, equally avid consumers.

Questions for Critical Thought

1. Are unbiased reporting and media possible? What would they look like?

2. Can you think of how your world view has been impacted by the media you consume?

3. Will the spread of the Internet encourage more diverse opinions or deter them? Why?

4. In this chapter, women on welfare was given as an example of conceptual entrapment. Can you think of any other examples?

5. What has been the effect of large media conglomerates replacing independent firms?

Recommended Readings

Fleras, A., & Kunz, J.L. (2001). *Media and minorities: Representing diversity in a multicultural Canada.* Toronto: Thompson Educational.

This book discusses the role of mainstream media in hampering Canada's perception of multiculturalism. By promoting the dominant ideology of society and defining what is socially acceptable and desirable, the media exclude many subordinate groups.

Freedman, J. (2002). *Media violence and its effect on aggression: Assessing the scientific evidence.* Toronto: University of Toronto Press.

Writing on a highly debated topic, Freedman disagrees with the assumption that violence has an adverse impact on children. However, he does think that advertising has a negative impact on viewers.

Seib, P. (2008). *The Al Jazeera effect: How the new global media are reshaping world politics.* Washington, DC: Potomac Books Inc.

This text examines modern foreign policy, public opinion, and international relations from the perspective of global media. It presents, explains, and applies the "Al Jazeera effect," which states that media can be both tools of conflict and of peace and that media transcend traditional borders in uniting citizens of the world in virtual communities.

Taras, D. (2001). *Power and betrayal in the Canadian media* (updated ed.). Peterborough, ON: Broadview Press.

Taras points out challenges to the Canadian media industry, including budget cuts, technological change, and ownership concentration. This book argues that these occurrences will narrow Canadians' access to diverse and good-quality information.

Wykes, M., & Gunter, B. (2005). *The Media and body image: If looks could kill.* London: SAGE Publications Ltd.

Combining research from sociology, gender studies, and psychology, this book addresses media representations of beauty standards and ideals as well as public interpretations and responses.

Recommended Websites

Canadian Radio-Television and Telecommunications Commission (CRTC)
www.crtc.gc.ca/

The CRTC is the Canadian government's regulative organization for mass media. It seeks to ensure fair access and equal content and to protect Canadians from misleading content. Its regulations and goals provide an interesting perspective on the media.

Media Smarts
http://mediasmarts.ca/

This website is run by a Canadian non-profit organization committed to providing people with the tools they need to engage media dynamically and critically. They seek to educate people on media use and to improve media literacy for all ages.

Net Neutrality
www.netneutrality.com/

This website focuses on the issue of net neutrality and fights to stop cable companies from dictating if a website gets connection priority over another. Net neutrality is one of the biggest issues currently facing the development of the Internet.

RadioLab: Trust Engineers
www.radiolab.org/story/trust-engineers/

This is a podcast about Facebook and its study of social control through emotional manipulation on social media—for example, seeing whether Facebook can get more people to vote by showing or not showing notifications that your friends have voted.

Government, Politics, and Ideology

Learning Objectives

◎ To define the concept of a "state" and from where it gets its authority

◎ To think critically about how ideology is used to maintain social control

◎ To understand how globalization is affecting different governments' ability to administer social control

◎ To identify differences in how Canadians and Americans understand their relationship to their governments

◎ To be familiar with theories of social capital, the civilizing process, and legal consciousness

---

Introduction

Our focus so far in this book has mainly been on *informal* agents of social control, in connection with appearance norms, socialization, religion, and the media. All of these agents of control are "informal" in the sense that they operate outside the realm of government and without governmental authority. In this chapter, however, we begin to focus on the more *formal* aspects of social control, beginning with the "state." Unlike the informal agents of control we have discussed so far, the state is unique in that it has the legal *authority* to impose severe sanctions on people. The laws and policies enacted by the state are so significant that they have the potential to affect every one of us, for better or for worse.

Of course, if we take a long historical scope, we have to start before the state to understand formal social control. In talking about social control and regulation before the modern nation-state, we would have to look at other dominant institutions that exercised authority and power, starting (for example) with the Catholic Church 2,000 years ago. We would have to discuss classical theology, philosophy, and law; then, with the Enlightenment, we would consider seventeenth- to nineteenth-century liberalism, and then nineteenth- and twentieth-century theories of social disorganization and pathology.

Along the way, we would examine the rise of Western science, knowledge, and discourse, especially the rise of medicine and psychiatry, two fields that are central to the Western constructions of normality/abnormality and morality/immorality today. In this context, we would discuss the dramatic shift from moral explanations of crime and deviance to medical explanations—the so-called medicalization of deviant behaviour. And, in fact, we *do* discuss some of these topics in this book: for example, we discuss the influence of religion in Chapter 5; and we discuss medicalization in passing in Chapter 9. The problem is, there is far too little space in this book to discuss all of these themes in the depth they deserve.

So, this chapter will limit itself to the following questions: What is the modern state? What are the state's functions, and what roles do politics and ideology play in social control by the state today? How, today, do people organize their lives *outside* the dominant norms and laws of the state, and how does this differ from lives organized *inside* the norms and laws of the state? How do state policies control the way people lead their lives? And finally, what are the mechanisms of social control present in a modern civil society, long considered by many to be an alternative to the power of the state?

What Is Social Contract Theory?

The concept of *social control* is inextricably linked with ideas about the *social contract*. So-called **social contract theory** discusses the relationship between the state and the individual. Specifically, it examines the authority of the state to impose laws that regulate people who have, knowingly or unknowingly, consented to be ruled by the state. To understand this social contract theory, it is useful to start, briefly, with the ideas of philosophers Thomas Hobbes, Jean-Jacques Rousseau, and John Locke.

Thomas Hobbes's *Leviathan* (1969 [1651]) is a classic work that deals with the logical underpinnings of state control. Here, Hobbes argues that, in effect, any state is better than no state. Without state protection and control, humans are likely to lead lives that are "solitary, poor, nasty, brutish, and short," according to Hobbes. That is because people are naturally self-driven, unjust, and dangerous. On the other hand, Hobbes notes that people are aware that maintaining peaceful relationships is to their benefit; in a state of chaos or war, people will be unable to achieve the well-being and satisfaction they desire. Therefore, notionally, people establish a society in which their rights and freedoms will be upheld.

A century later, Jean-Jacques Rousseau had a different view of the supposed social contract. In his book *Of the Social Contract, or Principles of Political Right* (1762), he describes humanity as naturally free and peaceful. It is only the imposition of personal wills by individuals that hinder the growth of the society as a whole. This is why, according to Rousseau, it is necessary for a General Will to replace personal wills, to offset individual, egotistic goals and direct us to more collective goals. According to Rousseau, the purpose of the state is to make laws that implement the General Will, thus fostering a society that serves all individual needs. Doing so will require the state to condition citizens to set aside their petty personal interests in the interests of a greater general good.

Finally, John Locke's *Two Treaties of Government* provide yet another perspective on social contract theory. Locke writes that the state of nature of man is characterized by "perfect freedom of acting and disposing of their own possessions and persons as they think fit within the bounds of the law of nature." (p. 106). In contrast to Rousseau, Locke emphasizes the rights of individual people. He notes that before a state is formed, people are considered amoral, and there is no basis for judging what is good or evil. In this context, the state serves as the impartial mediator in the affairs of its people, establishing clearly what is good and evil, moral and immoral based on The Laws of Nature: specifically, "No one ought to harm another in his life, health, liberty, or possessions" (p. 107). This is the beginning of all social control. If the ruler does not serve the people well, for example by making bad laws or failing to uphold good laws based on the Laws of Nature, the people have the right to choose another ruler.

The state controls a great many important resources, starting with the right to collect taxes and spend these taxes on social programs. No less important is a monopoly over the use of force. Social programs and enforced rules represent the two sides of state activism: roughly, the carrot and stick of state powers. Consider first the "carrot side" of this power: the duty of the state to regulate services that promote its citizens' well-being. **Social welfare** provides this necessary assistance that, at least in theory, satisfies a citizen's needs. This is a subtle form of social control because it rewards people for behaving in certain desired ways, rather than punishing them for behaving in certain undesired ways.

Social welfare consists of programs within the public sphere that provide education, health, or income support. In general, there are three categories of social welfare:

1. *Universal*: Universal social welfare is available to anyone within a specific jurisdiction. For example, every citizen within a province of Canada is eligible to receive publicly funded health care if they submit all required documents.
2. *Contributory*: Contributory welfare, on the other hand, requires people to contribute a certain fraction of their income to obtain social welfare assistance at a later date; this is characteristic of employment insurance and the Canada Pension Plan.
3. *Means-tested*: Finally, means-tested welfare provides support to people who need financial help to pay their living expenses. For instance, a single mom who is out of a job can get this type of social assistance.

For the most part, however, when we discuss the state in connection with social control, we look at the "stick" side of the equation: the power of the state to make and enforce laws, and to punish wrongdoers. But before we can discuss this in depth, we need to understand a little better what the state is all about.

What Is "the State"?

As is evident from the foregoing discussion, the **state** is an artificial entity—something that people create in hopes of improving their collective and individual lives. In part, they hope to do so by creating and enforcing wise laws: hence, the social contract implies the beginnings of formal social control. The state ideally gives people a wider range of ways to lead "better lives" within the framework of their own and society's limitations. In return for what Max Weber called "a monopoly on the legitimate exercise of violence" (Weber & Whimster, 2004, p. 119), the state supplies services that most people value: security from attack, health care, education, and a social safety net, among other things.

Max Weber, the first and most influential sociologist to analyze the workings of authority and the state, identified three types of *authority*, distinguished by the reasons those subjected to it accept authority: (1) traditional, (2) charismatic, and (3) rational-legal authority. Table 7.1 summarizes these types of authority.

Weber's notion of "legitimate authority" is, therefore, a critical idea in the history of sociology because it distinguishes authority from coercive power and notes that, most of the time, people follow society's rules because they have learned to believe that these rules are legitimate. Through legitimation, people acquiesce voluntarily in their own subjugation. But why do they do so?

Under traditional authority, long-held traditions and customs are the basis of legitimate power. In traditional states, people may feel that their rulers are appointed by God and that the ruling family possesses royal blood. Because of this royal blood, people think that power, obligation, and duty ought to pass down the royal family line, from one generation to another.

Table 7.1 Different Types of Authority

Type	Description
Traditional	• Power is founded on the basis of institutional custom. – Example: hereditary monarchy
Charismatic	• Power is founded on the charisma of an individual leader. – Example: revolutionary social movements
Rational-legal	• Power is founded on the basis of merit and rank. – Example: bureaucracy

Where traditional authority prevails, the power-holder is also supported and constrained by ancient traditions. Holding power through *dynastic inheritance*, the ruler inherits the legitimacy of a parent or kinsman who also held power. Traditional authority is most secure when it is based on the belief that a ruler's power is given by God and that challenging the ruler would amount to challenging God.

Under charismatic authority, on the other hand, tradition counts for nothing. Charisma relies solely on a leader's ability to influence others—thus, on the leader's exceptional qualities, such as the force of his or her personality. Charisma may draw its power from many different sources, including charm and presence, and we know it by its effects, not by its specific traits. The leader who possesses charisma can generate in others feelings of excitement and anticipation, and mobilize a mob of people toward almost any given goal. Charismatic leaders can charm their audience and deliver powerful messages that move people to action—even risky action. In fact, charismatic leaders can ignite people's passions and get them to do almost anything, simply out of admiration for the leader.

Many have said that Martin Luther King, Jr, was such a leader. He was able to mobilize a massive number of African-Americans to protest for their rights, despite the risks and costs involved. King's famous speech, "I Have a Dream," shows how a charismatic leader can motivate his followers by giving them the image of an alternative future. However, not all charismatic leaders motivate their followers for good purposes. Adolf Hitler, another charismatic leader, was able to incite hate against non-Aryans, persuading his followers to go to war and commit numerous crimes against humanity, including the mass murder of Jewish people, Roma people, people with left-of-centre political views, and homosexual people during the Holocaust.

Under the third type of authority, rational-legal authority, tradition and charisma are irrelevant; what counts are formally established rules and procedures. The right to exercise rational-legal authority in a particular matter is grounded in a person's formal position. Whoever fills the particular position of authority is obliged to treat everyone identically, in the way specified by written *rules*. Rational-legal authority is not only the basis of modern state organization, it is also the basis of the bureaucratic organization we can find in large business and military bodies. All modern societies apply this kind of authority, which is based on a system of written laws, rules, and regulations.

In this system, the distribution of authority is highly specialized, to ensure expert and professional attention to people's rights and responsibilities. The formal position held by an individual civil servant, for example, dictates the extent of that person's right to exercise authority, thus limiting his or her use of power. Similarly, the executive, legislative, and judiciary branches of the state each have their own duties and limitations, rules, and resources.

Of central interest to Max Weber is authority, not naked power as one might exercise at gunpoint. In his famous piece "Class, Status, and Party," Weber defines *power* as the ability of an individual or groups of individuals "to realize their own will in a communal action even against the resistance of others participating in the action" (Weber, 2009 [1946], p. 180). In this sense, power is akin to influence since it enables a person to control another person's behaviour. However, most of the time, power is exercised peacefully, through legitimate authority. In his work "Three Types of Legitimate Rule," Weber discusses how power is translated into authority.

Modern states, like modern business organizations, are organized around written rules that are based in law. This distinguishes them from states (and organizations) that run on tradition, charm, or personal relationships. The "rule of law" dictates that modern states (and the people who govern them) must follow strict rules to secure and preserve public legitimacy, and it ultimately gives people in authority the legitimate power over life and death in our society. "Rule of law," then, is enormously important in modern societies.

Interestingly, respect for the power of the state grows at the same time, and in connection with, the growth of private manners (including etiquette.) According to Norbert Elias's research, civility, polite manners, and state government all develop together. Together, these developments make up the so-called **civilizing process**. (See Box 7.1 for a recent example.) Good manners—for example, rules requiring that people urinate or defecate in private—historically begin with the aristocracy, then spread to the bourgeoisie, who to teach these manners to their children.

In time, the same manners spread further down the class structure, from class to class and generation to generation. Self-control—in the form of good manners, polite excretion, and private sexuality, for example—coincides with the rise of a strong state. It is through the rise of this state that a national culture of politeness develops—more evidence that "the social contract" indeed makes our lives less "nasty, brutish, and short."

Along similar lines, violence—both interpersonal and inter-state—declines with the rise of nation-states. Indeed, although there were a great many deaths in the twentieth century due to warfare and other state actions (e.g., genocide), the twentieth-century state was a safer place for ordinary people to live than the nineteenth- or eighteenth-century states (or earlier states) had been.

Types of States and Degree of Control

That said, some states are safer and more controlling than others. In particular, liberal-democratic states are safer, although less controlling, than authoritarian states, which, in turn, are less controlling than totalitarian states.

Authoritarian states typically forbid public opposition and use force to ensure compliance with the written laws. Often, authoritarian leaders

Box 7.1

Hezbollah and the Civilizing Process

Over the past two decades, the Lebanese paramilitary group Hezbollah has been showing an increased capacity for self-restraint, an important aspect of the civilizing process. Hezbollah receives much support from Iran and Syria and has military power within Lebanon that is possibly greater than the state itself. Hezbollah has been showing more restraint in its actions within Lebanon in an effort to gain legitimacy within the state. Co-operation with the Lebanese state can aid in Hezbollah's survival, and the more often that happens the more co-operative people tend to be (Saouli, 2011). Because of the sectarian and multi-ethnic nature of Lebanese society, Shiite Hezbollah is forced to cooperate at some level with other factions within the country.

Hezbollah needs to show the Lebanese people that it is more than an Iranian or Syrian proxy (Saouli, 2011). It has been accomplishing these goals by strengthening its core base of Shia supporters by building infrastructure and providing social services, such as waste collection and water supply. Hezbollah has also worked to integrate itself into the Lebanese state by running and sitting in parliament. This has allowed it to build connections with other parties and factions within the government and to win support from their constituents by representing them in parliament (Saouli, 2011).

force citizens to display public support of the state, in order to prove their loyalty. These authoritarian states exercise complete control over the society, with the cooperation of the military, the state church, and/or foreign multinational corporations.

Totalitarian states are even more controlling than authoritarian states. The totalitarian state, exemplified by Nazi Germany, intervenes in both public and private life. It demands complete loyalty and compliance, and it controls the distribution of rewards and punishments, according to centrally designated rules. A centralized power and ideology controls all people's lives. Some totalitarian states are said to be "far right," or fascist— for example, Nazi Germany—while other totalitarian states are "far left," or communist—for example, the Soviet Union under Stalin. Under a totalitarian government, freedom is severely limited. Total conformity and absolute loyalty are expected of all citizens, with torture or death as the penalties for those who deviate.

In totalitarian societies, ideology and propaganda are used extensively to brainwash the citizenry into conforming. For example, Benito Mussolini's fascist Italian state was driven by Italian nationalism (Ball & Bellamy, 2003).

Mussolini said "for the fascist, everything is in the state, and no human or spiritual thing exists, or has any sort of value, outside the state. In this sense fascism is totalitarian, and the fascist state which is the synthesis and unity of every value, interprets, develops and strengthens the entire life of the people" (Mussolini & Gentile, 1932, as cited in Kallendorf, 2009. p. 345). The totalitarian state of Italy required the unwavering loyalty of its citizens. Mussolini used propaganda to promote its national and political goals, and enlisted the educational system and mass media to teach the values of fascism to Italians of all ages.

The **liberal democracy**, a third kind of state, is quite different. In liberal democracies, such as Canada, people express their political views by electing representatives to a parliament, congress, or legislature. These representatives, meeting face-to-face, devise policies that they expect the electorate to support. If the electorate is displeased, it can vote its representatives out of power at the next election. "Democracy" literally means "rule by the people." Liberal-democratic states do not monitor people's every action and belief, nor do they suppress free speech and assembly, as authoritarian and totalitarian states do. In liberal-democratic states, social control takes a different form. Here, people are ruled by the powerful in less visible ways, to manipulate and influence their cooperation. Here, as well, persuasion rather than threat of force, is key.

How Political Values and Culture Affect Social Control

Liberal democracies, although similar to each other in many respects, differ in what they control, and how they control it, because they differ historically. Consider, for example, differences between Canada and the United States in their orientation to marijuana, abortion, same-sex marriage, imprisonment, and capital punishment. To understand the cultural differences between similar democracies, Seymour Martin Lipset, a prominent American sociologist and political scientist, compared the United States to Canada, Australia, and the United Kingdom.

Doing so, he was able to identify several key features that distinguished the US from the others, making it the country that it is today. These features included a revolutionary war and a commitment to liberty and achievement. In particular, because of more elitist values, the British and Canadians put less emphasis on equality of opportunity than did the Americans. Australia, more like the US in its emphasis on equality and achievement, differs from the US because it (like Canada) never had a revolution. As a result, Australia and Canada are less committed to liberty and wide-open competition than is the United States.

As a result, Lipset suggests, different "states of mind" exist in Canada and the United States. According to Lipset, Canada's "organizational principle"—its decision not to join the American Revolution in 1776 and break with England—left Canadians with the values and priorities of the Old World. That, according to Lipset, is why Canadians accept more state intervention in their daily lives—for example, higher rates of taxation and a larger social safety net. This reflects the view of Old World Tory conservatism that the whole is greater than the sum of its parts and, as such, that collective rights should prevail over individual rights. With this in mind, Canadians constantly try to accommodate competing interests within a framework of existing social institutions—a profoundly reformist (rather than revolutionary) ambition.

In Canada, there is a general acceptance of multiculturalism, variety, and fluidity. (See Box 7.2. for a comparison of attitudes toward homosexuality.) Canada's *lack of nationalism* is a distinguishing feature of the country, as compared with the United States. In addition, most Canadians continue to cling to the principle of a kinder, gentler society, in stark contrast to the social Darwinian ideology of the United States. Canadians want a sustainable social-welfare state that will leave Canada a more egalitarian place than the United States, but they, like Scandinavians and other northern Europeans, wrestle with the tax implications.

Box 7.2   Attitudes toward Homosexuality in Canada and the United States

One issue that has garnered significant attention has been the increasing acceptance of homosexuality in both Canada and the United States over the past 30 years. However, this acceptance has been much greater in Canada than in the US.

In Canada, significant legislation has guaranteed the rights of homosexual men and women, culminating in the legalization of same-sex marriage in 2005. In the United States, by contrast, the pattern is more mixed. Some US states have legalized gay marriage while others have refused to do so, sometimes even amending their constitutions to define marriage as exclusively heterosexual.

One of the biggest factors shifting public opinion in both countries has been the increased presence of gays and lesbians in the media and popular culture. There has also been a strong effort by social activists to bring these issues to the forefront of public thought. Both factors, however, are present in the United States and Canada and, therefore, do not explain the continued difference of opinion between the two where same-sex marriage is concerned (Andersen & Fetner, 2008). One possible explanation is the presence of a strong religious opposition in the United States and a lack thereof in Canada. The American religious right continues to oppose sexual equality and has no similarly powerful equivalent in Canada.

Political Ideology

The state, as we have seen, plays a significant role in formal social control, yet we would be wrong to think it is the only such institution to do so. As Michel Foucault has pointed out, all modern institutions are complicit in the business of social control. Recall that, for Foucault, the state is largely coercive and repressive; and its power is largely external to us. By contrast, non-state disciplinary power is largely internal to us, working on our motives and desires through what Foucault calls "techniques of the self." Through socialization—learning what Mead called "the generalized other"—we are disciplined to behave in socially appropriate ways without requiring external, coercive power.

This learning, as we noted earlier in the text, is exercised in modern societies through our experiences in families, schools, and workplaces; also, in total institutions such as hospitals, military barracks, and prisons. Families and schools are especially important in creating and disciplining our selves, as we have seen.

However, ideology is no less important a source of control. According to Antonio Gramsci (1978), the state and its institutions maintain their control not only through violence, threat, and coercion, but also through the manipulation of beliefs and ideologies. Gramsci defined *ideology* as a view of the world that is implicit in all works of consciousness: in art, law, economic activity, and every other part of individual life. And according to social theorist Herbert Marcuse, in liberal democracies capitalist ideologies have blinded us to class struggle, allowing one class to dominate and control all the others.

Under the spell of this ideology, the interests of the ruling class take precedence. Capitalist or "liberal" ideology holds that hard work will be rewarded with material wealth, thereby justifying the unequal distribution of wealth in society. People are viewed instrumentally, as part of the production system, and are, therefore, objectified (Marcuse, 1964). The comprehensiveness and pervasiveness of this belief keeps people from challenging the system or seeing society's problems (Marcuse, 1964).

Capitalist ideology accomplishes this by creating "false needs" that society forces on its members. "False needs" are material things that we think we need because society tells us to want them. These include the needs "to behave and consume in accordance with the advertisements, to love and hate what others love and hate" (Marcuse, 1964, p. 19). Because of our socialization, the fulfillment of these "false needs" makes us happy and, in turn, keeps us from realizing we are being oppressed. In this state of imagined freedom, we are free to choose between brands but not free to determine what we want from life—what we truly need (Marcuse, 1964).

This kind of one-dimensional thinking affects political debates about crime as well. In thinking about crime, people tend to imagine that it can be controlled by intensifying current practices rather than by solving the systemic problems that create crime in the first place (Kessler & Levitt, 1998).

Many put the blame on individual factors, not structural factors such as the cycles of poverty that push people toward criminal behaviour and divert attention from the *socio-economic* underpinnings of crime.

Multinational Corporations and Globalization

The efforts to implement systemic solutions to crime have, in recent years, been undermined by **globalization** and the shrinking power of nation-states, relative to multinational organizations. Multinational corporations are by definition at odds with the system of sovereign states within which they operate. The Westphalian state system (taking its name from the 1648 Peace of Westphalia) dictates that governments will have control over what transpires within their borders. With advances in technology, however, national borders have become more porous and the flow of people, resources, and money across borders, harder to regulate (see Figure 7.1).

Multinational corporations—which play an increasingly larger role in the world's economy—are decreasing the amount of control that states have over what happens within their territory, as they operate across and within the boundaries of many sovereign states (Hedley, 1999).

Multinationals achieve this freedom by "strategically [playing] off one country's set of rules against another" (Hedley, 1999, p. 225). Corporations look to do business in states with the fewest regulations, thus forcing states to continually reduce their regulations, in order to remain competitive. This "race to the bottom" erodes a state's control over the business practices within its borders. As a result, it allows multinationals to operate with little concern for the environment or for the rights of their employees.

The movement of large numbers of people from one country to another is both a cause and effect of globalization. Globalization encourages this movement to occur in large numbers, and migration, in turn, leads to the exchange of ideas that is the essence of cultural globalization. But migration also represents one of the biggest threats to national sovereignty, as it blurs the boundaries between countries and erodes their national identity. One result has been a wave of anti-immigration and anti-integration vitriol across Europe, as people have seen the state to be under threat from this globalization (Morris, 1997).

Globalization can also weaken a state's ability to control its own economy, independent of other countries. As the world becomes more economically integrated, each country's economic fortune becomes more heavily determined by events and policies in other countries.

The Neo-liberal State

In recent decades, the role of the state and, therefore, the social control by the state, has been transformed by an ideology called "neo-liberalism." The term *neo-liberalism* has been used in a variety of ways, for a variety

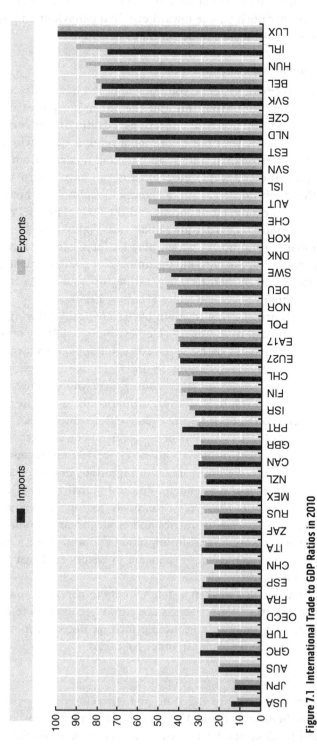

Figure 7.1 International Trade to GDP Ratios in 2010

Source: From OECD Factbook, 2011–12. Economic, environmental, and social statistics. Retrieved from http://www.oecd-ilibrary.org/sites/factbook-2011-en/04/01/01/04-01-01-g1.html?itemId=/content/chapter/factbook-2011-33-en&_csp_=991dd3505d336f07685f023bd9e02257

of purposes. However, people generally agree that neo-liberalism refers to the freeing-up of global markets, largely by reducing state power. In a neo-liberal society, the state is expected to intervene little in the economy. Controls are eased, free trade and free enterprise are emphasized, and markets are assumed to operate rationally—indeed, optimally—to provide the greatest good for the greatest number.

Under this system, people (supposedly) have the maximum freedom to pursue their private goals and, in doing so, they (supposedly) create the maximum prosperity for everyone. This point of view is most compatible with functionalist approaches to world organization, which emphasize equilibrium, efficiency, modernization, and integration.

From this standpoint, neo-liberalism is the economic and political belief (or ideology) that human beings are helped best through the free operation of economic markets. The neo-liberal ideology proposes that a free market allocates prices, goods, and services more efficiently than any other method. Ultimately, then, neo-liberalism rests on the assumption that humans can be economically rational and that markets operating freely, without state control, will maximize human well-being. From this standpoint, state intervention is unnecessary.

In the twentieth century, neo-liberalism fell out of favour for a time, then roared back into favour about 40 years ago and, since then, has continued to support capitalism throughout the world. During the period of the Great Depression, many of the world's economies came to rely heavily on central planning and governmental stimulation in order to recover from unregulated capitalism. However, neo-liberal ideas regained currency after World War II, in connection with the so-called Cold War, which pitted Western capitalism against Soviet communism.

Underlying this way of thinking is a kind of economic Darwinism that assumes that the greatest good will arise automatically through the workings of an uncontrolled marketplace. In this imaginary economic world, productive units will struggle for survival and transcendence; the less effective or efficient units will fail and become obsolete. The best will triumph and remain in place because no other economic system will prove to be more productive. Liberal capitalism will represent the "end of history" in the sense that there will be nothing more to strive for. Indeed, some neo-liberals propose that, with the fall of Russian communism, we have already come to the "end of history" (on this, see Fukuyama, 2004).

These neo-liberal ideas have been attacked from various standpoints: legal, philosophical, sociological, and otherwise. Neo-liberal policies, whether national or international, have tended to minimize the role of the state in economic activity by privatizing ownership and deregulating economic transactions. This extension of "free" markets was assumed to increase individual freedoms while producing national wealth that would trickle down from the top to the very bottom of the social class system. In practice, however, under continued neo-liberalism throughout the West, income inequality has increased, jobs have been outsourced to low-income countries, and the world economy was brought to near meltdown by the Wall Street collapse of 2008.

The paradox is that neo-liberalism has undermined and weakened the power of the state, in the interests of global trade and a free market. Yet the very same governments that have championed neo-liberal economic policies and smaller government—philosophically conservative governments—have tended to support traditional cultural values and a "law and order agenda," featuring more policing, more imprisonment, and fewer social programs to help people who are at risk of criminal activity.

So even while many neo-liberal governments, such as that of the Canadian Conservative Party under Stephen Harper, abdicated responsibility for economic regulation and a wide variety of social (not to mention environmental) programs, they have positioned themselves to spend liberally on prisons. Repeatedly, they have attempted to move social policy-making to the right but have been repeatedly thwarted in this effort by a more liberal Supreme Court. The Court, for example, has insisted that the government provide legislation to protect sex workers against violence; and more recently, it has insisted that people have the right to seek an assisted death, if they wish it.

This helps to remind us that the state is an important source of power and social control in society, as is the marketplace; yet, there are other sources of power: notably, the civil society and public opinion.

Civil Society and Social Control

The discussion of social control has so far been addressed at the macro level, looking at the role of the state. However, there are also implications of social control at a micro level, specifically when it comes to *civil society*. According to Walzer and Miller (2007, p. 115), civil society is a "space of uncoerced human association and a set of relational networks." Civil society offers people a way of organizing peacefully and nearly invisibly. In a sense, civil society offers people an alternative to the state and the economy: an alternate form of organization, cohesion, and control.

Civil society, from another angle, is the free accumulation of social relationships, creating vast quantities of social capital. Social capital theory posits that a network of voluntary associations and organizations, by creating communal solidarity, promotes trust between citizens and a high level of civic engagement. In turn, this creates the conditions for social integration, public awareness, and, in the end, *democratic stability*.

This is an old idea, although many think it is new. In *Community, a Sociological Study: Being an Attempt to Set Out the Nature and Fundamental*

Laws of Social Life (1970), Robert M. MacIver states that a community is an association where people in a certain area interact freely based on common interests. Similarly, institutions are devised to serve the common good. This means that institutions are created and controlled by the members of the community to achieve communal goals.

For example, a religious institution—such as a church—is composed of religious members and aims to spread its influence to other people. A political institution—for example, a party—mobilizes people to gain votes. These and other institutions also aim to modify behaviour. They do this through socialization and acculturation, among other things. In this way, people learn to behave differently in different institutional settings. For example, students at school have to interact in a respectful way with teachers and other classmates. They can only relax or play at specific break times, unlike at home, where they have more freedom to do whatever they want.

Similarly, our institutions create social laws that govern us. MacIver observes that there are many kinds of laws, depending on which context we are considering (MacIver, 1970): explicit laws that are imposed by the state as well as implicit laws imposed by the community. Since communities vary, their laws also vary. Robert Putnam (2000) has emphasized the importance of civic engagement and **social capital** for the maintenance of a strong sense of community. In Putnam's social capital theory, social *networks* are useful in providing access to information, shared values, as well as the *norms and rules* that govern social interaction (Muir, 2011).

Through networks and the build-up of trust, three types of social capital develop in any community (see Table 7.2). The first, *bonding* social capital, leads to the development of "strong ties" and a strong sense of communal membership, although it may also exacerbate "exclusive identities and homogeneous groups" (Putnam, 2000, p. 22). *Bridging* social capital, on the other hand, is more inclusive, bringing together people from a wide range of backgrounds and resulting in more "weak ties" to "more distant acquaintances" (p. 23). Finally, *linking* social capital "connects with those different levels of power or social status" (Muir, 2011, p. 961), such as civil society organizations, and state agencies. Equally, it connects people with high status and power to a wide coterie of people—protégés—with lower status and less power.

Table 7.2 Putnam's Types of Social Capital

Type	Description
Bonding	• A strong link between two or more homogeneous groups – Example: ties between gangs from the same area and backgrounds
Bridging	• A weak link between two or more heterogeneous groups – Example: a bowling league with teams from different states and backgrounds
Linking	• A relationship between two groups of disparate power – Example: A senator and a campaign volunteer

Sociologists, however, have not accepted these arguments at face value. Muir (2011), for instance, notes that the mere existence of social capital does not always mean that social contact is used in a positive manner, especially when it "excludes outsiders from local communities and encourages norms which are different from those of the wider society" (p. 961). For example, Putnam (2000) himself notes that, in the bombing of the Alfred P. Murrah Federal Building in Oklahoma City, Timothy McVeigh had a high level of social capital in the form of friends who were "bound together by a norm of reciprocity [which] enabled him to do what he could not have done alone" (p. 21). Along similar lines, Putnam (2000, p. 22) notes that the Ku Klux Klan used social capital to "achieve ends that are anti-social from a wider perspective."

James Coleman identifies three types of social capital: "obligations, expectations and trustworthiness in the social structure; information channels; and norms and effective sanctions" (Eriksson, Dahlgren, & Emmelin, 2009, p. 332). First, information is embedded in various social networks that can be passed along to others at meetings or through door-to-door engagement (Eriksson et al., 2009). This creates an "us-versus-them" mentality among those who are included and excluded, engaged and not engaged. There may even be *sanctions or punishments* for people who do not engage. Members of the community who do not engage in the "norms of reciprocity" that characterize the group are made to feel obligated to do so, if they want to be viewed as "good" and "responsible" community members (Eriksson et al., 2009).

Finally, citizens' engagement in community associations is also facilitated by the presence of strong leaders (Eriksson et al., 2009). Voluntary associations are essentially social constructs and are subject to the same hierarchical power structures and inequalities that exist in society at large. As a result, dominant groups and individuals have the power to exclude others (Eriksson et al., 2009). The people in the community with the most power are able to control others by delegating tasks and by deciding what strategies should be taken (Eriksson et al., 2009).

Conclusion

This chapter has been concerned with the state and its attempts to both control and support the national population. These two efforts—control and support—are connected since, as we have noted, state support is also a type of social control through social management.

How effective is the State at controlling and regulating behaviour through the laws it makes? This is a complex question, but a great many studies have been done on the effects of particular laws, and some of these have found, clearly and unambiguously, that laws *can be* effective in changing behaviour. That is, the state can control people's behaviour as it intends, through laws and punishments as well as through social programs and rewards. However, sometimes the side effects of a given law are quite unexpected. And, sometimes, laws have effects that are contrary to what the lawmakers intend.

The expectation that law will effectively control behaviour rests on the notion that threatened punishment for law-breaking will generally deter others from breaking the law. But is this expectation of "general deterrence" justified? Often, as we saw in Chapter 3 (which was concerned with government efforts to control substance use), states are unable to legislate changes in private behaviour—especially, private pleasure-seeking behaviour.

Along similar lines, consider the use of law-making to deter risky sex that might lead to HIV transmission. Consider for example the following study: Burris, Beletsky, Burleson, Case, & Lazzarini (2007) studied 490 men who have sex with men (some of whom also inject drugs) and are therefore at an elevated risk of HIV infection. Half of these men lived in Illinois, a state with an HIV-specific law explicitly requiring disclosure by HIV-positive persons before having sex. The other half lived in New York, which has no such law. The authors found that the respondents who lived in Illinois were little different in their self-reported sexual behaviour from the respondents who lived in New York. In short, the law made little difference.

The authors conclude, "Criminal law is not a clearly useful intervention for promoting disclosure by HIV+ people to their sex partners" (Burris et al., 2007, p. 3). They might have said that, at least in this domain, the law makes no difference to sexual behaviour. In large part, this is because many people subject to the law remain uncertain about the *meaning* of the law, whether and how it will be enforced, and how it squares with the subcultural values of their community.

As we saw in this chapter, different kinds of states, in different kinds of societies, use both controls and supports—sticks and carrots—in different ways. Some states are much more intrusive than others in their efforts to control the speech and action of their citizens. Some states are also much more inclusive than others in their efforts to support citizens through a social welfare net. In the midst of this all, classical debates continue about the bases of legitimate authority, social solidarity, and the role of the civil society in giving people a sense of social integration. No state has yet found the perfect solution, and each struggles with these issues in the context of a unique combination of cultural traditions and economic opportunities.

A current debate in Canada and other Western societies has to do with the rights and freedoms of minority (immigrant) populations who hold very different social, religious, and political views from the native-born population. This debate has been dramatically mobilized around concerns about terrorism—especially, home-grown terrorist acts that are carried out on local soil, not thousands of kilometres away. How to control such behaviour, and, more generally, how to integrate newcomers into Canadian society while regulating their views and desires, will be an ongoing problem for decades to come.

Questions for Critical Thought

1. What are the three types of authority identified by Weber? Explain the mechanisms, benefits, and drawbacks of each.

2. Compare the ideology of capitalism to that of communism. Which benefits whom? Which is more feasible and sustainable in the long run, and why?

3. What impact has globalization had on the power of the state to regulate its citizens?

4. Compare the political and moral values of Canada and the United States. Why do they differ? Present an argument for why we should or should not expect convergence between these two countries on key political values and moral attitudes.

Recommended Readings

Baer, D.E. (Ed.). (2002). *Political sociology: Canadian perspectives*. Toronto: Oxford University Press.
This is a collection of writings on political sociology in Canada. It effectively covers the basic topics of interest in this field, including political culture, the state, political movements, and more.

Bashevkin, S. (2009). *Women, power, politics: The hidden story of Canada's unfinished democracy*. Oxford, UK; New York: Oxford University Press.
In this important new addition to Canadian political sociology, the author argues that Canadians are unsettled by women politicians—in fact, by women in positions of authority in general. Exploring this discomfort, Bashevkin points out the many barriers and difficulties women face in politics.

Chappell, L., & Hill, L. (Eds.). (2006). *The politics of women's interests: New comparative perspectives*. London and New York: Routledge.
This is a comprehensive interpretation of political issues from a feminist perspective. It examines how political institutions both shape and reflect gender issues, and the current role of women in politics around the world.

Martin, R. (2002). *Propaganda and the ethics of persuasion*. Peterborough, ON: Broadview Press.
This book analyzes propaganda by first providing a historical outline of its development and then discussing its rise in the twentieth century. The author aims to increase public awareness of the construction and impact of propaganda.

Moore, B. (1966). *Social origins of dictatorship and democracy: Lord and peasant in the making of the modern world*. Boston: Beacon Press.
This classic work takes on a historical-comparative perspective, arguing that particular agrarian systems and ways in which industrialization occurs in societies later produces certain political systems, whether democratic, fascist, or communist.

Recommended Websites

Citizenship and Immigration Canada
www.cic.gc.ca/english/about_us/reports.asp
> This page contains many interesting statistics and resources about immigration to Canada. It not only provides useful insights into how governments control the migration of peoples but also the ways in which Canada is being affected by globalization.

The World Bank
www.worldbank.org/
> This website has information about the World Bank and its constituents. These resources can be useful in understanding how globalization shapes the decisions made by state and non-state actors and how it affects each of them differently.

Transparency International
www.transparency.org/
> Transparency International is a non-governmental organization (NGO) that focuses on exposing and fighting global political corruption. Its website has valuable information about how governments subvert and control their citizens to prevent social change.

Part III

Processes of Formal Control

8 Unequal Opportunities and Crime Prevention

Learning Objectives

◎ To identify the relationship between social inequality and crime

◎ To understand the effect of family structure on delinquency rates

◎ To appreciate how social inequality, crime, and law enforcement contribute to the cycle of disadvantage

◎ To recognize why the rate of punishment is distributed unequally among certain ethnicities

◎ To critically compare white-collar crime and street crime and recognize why they are treated differently

Introduction

This chapter will consider why people commit crimes. If we can reduce the reasons for crime, we can reduce and control crime more effectively. So, in this chapter, we will examine how social conditions increase and decrease the risk of criminal behaviour.

Many factors affect criminality, as we will see, but sociologists take a particular interest in the relationship between *crime and inequality*. Social inequality is among the most pervasive and important factors in determining crime levels. Around 70 years ago, Edwin Sutherland (1947) proposed that crime rates are lower in equitable societies and higher in unequal societies. One of the most common criminological findings is that disadvantaged people are more likely to commit common crimes than people with more socio-economic advantages (Rutter, Giller, & Hagell, 1998).

As a result, the more unequal a society is, the more often people will commit crimes and be victimized by crimes. But if inequality and disadvantage influence levels of crime, what are the mechanisms that explain or mediate this association? How do these mediating mechanisms vary in different social contexts and across various social institutions, such as the family and the formal education system? Finally, how is inequality perpetuated, maintained, and reinforced by a system of formal social controls imposed by the legal system on criminal offenders?

In general, we will argue that, if inequality tends to cause and perpetuate crime, we can control crime most effectively if we find ways to reduce inequality. The connection between crime and inequality, however, is far from straightforward. Indeed, we have not seen an increase in serious crime in Canada over the past 30 years, despite an increase in economic inequality. In short, researchers do not always see obvious links between inequality and crime in their data. This occurs in part because of the inter-correlation of variables that influence *both* inequality and crime. Factors like racism that affect inequality also tend to affect crime, so crime and inequality are spuriously linked.

Another difficulty involves determining the relative importance of, and connection between, *macro-level* (or societal) variables, such as social inequality, and *micro-level* (or personal) variables related to crime, such as age, sex, marital status, education, and income. In general, societal inequality is less directly influential than specific *individual experiences* of inequality, such as unemployment and poverty. However, both are important and in this chapter we will examine the complex relationship between inequality and crime.

Inequality and Incentives to Commit Crimes

Income inequality in Canada and the United States is high and has increased over the past three decades (Neckerman & Torche, 2007). In fact, among the 30 nations that comprise the Organisation for Economic Co-operation and Development (OECD), only Mexico and Russia have higher levels of income inequality than the US (Smeeding, 2005); Canada's levels of income inequality are far lower. That said, income inequality is also a significant problem in Canada, particularly when compared to Norway, Denmark, Finland, and Sweden, for example. Wealth in Canada is distributed more equally than in the United States, yet, according to the Canadian Centre for Policy Alternatives (McDonald, 2014), the top 20 per cent of income earners in Canada own roughly 70 per cent of the country's total wealth. What's more, this kind of inequality is far from unusual. As we can see in Figure 8.1, a high degree of income inequality is common throughout the world and, especially, in less developed countries.

Consider, first, the role of inequality on people's attitudes and values. Certain values like self-interestedness, more common in an unequal society, tend to promote criminal behaviour. In studying this, sociologist David Halpern (2001) looked for evidence that self-interested attitudes and values can help explain the occurrence of crime in capitalist societies. To find it, he used cross-national data from the World Values Surveys, an international set of surveys conducted periodically since the 1980s. Examining a set of 22 "morally debatable" value statements, Halpern found clustering among a

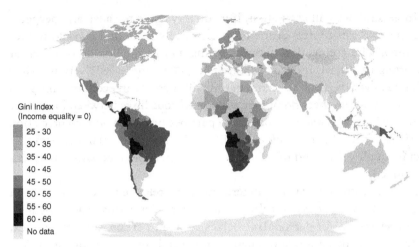

Figure 8.1 Worldwide Gini Index
Note: The Gini coefficient measures income inequality. The closer to 0 a country's coefficient is, the more equally its income is distributed.
Source: Data Source: Table 2.9 of World Development Indicators: Distribution of income or consumption. The World Bank (2014)

subset he characterized as "self-interested values." These included support for the following: keeping money you have found, lying in your own interest, cheating on tax forms if you have a chance, avoiding a fare on public transit, claiming benefits to which you are not entitled, and failing to report damage you've done accidentally to a parked vehicle.

Halpern found that societies in which people are more likely to endorse these self-interested behaviours are more likely to commit crimes and have crimes committed against them. He concluded that crime arises out of excessive self-interest and low social trust, both often found in the context of high social inequality.

Hagan and Peterson (1995), along similar lines, found that the same economic processes that influence day-to-day life tend also to influence crime. Everyday experiences of inequality, for example, create social disorganization, anger, and despair; and these, in turn, may lead to crime. For Hagan and Peterson, inequality creates *animosities* that can easily turn to feelings of frustration, hopelessness, and alienation, all of which can lead to crime. Formal mechanisms of social control—laws, police, courts, and prisons, among others—are unable to control crime under these conditions. Threats of punishment control people with a stake in conformity; they are much less likely to deter crime among social out-groups who feel they have nothing to gain by obeying the rules.

According to Hagan and Peterson (1995), the problem facing North American society is "capital disinvestment." In poor communities, people are so preoccupied with everyday issues—with just surviving—that they have little chance of developing the resources and skills that will help them do well in society. Long-term strategies like schooling and gradual career advancement make little sense to them; crime offers the promise of a quicker solution to their problem.

This is the kind of thing Robert Merton (1938) had in mind when he developed his idea of crime as an "innovative" response to disadvantage. His **anomie** (or strain) theory proposes that crime in North American society is a personal "adaptation" to social inequality. In modern industrial societies like our own, he notes, there is a gap between cultural goals and the means available to pursue these goals. As children in North America, we are taught to seek material success, often referred to as the "American dream." The mass media praise the "self-made person" who has achieved money and status through his or her own efforts in a highly competitive system. Supposedly, anyone can attain success if they "work hard enough." According to the rhetoric of the American dream, the only *legitimate*—that is, legal, honourable, and proper—way to succeed is through education and hard work.

However, some people are disadvantaged by their class, gender, race, age, citizenship status, ability, or sexual orientation. These people will have a harder time competing for the desired success. Some of them may respond to failure by working harder to succeed. Others may "drop out" or join other "failures" in fighting the system.

According to Merton, this gap between cultural success goals and the legitimate means of attaining success creates what he calls *anomie* or *strain*. Faced with this gap, people respond in different ways, choosing different "adaptations to anomie." The most common response, according to Merton, is **conformity**. By conforming, people do their best under the circumstances they are presented with, using the legitimate means available to them, even if success is slow in coming. A second way people adapt is by accepting the cultural goals—the desire for a nice big house and car, for example—while rejecting the accepted means of attaining them. Merton calls this response **innovation**, since these adapters find new and "innovative" ways to get what other people try to achieve through conformity. By this measure, Mafia gangs, for instance, are the ultimate innovators, devising complex systems of activity to attain wealth while avoiding imprisonment.

However, not all innovators are professional criminals. A great many ordinary Canadians are innovators, in the sense Merton meant. Consider tax evaders. According to the Canadian Revenue Agency (CRA), 40 per cent of Canadians are actual or potential tax evaders, looking for ways to avoid paying the taxes they owe, and readily justifying their actions. Rather than obeying the law and paying what they owe, these people invent ways to illegally keep more money in their own pockets.

As we can see, different theories emphasize different aspects of the link between inequality and crime. Halpern was concerned with self-interested values, Hagan and Peterson focused on the ineffectiveness of criminal sanctions, and Merton highlighted the gap between dreams and opportunities. What all these perspectives share, however, is the importance of *social inequality* for crime rates among different sub-groups in the population.

Crime in Urban Centres: Likely Groups

Sociologists have an interest in identifying which social groups are more likely to commit crimes, and *why* they are more likely to do so compared to other social groups. Crime in cities is particularly common and a source of great interest to sociologists and criminologists. Since the 1970s, poverty has increased in urban neighbourhoods and so, too, has crime (Jargowsky, 1994). As well, segregation based on race and class has concentrated poor minorities in inner cities, and it is there that we find the most crime (Lichter, Parisi, & Taquino, 2012).

According to William Julius Wilson (1987), poor urban areas have grown through a transformation of the "inner city." The extreme concentration of poverty and disadvantage in space creates a new kind of social structure: a disadvantaged community isolated socially, economically, and geographically from the mainstream society. According to Wilson, the isolation and concentration of disadvantage undermine the ability of communities to maintain their basic institutional structures (e.g., the family, schools) in good working condition. Isolation and disadvantage also undermine social control. As a result, people living in these neighbourhoods will be more likely to commit crime than people living in other neighbourhoods, other things being equal (Krivo & Peterson, 1996).

A version of Wilson's theory, *social disorganization theory*, originated with the Chicago school of sociology over 70 years ago. Shaw and McKay (1942, 1969) were some of the first researchers to map out rates of crime and juvenile delinquency by neighbourhood, finding these rates were highest in run-down city neighbourhoods. Shaw and McKay (1969) propose that as business and industry invade the downtown city core, surrounding neighbourhoods grow rapidly and social disorganization breaks down social controls. People in the city core are more likely than other people to witness crimes and have role models who are involved in criminal activity. On the other hand, they are likely to have less access to people who model conforming, non-criminal behaviour (Anderson, 1997). As a result, crime becomes normalized and intertwined with the activities of daily life.

This concentration of poverty in the inner city also results in fewer social networks of *informal social control* and fewer community-based institutions that discourage crime. In poverty-ridden areas, families, neighbours, and other groups are less likely to watch out for each other or to supervise the activities of young people. Disadvantaged communities also often lack the resources necessary to form security or "crime-tip" hotlines and neighbourhood crime watch groups (Garofalo & McLeod, 1989). Local organizations that normally foster inclusion and adherence to mainstream values, such as churches, schools, and recreation centres, may lack much influence in areas of concentrated disadvantage (Wacquant, 1993).

A classic study by Sampson, Raudenbush, and Earls (1997) illustrates this nicely. These authors applied the concept of **collective efficacy** to assess informal control in poorer neighbourhoods. "Collective efficacy," defined by how the members of a group perceive the effectiveness of their group, "influence[s] what people do as a group, how much effort they put into it, and their staying power when group efforts fail to produce results" (Bandura, 1986, p. 449). Sampson et al. (1997, p. 98) define collective efficacy with specific reference to neighbourhoods, as "the capacity of residents to control group level processes and visible signs of disorder," a capacity that ultimately helps to reduce the amount of crime in a given area.

Sampson et al. propose that collective efficacy relies on neighbourhood social capital—a people's willingness to intervene out of trust for one another and respect for the common good. This social capital can be built through reciprocal exchanges of favours and information, and through familiarity and network closure (e.g., where a child's parents also know the parents of the child's friends). As a neighbourhood begins to accumulate this kind of social capital, it is more readily able to intervene when crime or other inappropriate behaviour occurs in the neighbourhood. Accordingly, Sampson et al. (1997) find that as reciprocated exchanges and network closure increase, levels of crime decrease.

However, social control is lacking in disadvantaged neighbourhoods for other reasons as well: for example, because of a lack of police protection. In many disadvantaged neighbourhoods, prospective law-breakers are undeterred by the chance they will be arrested and punished because this chance is relatively slight. The police, moreover, are largely absent from such neighbourhoods. Taken together, these findings show that residents of disadvantaged communities often lack the institutional, financial, and social resources to prevent and fight crime effectively (Bursik & Grasmick, 1993).

As noted, low-income residents, especially racial minorities, tend to be highly segregated in areas of poverty, family disruption, high unemployment, and other forms of deprivation, compared to white, middle-class people (Massey & Denton, 1993). According to Wilson (1987), black inner city neighbourhoods become synonymous with disadvantage and crime. Wilson contends, however, that racial composition is *not* the key to understanding high levels of social disorganization in these communities. Rather, Wilson proposes that *extreme inequality and disadvantage* are the reasons for high crime rates in black communities. If similar conditions existed in white communities, we would find higher crime rates present there, too, he says.

This argument, however, has largely gone untested; white people rarely live in areas of such concentrated disadvantage, so it is hard to carry out a proper comparison.

In general, impoverished and socially disorganized social groups (Wilson, 1987; Krivo & Peterson, 1996; McNulty, Bellair, & Watts, 2012) are more likely than other people to commit crimes in urban centres. Much of this criminality is the result of a sense of relative deprivation. In large urban centres, people of widely varying backgrounds live in close proximity to one another, compare themselves with people around them, and notice disparities. Some studies suggest that, after moving to an urban centre, immigrants (Correa-Vélez & Onsando, 2009; Martinez, Lee, & Nielsen, 2004; Aoki & Todo, 2009) and students (Murray & Swatt, 2013 Willits,

Box 8.1 Terrorism or Insanity, or Both?

In the past 10 years, a number of violent criminal acts have occurred in various parts of the West, including France, Norway, Denmark, the US, the UK, and even Canada. In every instance, the criminal was a young male with a troubled personal history. In none of the cases was robbery a motivation. In every case, the criminals had a stated commitment to one or another ideology and access to one or more guns. In every instance, commentators later debated whether insanity was the best explanation. Consider the case of Michael Zehaf-Bibeau.

On October 22, 2014, shortly before 10:00 a.m., witnesses saw Zehaf-Bibeau arrive at the National War Memorial in Ottawa, Ontario, carrying a rifle. Dressed in blue jeans and a black jacket, with a keffiyeh (scarf) over the lower part of his face, he approached Corporal Nathan Cirillo of the Argyll and Sutherland Highlanders of Canada regiment. Corporal Cirillo was one of three unarmed *guards* posted at the Tomb of the Unknown Soldier. At close range, Zehaf-Bibeau shot Cirillo twice in the back, fatally wounding him. Two other soldiers on sentry duty tried to stop Zehaf-Bibeau, but they too were shot at and forced to flee to the other side of the memorial.

Zehaf-Bibeau then returned to his vehicle and drove a short distance to Parliament Hill, where he abandoned his vehicle. He carjacked a parliamentary vehicle and drove it to the Centre Block of Parliament. After wrestling with a security guard at the entrance, Zehaf-Bibeau ran inside, where he was killed by House of Commons Sergeant-at-Arms Kevin Vickers, after a shootout with Parliament security personnel.

Here is the background on this attacker: Michael Zehaf-Bibeau was a 32-year-old Canadian habitual offender and drug addict from Montreal. Several acquaintances reported he had mental issues. In 2004, Zehaf-Bibeau, who had a Libyan-Canadian

Broidy, & Denman, 2013) become more likely to commit crimes. As they come to see themselves as disadvantaged, they become more motivated to break the rules.

   This is particularly true of crimes against property. Crimes against persons—for example, violent acts such as assault or homicide—are harder to link to inequality and a rational desire to overcome disadvantage. One of the problems sociologists, criminologists, and jurists face is determining whether a particular violent crime is purposeful and rationally motivated— for example, an act of hatred, revenge, or terrorism—or is simply an irrational act resulting from some kind of insanity. This problem is discussed in Box 8.1, in connection with a recent violent attack on the Canadian Parliament.

father, had converted to Islam and visited Libya. At the time of the shooting, he had had plans to leave Canada for the Middle East; meanwhile, he was living in a homeless shelter in Ottawa. According to an RCMP official, Zehaf-Bibeau was angered by a delay in passport issuance.

   Was religious terrorism the cause? According to the RCMP, Zehaf-Bibeau had made a video prior to the attack in which he expressed his motives as being related "to Canada's foreign policy and in respect of his religious beliefs." He had previously expressed public support for jihadists in the Middle East; but in his mother's opinion, the attack was the "last desperate act" of someone with a mental disorder, who felt trapped.

   According to a CBC News report (2014),

   a chairperson at the mosque [Zehaf-Bibeau attended] said he did not know Zehaf-Bibeau and that he was appalled by the day's events. He emphasized that they work very hard to ensure radicalization does not happen. He said the measures included working with Canadian intelligence officers and even having Canadian military recruiters visit the mosque. The chairperson said the mosque even forbids small group discussions about the Qur'an.

   Yet the RCMP classified this as a "terrorist attack," perhaps because it took place a mere two days after a man used his car to run over two Canadian soldiers in Saint-Jean-sur-Richelieu, Quebec, killing one. The two incidents raised public concerns about the ability of police to prevent terrorist attacks and about the security measures in place at federal and provincial legislatures.

   In relation to our earlier discussion about how violent crime relates to inequality and incentives to commit crimes, we can see in this example that there may not always be a clear plan of action nor a clear benefit to the individual or his or her social group. Often, violence is an enactment of blind rage that, in many instances, is a result of personal experiences with social inequality and perceived social injustice.

Peer and Reference Groups

In general, the commission of crimes by disadvantaged people is a means of coping, a way of relating to the environment, and an attempt to surmount the disadvantages poor people face.

It's easy to understand why crime may seem sensible and attractive to disadvantaged people. Social disadvantage typically weakens access to, and achievement in, education and employment, making it hard for disadvantaged people to be eligible for non-criminal opportunities. As a result, disadvantaged people often compete with each other for limited opportunities. In this context, crime often becomes a means to negotiate or level the stratified playing field.

As well, disadvantaged people often learn criminality through interaction with one another. Sutherland's (1947) *differential association theory* helps to explain the link between socio-economic disadvantage and crime, in relation to people's peer or reference group. People who live in disadvantaged communities are often unaware of paths to success in the dominant society and have a higher level of exposure to criminal peers and environments (Fergusson, Swain-Campbell, & Horwood, 2004). As a result, they are more likely to learn criminal behaviour along with the attitudes, techniques, motivations, and rationalizations that make crime more likely (Sutherland, 1947).

In that sense, inequality provides differential access to *negative peer or reference groups*. Young people in many disadvantaged neighbourhoods are exposed to gang activity and learn their codes of conduct. According to Thrasher's (1927) ethnographic study of the topic, gang members pass on delinquent traditions to younger generations, especially the notion that status in gangs is often attained through violent and illegal acts. This kind of gang socialization persists today as a *"code of the street"* (Anderson, 1999). This code is based on traditional stereotypes of manliness, stressing strength, courage, physical prowess, an ability to endure pain, and an ability to hide one's weaknesses from others.

With these values in mind, boys are rewarded for showing aggression. During adolescence and beyond, male hierarchies develop, where aggression and physical prowess is key to gaining acceptance. In time, many men find alternative ways to attain status and respect (e.g., through getting a college degree, job, or getting married and having a family), but others do not.

Compared to other peer groups, delinquent peer groups are likely to be *neighbourhood based*, rather than based on school friends (Kreager, Rullison, & Moody, 2011). A lack of material resources often hinders the access of disadvantaged youth to easy means of transportation; and this limits their ability to participate in (non-criminal) extracurricular activities or to become friends with peers in other neighbourhoods (Harding, 2009). As a result, youth come to identify very strongly with their neighbourhood and adopt the neighbourhood codes of violence (Anderson, 1999).

However, as people age, their adolescent peer groups typically lose salience as other influential people, such as spouses and colleagues, come to replace the friendships made in adolescence (Warr, 2002). For Laub and Sampson (1993), gaining legitimate employment, entering the military, getting married, and having children all offer crucial opportunities to turn away from deviant behaviour. For example, parenthood may isolate the individual from associations with deviant people and a risky lifestyle. It may also provide past delinquents with a sense of pride in their new role as parent and caregiver (Edin and Kefalas, 2005). That said, peer groups can also lead youth on a path to crime and delinquency from which they never recover.

Family Variables

As Eitzen (1992) notes, income inequality increases the number of single-parent households, especially among racial minorities. This provides another link between inequality and crime: single-parent families are more likely to be poor, and children born into poor families are over three times more likely to commit a property or violent crime in their youth than children from wealthier families (Fergusson et al., 2004). Inequality also undermines parents' efforts to support and supervise their children, for not only are the single parents short of time, they also may suffer anxieties related to their economic status that detract from their parenting abilities. Research shows that a single parent, with his or her many commitments, tends to be more stressed than a pair of partners who can divide up the household, work, and child-care duties.

A single-parent household also generally has less income than a two-parent household, so the single parent may have to work longer hours to earn additional income. This may make single parents less capable of monitoring their children's activities effectively, with delinquency as one possible outcome. Canadian data show that while 18 per cent of youth living with two parents were occasionally delinquent, the figure rose to 25 per cent for youth from single-parent families. However, two parents at home are no guarantee of law-abiding behaviour. The same data show that 35 per cent of youth with stepfamilies were occasionally delinquent (Public Safety Canada, 2014).

The best parenting strategies—termed *authoritative parenting*, as we discussed in Chapter 4 (Baumrind, 1966)—provide children with a good balance of support and structure, whether two parents are present, or only one. Such parenting strategies give children an appreciation of the consequences of their actions, while building self-confidence and independent thinking (Gray and Steinberg, 1999). However, some research suggests that single-parent mothers provide their children with less supervision and control, and more freedom, than other parents. This excess freedom contributes to disruptive, impulsive, and self-destructive behaviours, and an increased susceptibility to the influence of deviant peers (Florsheim, Tolan, & Gorman-Smith, 1998). Sometimes, this may be balanced out by the presence of an aunt, grandparent, or other concerned adult, however (Florsheim et al., 1998).

At the same time, Florsheim et al. (1998) urge us to remember that family arrangements that undermine parental supervision, discipline, and control have the same effect in *both* single-parent and two-parent households. As a result, although single-parent families may face many challenges, single-parenthood, on its own, *does not* explain delinquent behaviour. The evidence shows that many single-parent families are able to parent effectively, while many two-parent families are not.

Chronic social disadvantage contributes to delinquency and crime, in part, by increasing family stress. When this stress leads to strained relationships, and harsh, uninvolved, and inconsistent parenting, behavioural problems are likely to emerge in children (McLanahan & Percheski, 2008). Youths of low socio-economic status (SES) are also more likely to be punished harshly by parents; this increases the likelihood that such youths will learn codes of violence from their peers, which promotes higher levels of future violence (Heimer, 1997).

The tradition of using physical punishment to discipline disobedient children has come under heavy scrutiny in recent decades. Research suggests that this is another source of criminal violence in our society. Murray Straus (1991) proposes that physical punishment in the family, school, and community increases the risk of criminal violence by young people. Physical punishment by parents and teachers may produce conformity in the immediate present, but tends to increase the risk of deviance in the future. So, delinquency in adolescence can take the form of wife beating, child abuse, and other crime (such as assault, robbery, and homicide) as an adult. Following Straus (1991), many studies suggest that physical punishment during childhood increases the likelihood that a person will commit crimes later on in life (Currie & Tekin, 2012; Fergusson & Lynskey, 1997; Fagan, 2005).

The practice of physical punishment begins with beliefs about the effectiveness of such punishment. Parents who believe in the efficacy of physical punishment not only hit more often; they may also go beyond ordinary physical punishment and assault the child in ways that carry a higher risk of serious injury to the child, such as punching and kicking. Given findings like these, it is no surprise that many attempts have been made in Canada to strike down laws that permit physical punishment, such as Canadian Criminal Code Section 43. This section allows parents to use a "reasonable" amount of force on their children for corrective discipline, although the meaning of "reasonable force" is purposely left vague (Barnett, 2000; Blanchfield, 2012). To date, attempts to strike down Section 43 have all failed (Government of Canada, 2014). To clarify, the existence of Section 43 does not justify child abuse but justifies reasonable or moderate physical punishment that is intended to correct a child's behaviour. The problem is, some parents take these practices too far.

Whatever the intent, physical punishment tends to have negative consequences. Many researchers find that children who are physically punished are more likely to break the social rules later in life, and are, therefore, more likely to commit a crime (Currie & Tekin, 2012; Straus, 1991; Fergusson & Lynskey, 1997; Fagan, 2005). People who were physically punished in childhood are significantly more likely as adults to engage in both violent crime *and* property crime. They also have a higher likelihood of developing substance abuse problems and mental health disorders in adulthood (see, for example, Fergusson & Lynskey, 1997).

Lack of Education

Education is sometimes referred to as "the great equalizer" because it tends to have a positive effect on future wages, as well as other social and health outcomes. Not surprisingly, therefore, graduation from high school is associated with a significant reduction in the likelihood of delinquency, arrest, and imprisonment (Lochner and Moretti, 2004).

However, access to the benefits of education, although free of charge, is nonetheless shaped by class origins. Students from disadvantaged backgrounds often feel alienated from school, and for this reason may fail to develop high educational aspirations or internalize school norms for use in their everyday life. They tend to under-invest themselves in their own education and, for this and other reasons, are at increased risk of committing crime and being imprisoned in the future (Hirschi, 1969).

According to William Julius Wilson (1997), school is a site where children from different socio-economic backgrounds begin to form friendships along class lines. They tend to associate with children who are similarly advantaged, such that children from poor and working class backgrounds are more likely to associate with peers of the same status. From their peers, they learn "oppositional scripts," which encourage distrust and suspicion of people in authority. Some students perform these scripts by skipping classes, acting in disrespectful ways toward their teachers, and avoiding interaction with students who conform to the norms of the school.

Schools in disadvantaged neighbourhoods often lack the resources to provide children with a good educational experience, when compared with schools in more affluent areas. Partly as a result of this, students in low SES areas tend to have poor results on standardized tests and to drop out of school at higher than average rates (Arum, 2000). Children who attend these schools may not have easy access to extracurricular educational activities, or educational resources to overcome learning disabilities (Lareau, 2002). As a result, these children tend to develop a weak attachment to school, leading them to under-invest effort in their schoolwork. Poor grades get worse, and a steady stream of disappointing school results often leads to delinquency.

In sum, then, although schools can be sites of opportunity for students to develop skills for success through legitimate means, schools also contain several mechanisms that reproduce inequality and facilitate future crime.

Under some conditions, schools themselves—especially, secondary schools—may even be breeding grounds for delinquent association and criminal behaviour (Willits et al., 2013; Murrary & Swatt 2013). Schools try to regulate student's daily activities and keep them supervised, but they are rarely free of violence and crime, especially in disadvantaged neighbourhoods. In the US, fully 85 per cent of public schools recorded that one or more crimes occurred on school property or at school events during the 2009–10 school year (Robers, Rathbun, Snyder, & Morgan, 2013). Totaling an estimated 1.9 million crimes, this translates to a rate of 40 crimes on school property per 1,000 students per year (Robers et al., 2013).

To a large degree, crimes hatched or perpetrated at school are responsible for much of the delinquency and crime in any given neighbourhood. The main perpetrators are secondary school students. Compared to elementary school students, who are more heavily supervised before, during, and after school (Murray & Swatt, 2013), middle and high school students are relatively unsupervised, leading to higher rates of delinquency and crime. Indeed, unsupervised adolescent peer groups are "perhaps the best predictor of community crime rates" in a neighbourhood (Osgood & Anderson, 2004, p. 519).

In *private* middle schools and high schools, crime rates are somewhat lower (Murrary & Swatt, 2013), and this is because the children there tend to be better supervised. Private schools are usually located in better neighbourhoods, where children receive greater supervision from parents, teachers, and the police. As well, teachers in private schools report less student misbehaviour (22 per cent) than public school teachers do (41 per cent) and are slightly more likely to enforce school policies (77 per cent) than public school teachers are (68 per cent) (Robers et al., 2013).

To conclude, neighbourhoods with unsupervised adolescents tend to have higher crime rates than both neighbourhoods *without* schools and neighbourhoods *with* supervised adolescents and young students (Murrary & Swatt, 2013; Willits et al., 2013). That said, nothing is quite as unsupervised—hence, as delinquent—as adolescent life on the streets, as we see from the discussion of homelessness in Box 8.2.

Inequality, Disadvantage, and Punishment

Inequalities can also be found in the legal system here in Canada, just as in other countries. Consider the problem of racial discrimination and the over-representation of racial minorities in our prison system. Canadian jurisdictions

Box 8.2   Mean Streets and Main Streets

In *Mean Streets: Youth Crime and Homelessness* (1998), sociologists John Hagan and Bill McCarthy examine how and why youths leave home for a life on the street. The study sheds light on the daily toils and survival strategies of nearly 500 street kids in Toronto and Vancouver.

In designing their study, the authors went against most current criminological research on youth crime, which "has been almost exclusively based on the work of 'school criminologists,' academics whose work is based on the self-reports of young people living at home" (Uggen & Piliavin, 1998, p. 414). Instead, the authors focused on a particularly deprived, crime-ridden group of young people who lived away from home: specifically, on the street. The study began by identifying the risks facing young people who come to live on the street. For many young people on the street, their problems began at home with parental abuse and neglect, typically in impoverished neighbourhoods where their parents were experiencing unemployment.

Many of the youths, especially boys, were subjected to violent outbursts by their depressed or angry parents, who, for their part, had become frustrated by a low or insecure income. Gradually, these youths lost interest in school; their schoolwork began to slip, and a combination of poor grades and conflict with parents and school administrators led many of them to drop out. Lacking social and economic capital, the street youths learned to get by on criminal capital—a combination of criminal knowledge and skill with social embeddedness in a community of young people for whom crime is a necessary way of life.

Few of these young people remain on the street forever. In fact, a majority of these young people "age out" of homelessness and petty crime. This is true of juvenile delinquency generally: opportunities to make good, and important new social attachments gradually turn troubled youth into productive citizens. Yet our society spends far more on arresting and imprisoning young lawbreakers than it spends on remedying their early disadvantage and keeping them off the street in the first place.

do not regularly keep or publish criminal justice statistics about the representation of all racial groups in Canadian jails and prisons, but available studies show that some groups are more likely to be imprisoned than others.

In particular, Aboriginal people and Canadian blacks are over-represented in Canadian jails—a trend that has received scholarly attention for quite some time. In 2007–8, Aboriginal people accounted for about 3.1 per cent of the adult Canadian population, but 18 per cent of all admissions to Canadian jails and prisons (Perreault, 2009). These Aboriginal offenders are often younger, less educated, less likely to be employed at the time of their admission to prison, and more likely to reoffend than non-Aboriginal inmates. In many cases, they also struggle with substance abuse problems.

At the same time, Aboriginal people are also more likely to be victims of crime, particularly violent crime, than non-Aboriginal people. On-reserve crime rates are three times higher than crime rates in the rest of Canada, and rates of on-reserve violent crime are eight times higher (Brzozowski, Taylor-Butts, & Johnson, 2006).

In large cities like Toronto, people are rightly concerned about gang violence, and many of the young people involved in this violence are racial minorities and/or recent immigrants. Since the beginnings of gang research, scholars have viewed the gang as a social problem that reveals the social and personal disorganization of inner-city minorities. In this context, Frederic Thrasher's seminal work *The Gang: A Study of 1,313 Gangs in Chicago* (1927) is often cited as the first sociological investigation of urban street gangs. Yet Thrasher's analysis ignored aspects of street gang activity that have since become central to modern sociological research; in particular, it ignored the violence often associated with gang activity.

Present-day gang research is more concerned with examining the organization (not *dis*organization) of street gangs and the communities in which they function, and with their criminal activities, not their role as a substitute family. Much of the current research is also concerned with how race and gender influence modern gang structure. US law enforcement agencies report that anywhere from 50 to 90 per cent of gang members currently come from minority racial and ethnic groups (Egley & Major, 2002; Curry & Spergel, 1992). Canadian research by Scot Wortley (2003; see also Wortley & Tanner, 2004) suggests a similar pattern. Racial and ethnic distinctions are often, although not always, based on different residential patterns, and often gangs from one neighbourhood (and ethnic background) fight gangs from other neighbourhoods (and ethnic backgrounds) for dominance.

A current focus on female gang members is perhaps the newest and most path-breaking area of gang research. Earlier research tended to assume that female gang members were subordinate to male members and that their participation in gang activities was insignificant (Miller, 2001). Today, researchers estimate that females make up about 30 per cent of the overall gang population, although the exact number varies across studies. That said, researchers agree that female and male gang members commit violent offences with different frequencies.

In short, females—in gangs and otherwise—commit violent crimes less often than males and are generally involved in less violent crimes (Esbensen, Deschenes, & Winfree, 1999). Some researchers suggest that females avoid participating in especially risky or violent behaviour, although doing so often results in their having a lower status within the gang hierarchy (Miller, 2001). Most research on gangs is still carried out in poor and minority neighbourhoods. Yet gangs have been identified in suburban and rural areas, too (Evans, Fitzgerald, Weigel, & Chvilicek, 1999), and some studies report that gang membership is growing at a higher rate in these outlying areas than in the central cities (Egley & Major, 2002).

Many gang members and other young criminals end up in jail. For many youth, imprisonment is the turning point in their "criminal career." The collateral consequences of imprisonment—interruption of education, work, and family formation—undermine their successful integration into society and the possibility of upward mobility. Instead, the consequences of imprisonment serve to maintain racial and class disadvantage, thereby trapping people in a **cycle of disadvantage** that may well lead to other criminal behaviour. Prior imprisonment even tends to reduce a person's ability to get married and to support and parent children (Western, 2006). Thus, imprisonment even affects other members of the offender's community.

Family members suffer a particularly heavy cost. For example, daughters of fathers who had been imprisoned are found to be at an increased risk of physical and sexual abuse, of homelessness, and of future contact with the formal criminal justice system (Foster & Hagan, 2007). They are also likely to achieve lower levels of education. Unsurprisingly, a father's imprisonment is associated with significant reductions in the amount of financial support he can provide to his children (Geller, Garfinkel, Cooper, & Mincy, 2009), and this results in less education and higher levels of aggression in boys (Wildeman, 2010).

To minimize these collateral costs, Canadian courts have often attempted to address people's social disadvantage when sentencing them. As an example, consider Aboriginal offenders, a group with arguably the most social disadvantage in Canada: a judge is expected to determine whether the systemic disadvantage that Aboriginal peoples face has contributed to a criminal defendant's actions (Ives, 2004). Social disadvantage was considered in two criminal cases in 2003, when African-Canadian offenders' sentences were eased to reflect the effect that systemic racism and disadvantage had had on their lives (Ives, 2004). Many feel that the resulting moderate punishments are fairer, more just, and more effective.

White-Collar Crime—How Is It Different?

Our focus so far has been to consider the effect of inequality on "street crimes." In this section, we consider white-collar crimes, typically committed by people who occupy social positions of advantage. White-collar crimes differ significantly from street crimes.

First, Sutherland (1940) notes that traditional theories about crime focus on poverty and lack of opportunity; and these factors are insufficient to understand the incidence of white-collar crime. Still, Sutherland urges us to understand that all crime—including corporate crime—has an important cultural aspect to it. All criminals learn to hold criminal values and develop their criminal skills, whether they are safecrackers or Wall Street financiers. But they learn them in different ways and different social contexts.

Second, the characteristics of the perpetrators and victims of white-collar crime and the amount of money involved differ significantly. The people most likely to commit street crimes are youths who are unemployed or have low status, unskilled jobs, or low income (Farrington, Gallagher, Morley, St. Ledger, & West, 1986). By contrast, the people most likely to commit white-collar crimes are highly skilled people in high-income jobs, such as lawyers, politicians, and business executives (Friedrichs, 2011; Sutherland, 1945). Of course, not all perpetrators of white-collar crimes are employed in high-paying, high status jobs. Still, the commission of white-collar crimes depends on the specialized skills and unusual opportunities that come with professional and managerial jobs. By contrast, street crimes require few skills, so almost anyone is sufficiently skilled to commit them.

Examples of white-collar crime include money laundering, misuse of public funds, and embezzlement (Collins & Schmidt, 1993). Both kinds of crime—street crime and suite (or white-collar) crime—are harmful and victimize people. White-collar crimes victimize social institutions such as businesses, financial institutions, governments, religious organizations, and the general public (Collins & Schmidt, 1993). They cheat their customers and the public at large. In fact, white-collar crimes victimize so many people that it is often hard for the victims to realize they have been victimized: often, their individual losses are low (Friedrichs, 2011).

This is one reason why many white-collar crimes go unreported to law enforcement (Kane & Wall, 2006). Indeed, the reporting rate of white-collar crime is far lower than the reporting rate of street crime. A 2005 public survey found that white-collar crime has a 30.1 per cent report rate to law enforcement (Kane & Wall, 2006) compared with street crime, which has a 48 per cent report rate to law enforcement and a 34 per cent report rate to other officials, such as school administrators (Langton, 2012). In large part, this is because many victims do not see white-collar crimes to be as serious as violent street crimes (Langton, 2012; Kane & Wall, 2006).

Ironically, white-collar crimes are far more harmful to society than street crimes are. The average loss due to embezzlement is about one million dollars ("The Marquette Report," 2009, as cited in Payne, 2012). Compare this to the average robbery profit of $1,153 and the average burglary profit of $2,185 (Federal Bureau of Investigation, 2012). This difference results from the ability of white-collar criminals to steal from many victims at once. Whereas street criminals can take $1,000 from one gas station, white-collar criminals hacking into a bank information system (for example) can take $100 from each of a million people, resulting in a much higher yield. Kane and Wall (2006) report that white-collar crimes cost the United States an estimated $300 billion to $600 billion in losses each year, and Friedrichs (2011) believes this amount may reach up to a $1 trillion dollars annually. No comparable Canadian statistics are available.

Yet street crimes are usually punished far more harshly in criminal court. The sanctions imposed on low-status offenders can often be stigmatizing, even when only small amounts of money are involved in the crime (e.g., a burglary case). By contrast, white-collar crimes are often administered in civil court or professional administrative hearings (convened, for example, by the Law Society or Medical Association of a given province) and are only mildly sanctioned, even in cases where millions of dollars are involved (e.g., anti-trust cases, fraud). The clearest evidence of this followed the 2008 meltdown of financial institutions on Wall Street, where many reckless financial speculators—friends of the lawyers and politicians who prosecuted them—were bailed out, rather than locked up. Almost no criminal investigations or prosecutions resulted from an economic crisis that deprived hundreds of thousands of people of their homes and life savings.

Sutherland (1940) proposed two reasons to explain why white-collar crimes tend to be punished less harshly. First of all, white-collar crimes are less likely than street crimes to involve angry victims. That's because many corporate crimes lack a clear victim. Second, and more significantly, corporate actors wield an immense amount of power in a free-market economy and often use their political influence to get prosecutors to bend the rules.

Politicians in positions of great authority often depend on donations from large corporations, and this makes them susceptible to the influence of wealthy donors. As a result, crimes committed by people in positions of socio-economic privilege are not only different in nature from crimes committed by disadvantaged people, they are also unequal in punishment. In Table 8.1, we summarize the more important differences between white-collar and street crimes discussed in this chapter.

Table 8.1 White-Collar Crime vs. Street Crime

	White-Collar Crime	**Street Crime**
Perpetrators	• People in professional or managerial jobs – Example: lawyers, accountants, politicians	• People with low incomes and few job prospects

Victims	• Large social institutions
	  – Example: banks, companies
		• Individuals
		  – Example: a store owner

Damage	• Usually in the hundreds of thousands of dollars, if not more	• Usually in the thousands of dollars, if not less
Likelihood of reporting	• Less than one-third of white-collar crimes are reported.	• Nearly half of street crimes are reported.
Prosecution	• Civil courts	• Criminal courts
Examples	• Embezzlement • Fraud	• Mugging • Vandalism

Conclusion

In this chapter, we have seen that social inequality is one of the most important factors driving people to crime. Social inequality also influences the amount and type of punishment people receive for their crime. Everyone is aware of the unfairness in all of this, but most of us are taught to turn a blind eye and to resign ourselves to the "system of justice." We are also taught to stereotype certain types of people as good or bad, moral or immoral, worthy or unworthy of punishment.

However, we have also noted that there is not a clear linear relationship between inequality and crime. As noted earlier, in the past 30 years we have seen continued decreases in the official crime rate despite continued increases in the level of income inequality. Likely, the effects on crime of increasing inequality have been masked in several ways. First, the proportion of young men in the population—those who are most likely to commit street crimes—has been steadily decreasing. Second, the proportion of middle-aged people in the population—those who are most likely to commit white-collar crimes (which are rarely charged or prosecuted)—has been steadily increasing. Third, rates of alternative "adaptations to anomie," such as addiction and mental illness, have been increasing, as Merton might have predicted.

So, we cannot rule out the importance of social inequality for crime and other deviant behaviour. Crime remains a serious and costly problem in our society. If we could reduce the amount of crime in society, we could also reduce the amount of costly punishment. And both could be accomplished by reducing the amount of inequality. So, one important strategy of social control—one that would likely be highly effective—would be to reduce social inequality. Yet, for obvious reasons, people of wealth and power are unlikely to relinquish their advantage willingly; they have too much to lose. And the rest of the population, duped into thinking that some people are naturally "bad" or "criminal," go along with the agenda of more punitive law-making, more police enforcement, and more imprisonment of the socially disadvantaged.

What we have seen, in this chapter, is the way a society settles for highly ineffective social control in order to avoid the discussion of a topic that would likely bring about more effective social control: namely, the topic of social inequality.

Questions for Critical Thought

1.   Why do you think white-collar crimes are reported and prosecuted less than street crimes? What strategies can be used to address this?

2.   How does your parents' education affect your own education? How is this related to the cycle of disadvantage discussed in this chapter? What can be done to address this?

3. In this chapter we looked at many aspects of social inequality that are related to crime. Do you think these factors increase when impoverished neighbourhoods are more remote from wealthier ones? Why or why not? How can this issue be addressed?

4. What impact do you think private elementary and high schools have on inequality? On criminality?

5. Why do you think social inequality has been increasing in Canada and the United States over the past few decades? What can be done to address this?

Recommended Readings

Britt, C.L., & Gottfredson, M.R. (Eds.). (2003). *Control theories of crime and delinquency.* New Brunswick, NJ: Transaction Publishers.
In this book, contributors discuss the notion of learning, or socialization, in the context of control theory and the effects that families, peers, and criminal justice have on self-control, social ties, and criminal behaviour. Part III looks at crime cross-nationally.

Doob, A., & Cesaroni, C. (2004). *Responding to youth crime in Canada.* Toronto: University of Toronto Press.
This book dispels various myths—for example, that youth crime is on the increase, that females are becoming more violent, and that the gang problem in Canada is out of control. The authors argue that effective programs to deal with youth crime will most likely operate in preventive or diversionary institutions.

Laub, J.H., & Sampson, R. (2003). *Shared beginnings, divergent lives: Delinquent boys to age 70.* Cambridge, MA: Harvard University Press.
Earlier longitudinal research on criminal activity has not followed delinquents much past the age of 30. This book, following 500 delinquent boys up to age 70, uses both qualitative and quantitative data to identify patterns of crime and profiles of criminal careers.

Sjogren, H., & Skogh, G. (Eds.). (2004). *New perspectives on economic crime.* Northhampton, MA: Edward Elgar.
Economic crime is crime committed to gain profit within an otherwise legitimate business. The victims of such crimes may be private citizens, businesses, or the state. Key areas examined in this book include the economics of corporate crime, problems with enforcing rules, and the history of economic crime.

Thornberry, T.P. (2003). *Gangs and delinquency in developmental perspective.* Cambridge, MA: Harvard University Press.
The findings of this book show that multiple developmental deficits lead youths to join gangs, but membership, in turn, leads to an increase in delinquency and violent behaviour, further disrupting normal adolescent development.

Recommended Websites

Canadian Social Research Links
www.canadiansocialresearch.net
This comprehensive website of Canadian social research links is kept by a retired federal civil servant. It has government and non-government links as well as

thousands of links sorted by social theme. It's an excellent gateway for any Internet research.

Center on Juvenile and Criminal Justice
www.cjcj.org/index.html

The Center on Juvenile and Criminal Justice is a private American service, although its website provides a focused and academic investigation of the social issues surrounding juvenile crime. The website provides information and links on a great many issues, including government and non-government agencies, professional associations, and media sites.

Department of Justice
www.canada.justice.gc.ca

The Canadian Department of Justice website is a great starting point for deviation research. It contains up-to-date information on laws and policies. The website also provides various publications, such as reports, working documents, and policy papers.

9

Sources of Control: Force and Punishment

Learning Objectives

◎ To understand the purposes of punishment

◎ To examine the different types of commonly used punishments

◎ To see how punishment reflects politics and ideology, not merely crime

◎ To study the history and effectiveness of imprisonment

◎ To consider the reasons mass imprisonment is particularly ineffective

◎ To consider alternatives to imprisonment

Introduction

As we have seen throughout this book, the state is only one source of social control in Canadian society, and perhaps not even the most powerful one. That said, the state does enjoy a monopoly on the legitimate use of force and violence in our society. Unlike any other social group, institution, or organization, the state can collect taxes; and it can use that money to put people in prison for breaking the rules it has made.

One might imagine that the power to imprison is an important type of social control in society. Obviously, few if any Canadians would like to be in prison or suffer the stigma of having been imprisoned. Yet imprisonment, in Canada and elsewhere, generally fails to achieve the goals of social control. True, imprisonment keeps some dangerous people off the streets for a fraction of their lives, and in that way, it protects the rest of us from potential misbehaviour. But the rates of recidivism, in Canada and elsewhere, are extremely high among people who have been imprisoned. People released from prison are likely to commit further crimes, and, indeed, after imprisonment people are even more capable criminals than they were before imprisonment.

So, from this standpoint, imprisonment is an unsatisfactory form of social control. It doesn't appear to rehabilitate people or to deter people from crime, in the long run. In addition to its ineffectiveness, imprisonment is expensive to society and disruptive to individuals, families, and communities. From this standpoint, imprisonment has more symbolic than instrumental significance as a form of social control in our society: an unmistakably costly failure that masquerades as social engineering.

Our thinking about punishment has changed dramatically over time, and so have punishments. Today, most people in developed societies assess punishments in terms of their effectiveness, not their moral intention. Sociologists, for their part, are interested in a few main questions in connection with punishment: Which punishments will work best to prevent crime? Which will reduce the likelihood of recidivism? And, finally, which will make society safer in the long run?

Let's start by identifying what punishment is. Philosopher Antony Flew (1954) proposes that, to qualify as a punishment, an action must have the following features:

- It must be unpleasant.
- It must result from, or follow, an offence.
- It must be imposed after a formal process of fact-gathering, detection, arrest, and trial.
- The person punished must be the offender.
- The punishment must occur in this world, not the afterlife.
- Finally, to distinguish it from revenge or remorse, punishment must be exacted by a person in authority—not by the victim him or herself.

We can see these intentions evident in the earliest known example of codified punishment, the Code of Hammurabi (circa 1754 BCE), which is excerpted below in Box 9.1. Note the preponderance of death penalties in this code of behaviour. We are left with little doubt about how the crime and the wrongdoer were viewed in this legal system.

The Goals of Punishment

As we see in the Code of Hammurabi, one of the oldest goals of punishment is retribution, literally "payback" for harm done, or "an eye for an eye." The idea of retribution continues to have public appeal, especially when applied to punishments for serious crimes, such as kidnapping or murder. However, retributive punishments do not address two of the key concerns that many people today have about crime: prevention (deterrence) and harm reduction. (See Table 9.1 for a summary of the types of punishments.)

Retributive punishment seeks to restore justice—or, at least, moral balance—by harming the offender. When someone breaks a law, he or she challenges the legal system that designates the forbidden act as criminal. Breaking a law is an affront against the sovereign, damaging the authority from which the law has issued. That is why only the state—through its public prosecutors or Crown counsels—can lay a charge and bring a lawbreaker

Box 9.1   The Code of Hammurabi (excerpt)

1. If any one ensnare another, putting a ban upon him, but he cannot prove it, then he that ensnared him shall be put to death.
2. If any one bring an accusation against a man, and the accused go to the river and leap into the river, if he sink in the river his accuser shall take possession of his house.
3. If any one bring an accusation of any crime before the elders, and does not prove what he has charged, he shall, if it be a capital offence charged, be put to death.
4. If any one steal the property of a temple or of the court, he shall be put to death, and also the one who receives the stolen thing from him shall be put to death.
5. If any one steal the minor son of another, he shall be put to death.
6. If any one take a male or female slave of the court, or a male or female slave of a freed man, outside the city gates, he shall be put to death.
7. If any one receive into his house a runaway male or female slave of the court, or of a freedman, and does not bring it out at the public proclamation of the major domus, the master of the house shall be put to death.
8. If any one find runaway male or female slaves in the open country, [and] if he hold the slaves in his house, and they are caught there, he shall be put to death.
9. If any one break a hole into a house (i.e., break in to steal), he shall be put to death before that hole and be buried.
10. If any one is committing a robbery and is caught, then he shall be put to death.

Source: Translated by L.W. King. (2014). *The Code of Hammurabi*. Netlancers Inc.

Table 9.1 Goals of Punishment

Goal	Description	Example
Retributive justice	• Harming the offender as reprisal for the crime he or she committed	• An eye for an eye
Restorative justice	• Repaying the victim for the damages they incurred due to the crime	• Repaying a shopkeeper for stolen goods
Rehabilitation	• Making the offender less prone to committing crimes	• Giving offenders a job so they don't resort to crime for income
Incapacitation	• Physically preventing the offender from committing more crimes	• Prisons, stockades, capital punishment
Deterrence	• Making future criminals less likely to commit crimes for fear of punishment	• Heavy fines or long minimum sentences

to justice. Only in punishing the criminal is the sovereign's power thus restored. Retributive punishment occurs without any necessary input from the offender: in a strict sense, it doesn't matter if she or he accepts the blame or expresses regret over the crime. Justice is restored only with the act of punishment. And that is why strict, traditional punishments—such as prison or the death penalty—are consistent with this "just deserts" view of punishment (Wenzel & Thielmann, 2006).

Restorative justice, on the other hand, views the goal of punishment as reasserting the values and norms of the community after they were transgressed by a criminal act. In this viewpoint, justice is a co-operative enterprise that can only be achieved when the community's moral consensus is reaffirmed. It is not the act of punishment but the confirmation of social norms that restores justice. So, a major difference between retributive and restorative justice is that in the latter, the offender's sense of guilt and repentance plays a significant role. If the offender accepts blame and recognizes his or her behaviour as having violated the social consensus, then justice has been restored. This understanding of justice is much more in line with the ideal of rehabilitation as the preferred goal of punishment (Wenzel & Thielmann, 2006).

As noted earlier, there are other goals of punishment, and these also relate to retributive and restorative justice in various ways. **Deterrence theory**, for example, suggests that a primary goal of punishment is to use fear to prevent further rule-breaking. Punishment is intended to dissuade people from committing crimes by showing them that if they do, they will be caught and painfully punished.

Punishments aimed at deterrence may be "specific" (i.e., aimed at deterring the particular criminal being punished from committing new crimes), "general" (i.e., aimed at deterring others from committing crimes), or both. The great classical criminologist Cesare Beccaria (1738–1794) thought that people would act rationally to avoid the unpleasantness of punishment if they were shown the clear consequences of rule-breaking. With this in mind, it follows that, to be effective, punishments must not only be unpleasant, they must also be certain, swift, and publicly observable. Along similar lines, punishment motivated by **incapacitation** uses imprisonment to keep offenders from committing even more crimes. Both of these views—deterrence and incapacitation—take a pragmatic view of punishment, ignoring the immorality of the crime and aiming only to prevent further crime, not restore justice. Both are also forms of retributive justice, although proponents claim that they are effective, and not merely symbolic (unlike some forms of retribution.)

Incapacitation, then, is a practical outlook on punishment and it aims to de-commission people who have not only inflicted harm but are also thought to be a continuing danger to society. Banishment and execution have accomplished this goal in the past; but today, most modern societies rely on imprisonment.

Many think of long-term imprisonment as a fearsome form of punishment—which it is—and one that, for this reason, should effectively deter crime. Separating rule-breakers from the world at large and confining them to a narrowly routinized, continually regulated lifestyle would seem frightening to the average person. Yet research has shown that inmates vary in their perceptions of prison. People with a long history of institutional confinement—whether in prisons, hospitals, orphanages, work camps, or otherwise—view imprisonment with less than average dread. Black people reportedly tend to prefer prison to probation, citing institutional racism on the part of probation officers as the main reason (Crank & Brezina, 2013). On the other hand, convicts with spouses and children tend to hate prison as it deprives them of family life; and their children, of a parent.

Generally, convicts who have already embraced a **criminal lifestyle** (i.e., a career in crime) are least likely to find imprisonment disagreeable. In fact, "the attitudes and values of lifestyle criminals effectively neutralize the intended punitive effect of prison" (Crank & Brezina, 2013, p. 787), for three main reasons:

1. Career criminals consider a "normal" life—for example, a 9–5 job and a consumerist lifestyle—to be boring. For them, occasional prison terms are necessary if they are to avoid such uneventful, middle-class lives.
2. Through long acquaintance with other criminals, the criminal lifestyle prepares people for imprisonment, thereby lessening the perceived severity of punishment.
3. Imprisonment enhances a reputation and "street cred" (Crank & Brezina, 2013).

As you can imagine, this is extremely problematic for the penal system, for, "if offenders do not view imprisonment as punitive, then it is highly unlikely that imprisonment will serve as a meaningful deterrent" (Crank & Brezina, 2013, pp. 782–3). And this observation agrees with empirical research showing that imprisonment has only a minor deterrent effect on repeat offenders (i.e., career criminals) (Bhati & Piquero, 2007). As well, other research has shown that even the harshest forms of punishment, including the death penalty, also fail to deter future criminals (Sorensen, Wrinkle, Brewer, & Marquart, 1999).

The observed failure of deterrence may contribute to widespread efforts to find other ways of dealing with criminals: for example, using strategies of rehabilitation. **Rehabilitation** means turning convicted criminals into law-abiding members of society. In earlier centuries, many prison reformers were Quakers, who thought that all human beings can reform by "coming to God" through repentance. This would mean focusing on ways to ensure that offenders take responsibility for the harm they have caused. Rehabilitation

Box 9.2   The Police and Use of Force

Some deviant acts are controlled with force. For instance, the police are required to handle a variety of peacekeeping and law-enforcement tasks that include settling disputes, removing drunks from the street, aiding the sick, controlling crowds, and pursuing criminals.

The capacity to use force is at the centre of the police mandate, but sociologists wonder, *How do police officers learn to use it properly?* Jennifer Hunt's (1985) research explores the way police themselves classify and evaluate acts of force as either legal, normal, or excessive. Hunt defines *normal* (or legal) force as the coercion needed to subdue, control, and restrain a suspect, in order to take him or her into custody.

It is in the formal police academy that recruits first learn to use *normal* force. In the academy, police recruits are trained to use regulation instruments to subdue,

falls under the restorative model of justice, although not all rehabilitative strategies enlist the co-operation of the victim and community.

While not all rehabilitative justice requires restitution and not all restorative justice requires repentance, in general the two strategies are congruent: both strategies aim at moral and behavioural improvement and involve direct communication between the offender and the victim. Also, both believe that moral (and behavioural) improvements are more likely to deter future criminality than mere imprisonment and harsh punishment. (See Box 9.2 on the use of police force.)

Imprisonment: Retributive Punishment

In Canada and most other present-day societies, punishments such as imprisonment come at the end of a long deliberative process—a process that is (rightly) slow, complex, and costly. Criminal cases are numerous: adult criminal courts in Canada heard about 385,000 cases in the last year for which statistics are available (2011–12), and these involved more than one million charges (Statistics Canada, 2013). Criminal cases are slow proceedings. The amount of time it takes to dispose of a case in adult criminal courts averages over 100 days.

The legal system of Canada stems from two main legal traditions: the English common-law tradition and the French civil-law tradition (Department of Justice Canada, 2013a). In the common-law tradition, an control, and restrain a suspect. Through both observation and instruction, rookie cops gradually learn to apply force and account for its use. However, much of what rookie cops learn is learned in the "informal world" of the street. When rookie cops enter police duty, they are encouraged by veteran colleagues to buy more powerful weapons than the department has issued them. In school, recruits are taught to avoid hitting a person on the head or neck because it can cause lethal or permanent damage. But on the street, rookie cops learn to hit wherever it causes the most damage, to incapacitate suspects and prevent them from doing any (further) harm.

The on-the-job use of excessive force is motivated by a desire to belong. New officers quickly learn that they will earn the respect of their co-workers by being "aggressive" and using whatever force is needed in a given situation. Female rookies are especially called on to prove their toughness. Unlike male rookies, female rookies are thought to be physically weak, naturally passive, and emotionally vulnerable. Females, then, run into special problems in learning to use normal force. Women rookies must display their physical abilities to overcome sexual bias and gain acceptance from veteran police officers. They are encouraged, informally, to act even more aggressively, and to display even more machismo, than male rookies.

emphasis is placed on legal precedent—that is, on the results of past cases. So in all the Canadian provinces except Quebec, disputes are settled by looking at (and trying to apply) previous decisions. The final verdict of a case will typically follow the same logic of the related case, a principle called *stare decisis*. However, this process is not as rigid as it seems. If a case is markedly different from former cases, the judge in authority can create legal precedent him- or herself.

Criminal cases in Canada follow procedures and precedents outlined in the Criminal Code. Crimes are categorized into three categories: (1) summary offences, (2) indictable offences, and (3) dual-procedure electives (sometimes called hybrid).

Summary offences require the accused person to "appear before a provincial court judge for a trial that will normally proceed 'summarily,' that is without further procedure" (Department of Justice Canada, 2013b). If found guilty, people may be fined up to $2,000, imprisoned for six months, or both. Trespassing, disorderly conduct, and theft of property valued under $5,000 are all examples of summary conviction offences (Criminal Code of Canada, 2010).

On the other hand, **indictable offences** constitute more serious charges that include such crimes as homicide, rape, and violent behaviour (Criminal Code of Canada, 2010). Unlike summary offences, indictable offences may require multiple hearings. People charged with an indictable offence may appear before a provincial court judge, a superior court judge, or a superior court judge with a jury.

Imprisonment Rates in Canada and Internationally

Countries vary significantly in the number of people they imprison and the length of time they imprison them for similar offences. Canada and the United States, for example, are similar in many respects, but they differ in the ways they punish rule-breakers. In particular, the United States has far more prisoners per capita and far more punitive court outcomes than Canada.

The US imprisonment rate, which has exploded over the past 35 years (see Figure 9.1), is now more than five times higher than it was in 1970. Over the last few years, Canada's imprisonment rate has varied from between 105 to 120 prisoners per 100,000 of the population, compared to an imprisonment rate of 716 per 100,000 in the United States (Walmsley, 2013). The growth in imprisonment in the United States continues unabated: Americans now imprison more of their citizens (per capita) than any other nation on earth.

Other high imprisonment rates are found in Russia, China, Singapore, and some rapidly developing nations, such as South Africa and Brazil. By contrast, imprisonment rates far lower than Canada's prevail in Japan and the Scandinavian countries (Norway, Sweden, Denmark, and Finland), which range from between 50 to 70 prisoners for 100,000 people.

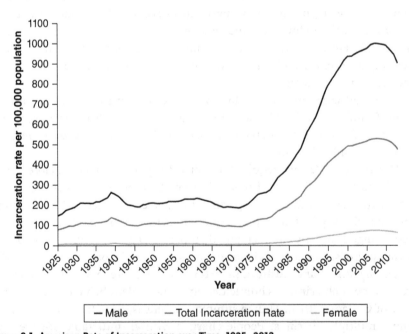

Figure 9.1 American Rate of Incarceration over Time, 1925–2013
Source: Wikipedia, citing the United States Bureau of Justice. (2010, 5 January). US incarceration rates 1925 onwards. Retrieved from http://en.wikipedia.org/wiki/File:U.S._incarceration_rates_1925_onwards.png

Imprisonment rates do not always vary in direct proportion to crime rates, however. They are also reflections of cultural attitudes toward the punishment of crime. That is, imprisonment rates reflect prevailing political and ideological beliefs about punishment. Low, stable imprisonment rates in Canada result, at least in part, from Canadians' desire to distance the country from the punitive excesses of their American neighbours.

Race and Imprisonment

As we saw in Chapter 8, disadvantaged people are more often involved in crime than people in more advantaged social positions, whether we measure advantage in terms of class or race. For instance, homicide rates are six times higher for young black men than for young white men. That said, sociologists are interested in *why* minority offenders are punished more harshly for the same crime and why the law is enforced more aggressively against disadvantaged people (see Figure 9.2). For instance, blacks and whites use drugs at similar levels, but police focus on black drug users, thereby producing racial disparities in drug possession arrests (Beckett, Nyrop, & Pfingst, 2006).

In deciding how to treat offenders, law enforcers are influenced by their perceptions of the threat that each group may pose. In a systematic way, these perceptions influence the routines and rules of the criminal justice system. As a result, law enforcement officials inflate small differences in crime rates into large disparities in punishment. According to Wortley (2003), black people are highly over-represented in certain offence categories—including drug possession, drug trafficking, and serious violence. Wortley (2003) ascribes this finding to *racial profiling*, such that minority offenders

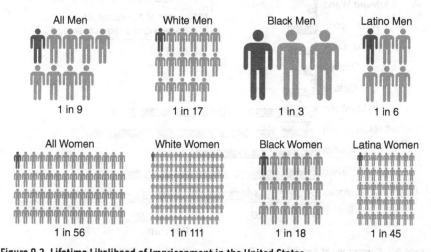

Figure 9.2 Lifetime Likelihood of Imprisonment in the United States
Source: The Sentencing Project. (n.d.). Racial disparity. The Sentencing Project: Research and advocacy for reform. Retrieved from http://www.sentencingproject.org/template/page.cfm?id=122

are more likely than white offenders to be arrested and to be treated harshly after arrest.

This racial profiling is evident in a variety of venues. For example, black people going through customs at the border are more likely to be searched for illegal items (Weatherspoon, 2004); in court, they are less likely to be granted bail by court judges (Schlesinger, 2005).

Like black people, Aboriginal people are over-represented in Canadian jails (see Figure 9.3). According to Statistics Canada (2012), 27 per cent of adults in provincial and territorial custody and 20 per cent of those in federal custody are Aboriginal, which is much higher than the proportion of Aboriginal people (3 per cent) in the Canadian population as a whole. This over-representation is especially marked in the western provinces. For example, in Saskatchewan, Aboriginal people comprise close to 80 per cent of the prison population but only 10 per cent of the adult population. Compared to non-Aboriginal offenders, these Aboriginal offenders are also younger, less educated, less likely to be employed at the time of their admission to prison, and more likely to re-offend. Finally, over 90 per cent of all Aboriginal offenders in Saskatchewan are also found to have a substance abuse problem.

Like black people in the US, Aboriginal people in Canada are less likely than average to be granted bail and more likely to have their sentences extended (Stenning & Roberts, 2001). Similarly, both groups have limited economic mobility and access to services. As a result, imprisonment reinforces

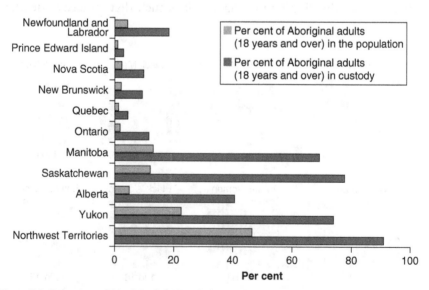

Figure 9.3 Percentage of Aboriginals in Population vs. Percentage Imprisoned
Source: Statistics Canada, Canadian Centre for Justice Statistics. (2015, 31 May). *Integrated Correctional Services Survey.*
Retrieved from http://www.statcan.gc.ca/pub/85-002-x/2012001/article/11715-eng.htm#a7

large race and class disadvantages. Media portrayals of crime, suggesting that most criminals are people of colour, reinforce the stigmatization of these groups.

Health Aspects of Imprisonment

Imprisonment is also associated with both short- and long-term health risks. Let's start with the fact that the proportion of mentally ill prisoners is much higher than in the population at large: for example, the number in US prisons is five times the number of those in mental hospitals. As well, large numbers of inmates carry and pass on communicable diseases while in prison, most commonly hepatitis, human immunodeficiency virus (HIV), and tuberculosis (Beckwith, Zaller, & Rich, 2006). In fact, the prevalence of infectious disease and chronic disease is significantly higher in the prison population than in the national population as a whole (Golembeski & Fullilove, 2005). Eventually, most of these inmates are released into the community, spreading disease into the general population.

Efforts to eradicate these problems are often unsuccessful, given the large and diverse number of people who are imprisoned. According to Smith (2000), different groups require different approaches in tackling health-related issues. For example, the needs of women are different from the needs of men. In the end, prisoners and ex-prisoners are held largely accountable for their own health.

Children and wives of ex-prisoners are also drawn into the orbit of the penal system through the disruption of family life and the contagious stigma of imprisonment. Relationships are disrupted when an offender is imprisoned. Children and spouses of offenders suffer when imprisonment occurs. Some research has shown that formerly imprisoned men experience lower marriage rates and increased risks of divorce (Pettit & Western, 2004).

Imprisonment tends to separate people from their families and friends. As a result, imprisonment affects other people besides the convict, often resulting in loneliness, isolation, difficulties in maintaining contact, deterioration in relationships, and extra burdens of child care; and these can compound a sense of loss and hopelessness among prisoners' partners (Murray, 2005).

Women and Imprisonment

Today, more women are being imprisoned than in the past. As a result of this, even more families are suffering the collateral damage of formal punishment. In Canada, the surge in female inmates is particularly marked among Aboriginal populations, for a variety of offences (including drugs.) Most women that are imprisoned are charged with non-violent crimes, and between 70 to 80 per cent of female inmates are single mothers who committed "poverty-induced" crimes (Chesney-Lind, 1997, pp. 158, 179; Jacobsen, 2008).

Once in prison, many women—like men—face sexual assault, harassment, and medical neglect (Chesney-Lind 1997, p. 4; Jacobsen, 2008). Prisons and jails are male-dominated realms that have the tendency to perpetuate misogynist and sexist sentiments. Most prisons, in fact, lack facilities that cater to women. According to Bertrand (1996), criminal justice systems do not tend to prioritize making prison a humane experience for women.

Hannah-Moffat and O'Malley (2007) write that women are regularly thought of as "correctional afterthoughts." Women tend to commit less serious crimes than men, but less thought is given to rehabilitating them and preparing them for life after prison. Gender-specific approaches present complex challenges, it is true, but so far, little effort has been made to solve this problem. The rate of female recidivism is low, but many women offenders, like male offenders, are stuck in the cycle of poverty, stigma, and hopelessness after their release from prison.

In particular, they suffer from a disruption of their family bonds. An estimated 63 per cent of imprisoned women have one or more minor children, and most report having lived with their children before imprisonment. In adulthood, the children of imprisoned mothers are more likely than average to be convicted of a crime or sentenced to probation. We can ascribe this, in part, to the enforced separation of these children from their convicted mother during an important period in their lives.

Life after Prison

After imprisonment, people's lives are changed forever. In many cases, after prison release, men and women are prevented from entering licensed and public-sector occupations. As a result, a great many ex-convicts have to rely on family and friends for income after release (Visher, Debus, & Yahner, 2008).

Once they are back in the community, according to Harding, Wyse, Dobson, and Morenoff (2011), "former prisoners are at high risk of economic insecurity due to the challenges they face in finding employment and to the difficulties of securing and maintaining public assistance while imprisoned." (p. 440). A reported four out of five ex-convicts spend a long time seeking a job upon release from prison. Unsurprisingly, a criminal record hinders their ability to get a steady job. Many employers, believing the ex-convicts have not yet paid their debt to society, discriminate against hiring them.

In Canada, as elsewhere, there are programs that try to help prisoners find a job after serving their sentence. However, recent documents show that these programs are far from adequate. According to Mackrael (2013), such programs prepare prisoners to enter industries that are dwindling or where job vacancies are scarce. Some ex-convicts are able to return to a previous employer. Ex-convicts who succeed in finding secure, well-paid employment are dramatically less likely to return to prison in the first year out.

Prisonization Theory

What happens when large numbers of young men are arrested, charged, convicted, and thrown into prison by a fearful, punitive country? The result is not good because prisons are neither benevolent nor rehabilitative. By their nature, prisons capture people, take away their rights, and degrade them. In short, they are institutions that dehumanize human beings. This process re-shapes inmates' character and makes them less prepared for the outside world.

Sociologist Donald Clemmer developed **prisonization theory** to describe and explain this process. His goal was to explain why prisons tend to debilitate people, rather than rehabilitate them. In short, prisons are obliged to handle large numbers of young, unruly people under harsh conditions of continued surveillance. This treatment, which keeps peace in the prison, also has unintended and undesirable effects: it alienates prisoners and unites them against the prison administration. A prison subculture, growing out of everyday prison life, reflects and hardens this alienation.

Prisoners quickly learn this prison subculture, especially its anti-administration values and codes of conduct. Through contact with more experienced inmates, prisoners gain new criminal skills, learning to behave in even more undesirable and violent ways. The theory of prisonization suggests that being imprisoned for a long period of time forces people to adopt the norms and standards of a prison environment, often making prisoners incompatible with life on the outside. Prisonization may also make non-violent offenders more likely to commit violent crimes upon their release, which calls into question the effectiveness of the penal system as a whole. If going to prison will make a non-violent offender more likely to commit violent crimes, then the experience is having the opposite of the desired outcome (Stevens, 1994).

And violence is a part of everyday life in maximum- and medium-security prisons. An unfortunate reality there is that "survival for most inmates depends on how violently they behave towards others" (Stevens, 1994, p. 140). Violence is used to establish and maintain one's reputation and to protect oneself from the violence of others. What's more, violence in prison usually goes unpunished. In effect, this means that prisoners can expect different standards and rights than society at large.

Many theories try to explain why prisons are so violent and why prisonization occurs. For one, **deprivation theory** suggests that prisoners are united by their shared experience as inmates, lacking property, freedom, privacy, and romantic partners. These factors, in close living quarters, undermine normal behaviour, making prisoners more prone to violence more prone to violence (Stevens, 1994). **Importation theory**, on the other hand, suggests that the violent culture is imported from the disorganized, low-income communities that the majority of prisoners come from. **Interaction theory**, finally, proposes that power inequalities, both among prisoners and between prisoners and administration, are responsible for violence in prisons. On the one hand, tight budgets and heightened stress make guards unlikely to treat prisoners with kindness, leading to violence; on the other hand, gang life and prisoner politics also lead to violence (Stevens, 1994).

For all of these reasons, prisonization has a strong effect on inmates. Consider this: over 30 per cent of maximum-security prisoners and 40 per cent of medium-security prisoners are indicted for non-violent offences. Yet while experiencing imprisonment, many of them openly admit they would likely commit violent crimes upon release. Living in a prison environment makes people aggressive and more prone to violence, regardless of their earlier views and inclinations. In essence, "belonging to an organisation [like a prison] can by its nature turn non-violent offenders into killers" (Stevens, 1994, p. 151).

This process leads to **recidivism** or the "**revolving door**," mentioned earlier. Recidivism means returning to criminal behaviour even after having suffered punishment for earlier crimes. Recidivism is not inevitable, however, and, according to Andrews (1989), rates can be reduced, depending on how we deal with crime. But in the North American context, there is a high recidivism rate. In Canada, for example, "the most recent data from the last three months of 2007 shows 75% of adult inmates released from provincial jails were charged with another offence within two years of completing their sentence" (Brodbeck, 2010, p. 1). More surprisingly, according to data collected from April to June of 2006, *100 per cent* of the youths that were released reoffended within two months.

So, North American ways of dealing with crime are evidently ineffective in curbing high rates of recidivism. A punitive approach to deterring and correcting crime is apparently a weak form of social control, as opposed to the restorative justice paradigm of Scandinavian countries, where recidivism is much lower.

Rethinking Imprisonment

Rapidly rising cost is one of the reasons people are rethinking their support for prison building. A huge amount of taxpayer money is needed to establish, maintain, and staff jails. According to government reports, "the cost of the federal prison system has risen 86% since the Harper government took over in 2006" (Davis, 2011, p. 1). The cost of the ever-growing prison system is taking a financial toll on society. Tough-on-crime initiatives, such as mandatory minimum sentencing, extend prison sentences and increase the number of imprisoned people, adding to overall costs. A study published in 2014 reports that each prisoner in Canada's 54 federal penitentiaries costs taxpayers approximately $117,788 to keep there (Thibault, 2014). If we compare this to the amount spent on an average Canadian retiring at the age of 65, it appears the offender charged with a heinous crime is considered worth more than 10 times what a retiree is worth (Platt, 2012).

While the costs of imprisonment in Canada are much more modest than they are in the neighbouring US, there can be no doubt that large-scale imprisonment poses a huge fiscal burden for government budgets. By contrast, probation, parole, and community service are cheaper and more effective approaches; however, none of these options is cheap and none is *perfectly* effective. Better support for families and schools would produce Canadians who are less likely to commit serious crimes and, therefore, less likely to need costly, lengthy punishment in adulthood.

Likewise, better support for addiction prevention programs and addiction therapy would cut the costs associated with arresting and imprisoning drug offenders. Eighty percent of violent crimes occur while an offender is on drugs or trying to get drugs; thus, drug use has a significant influence on crime rate. Despite this, treatment for substance abuse in correctional facilities is far from adequate. As well, treatment rarely continues after a prisoner's release, and this causes a high rate of relapse and recidivism. By contrast, studies have found that "every dollar spent on treatment results in seven dollars in savings on reduced crime and health care costs" (Shrum, 2004, p. 227). So, instead of paying to lock up offenders for lengthy sentences, we should be spending the same (or less) money to rehabilitate prisoners and keep other people from getting into trouble.

More spending on education would have a similar preventive effect. Large numbers of convicts have not completed high school, and this has important implications for recidivism. Research shows that recidivism rates decrease drastically with each additional year of education completed, and especially with the completion of a high school equivalency certificate (Shrum, 2004). Despite this, public opinion continues to demand that penal systems be "tough on crime." Budgets for prisoner education programs are the first to be cut, even though they make up only a tiny fraction of the overall justice system budget (Nally, Lockwood, & Knutson, 2012). Prisoner education has been shown to be an effective means of reducing recidivism, yet right wing administrations in both Canada and the United States clamour for more and longer sentences.

By educating convicts and treating their drug problems, we can make it much easier for offenders to reintegrate into society and break the cycle of poverty. Convicts with higher levels of education are more likely to find jobs after their release, and this makes their children less likely to be imprisoned in the future. There is no societal advantage to lengthy prison terms, as it has been shown that "additional time served in prison has little influence on recidivism" (Shrum, 2004, p. 232).

How Scandinavian Countries Punish

Compared to North America, Scandinavian countries have been at the forefront of providing *rehabilitation* for offenders. In this sense, they have achieved a higher level of understanding when it comes to crime prevention. Their favoured approach is restorative justice, which we discussed earlier in this chapter. One example of this—the so-called Alternative project—is funded by the European Commission. In this model, every stakeholder discusses the crime, possible sanctions for the offender, and, most importantly, the best ways of reintegrating the offender back into society. The main idea behind restorative justice is finding ways to encourage and support the offender, an idea not usually present in punitive justice.

Unlike the conventional sense of justice in Canada and the United States, restorative justice establishes a system that is fair to everyone and benefits everyone. The result is significantly reduced rates of imprisonment and recidivism. As one commentator notes, "Norway has only 74.8 people imprisoned per 100,000 residents . . . [and] only 20 percent of Norway's ex-cons commit repeat offenses within two years, versus 50 percent in Britain and 60 percent in the U.S." (The Week, 2012).

The Medicalization of Mental Illness

At the opposite end of the spectrum from imprisonment is **medicalization**. According to Peter Conrad, "medicalization describes a process by which nonmedical problems become defined and treated as medical problems, in terms of illness or disorders" (1992, p. 209). This process involves using medical terminology to describe the problem, medical methods when dealing with it, and a medical viewpoint when thinking about it. A few of the behaviour patterns, previously outside the purview of medicine, that have been medicalized include alcoholism, overeating, and hyperactivity.

Conrad points to two social trends to explain the growth of medicalization. First is the rise of medicine as a "dominant, prestigious, and successful profession" (Conrad, 1992, p. 262). Medicine has become so important and respected in our society that linking an issue or treatment to medicine creates an air of legitimacy for it. Second, secularization has allowed medicine to fill the void created by a decline of religious faith. Many acts once viewed as sins are now being viewed as symptoms of sickness. Attempted suicide, for example, was once counted as a sin but is now viewed as a medical problem.

As a consequence, public opinion has shifted away from viewing deviance as "badness" to viewing it as "sickness" (Conrad & Schneider, 1992). What this means, in practice, is that criminals are no longer considered responsible for their behaviour. When viewed as "sick," they are absolved of moral and legal responsibility. Today, the "medical model" has been applied to many categories of deviant behaviour. As illnesses, they are still viewed as negative and harmful, but the wrongdoer is no longer considered blameworthy in the same way.

Calling something an "illness" affects people's behaviours, the attitudes they take toward themselves, and the attitudes others take toward them. Talcott Parsons recognized that both crime and illness are designations for deviant behaviour. Both are violations of norms and, as such, can disrupt social life; but the attributions of cause are different. Deviance considered voluntary or "wilful" we still tend to define as a crime. Deviance that is seen as involuntary or unintended, on the other hand, tends to be defined as illness. In turn, these social definitions lead to very different social responses. Criminals are punished, with the goal of altering their behaviour, excluding them from the normal population, and deterring others. Sick people are "treated," with the goal of altering the conditions that prevent their conventionality.

In this moral drama, the physician acts as a social control agent in legitimating the **sick role**. Because the sick person is unable to function normally, her behaviour must be considered deviant. That said, we are sympathetic to the sick person. Thus, the sick role is a type of "forgiven deviance." Similar thinking applies to all kinds of medicalized deviance, meaning that people deemed blameless for reasons of sickness are excused from social expectations and released from normal responsibility.

Today, we continue to witness the "medicalization of deviance." As a result, not only have conceptions of deviant behaviour changed, but also agencies mandated to control deviance have changed. As well, with medicalization, sanctions for deviance have changed from punishment to treatment or rehabilitation. Law-breakers deemed "normal" or garden-variety criminals are fined or sent to jail. Law-breakers deemed "ill" are sent for treatment.

Measures of Effectiveness

People hold various, conflicting ideas about the purposes of punishment and the permissible range of punishments. Capital punishment is one of the oldest forms of punishment and was much favoured by Hammurabi, as we saw earlier. While used much less frequently today than it was in past centuries, capital punishment remains in use even in some developed societies such as the US. Corporal punishment, also, remains in use in many countries of the world, although it too has been banned in many countries. In particular, many developed countries have taken firm steps to nullify any justifications for the corporal punishment of women, children, or institutionalized people. Even corporal punishment in schools is largely outlawed today.

That said, torture—which once was much more common—continues to receive justification by both developed and less developed societies. Often torture is justified by referring to matters of terrorism or matters of national security. Whether we view torture as a means to securing information, or an end in itself to symbolize contempt for captive populations, many experts doubt that torture is effective in achieving its desired goals and may even, like other severe controls, have the opposite effect to what is desired.

Progressive people everywhere have sought liberal, enlightened alternatives to death, corporal punishment, torture, and imprisonment, and some have come to embrace the notion of restorative justice. Here the goal of punishment is not to inflict pain but to reintegrate the offender and help the victim. Such punishment needs much tolerance and co-operation from the community. We do not know yet whether this approach yields better results, but early findings suggest that restorative justice is indeed better for victims, communities, and offenders than the other alternatives discussed here. That said, many victims continue to harbor a wish for revenge.

So far, we know relatively little about the effectiveness of restorative justice. That said, we know that some of the alternatives, like lengthy and severe imprisonment, are far from effective as well as being costly to society in economic, social, and moral terms.

Conclusion

As we have seen in other chapters, the topic of punishment—like other topics associated with social control—allows for various competing interpretations. This is important because conceptions of "justice" shape the ways people dole out punishment.

We have not said much about the treatment of women in this chapter, since women are relatively less likely to suffer many of the punishments we have discussed here. However, it is worth noting that sometimes women are, inappropriately, treated differently from men; and sometimes women are treated inappropriately in the same way as men are. Likewise, one might say the same about the treatment of people with mental problems, disabilities, and other characteristics. The law has always had to walk a fine line between standardization of decision-making and individualization of decision-making. It is not only the crime that is being punished: it is also the person, and rule-breakers vary widely in their motives and capabilities.

Some would say this fundamental problem—standardization versus individualization—shows the bizarre particularities and illusions of social organization, and the complexity of doing justice. To be sure, in this chapter we have seen that strong urges to punish wrongdoers often lead to extreme behaviours, with extreme and dysfunctional social outcomes. This itself tells us something about the sociologically unusual nature of social control.

In the next and final chapter, Chapter 10, we will continue this theme by considering victimization. As we will see, the law can victimize people, but it can also protect and help them—an important fact for society's most vulnerable members.

Questions for Critical Thought

1. Why do societies need procedures of formal punishment to deter crime and other deviance? Why aren't informal types of control and punishment (e.g., shame, guilt, social exclusion) good enough?

2. What are the pros and cons of alternatives to capital punishment: for example, life in prison without the chance of parole? Consider other alternatives, too.

3. What differences would you imagine exist between probation and parole? How would they be reflected in the different qualities required of probation officers and parole officers?

4. "Imprisonment often does more harm to people left on the outside than it does to the people who have been imprisoned." Discuss the merits of this statement.

5. Should victims be allowed to influence decision-making in criminal courts or parole deliberations? Why or why not?

Recommended Readings

Gottschalk, M. (2006). *The prison and the gallows: The politics of mass imprisonment in America*. New York: Cambridge University Press.
This book argues that feminists, the victim's rights movement, prisoner rights advocates, and death penalty opponents all contributed to the push for mass imprisonment, by promoting policies that are attractive to conservatives. Gottschalk urges us to favour (instead) citizenship, rights, and the protection of children and families.

Western, B. (2006). *Punishment and inequality in America*. New York: Russell Sage Foundation.
This book explains some of the reasons behind the explosion in imprisonment rates over the past 30 years. It focuses attention on the economic and social consequences of mass imprisonment over time, especially with regard to the poor economic prospects of former inmates, the effect their imprisonment has had on their family life, and how it has perpetuated the cycle of crime.

Whitman, J.Q. (2003). *Harsh justice: Criminal punishment and the widening divide between America and Europe*. Oxford, UK: Oxford University Press.
The author argues that America's susceptibility to degradation and harsher punishment practices is precisely linked to America's historic lack of an aristocracy. He argues that both Tocqueville and Durkheim failed to understand the link between traditions of social hierarchy and the dynamic of degradation in punishment.

Zimring, F.E. (2003). *The contradictions of American capital punishment*. Oxford, UK: Oxford University Press, 2003.
Zimring asks, *Why is the US the only developed Western nation to currently have the death penalty?* And what is it about US history and culture that supports

Americans' affinity for this ultimate use of government power? He suggests that the reason for the predominantly Southern character of the American death penalty is cultural. The death penalty culture of the contemporary South, he argues, comes from the same culture of vigilante justice that once led to lynchings.

Recommended Websites

Death Penalty Focus
www.deathpenalty.org
> Dedicated to ending the death penalty in US states—especially California—this website provides important resources about capital punishment and progress reports about various projects that include increasing the visibility of opponents of the death penalty; energizing and mobilizing clergy and faith communities; and giving voice to men and women who were wrongfully convicted.

Parole Board of Canada
www.npb-cnlc.gc.ca
> This website explains the mission, goals, and legislation underlying the work of Canada's Parole Board and provides a capsule history of its development.

The Pew Charitable Trusts: State Policy
www.pewcenteronthestates.org
> In addition to providing information about research on the death penalty, this website examines research on soaring prison budgets and whether imprisonment is the best path to public safety. Pew's Public Safety Performance Project helps states advance fiscally sound, data-driven policies and practices in sentencing and corrections that protect public safety, hold offenders accountable, and control corrections costs.

10 Social Control and Victimization

Learning Objectives

◎ To learn the different ways in which people can be victimized

◎ To understand the leading theories about criminal victimization

◎ To see the special importance of location (place) for victimization

◎ To recognize that vulnerable populations are at highest risk

◎ To focus on the dangers facing homeless people, sex workers, and Aboriginals

---

Introduction

As we said in the Preface, this book is about social control of various kinds: social control that achieves integration and social control that achieves regulation; microsociological control and macrosociological control, and, most especially, social control that operates from inside the person, as Foucault has described. From Foucault's standpoint and our own, informal social control—discussed in the first half of the book—is far more pervasive and important than formal social control, discussed in the last few chapters.

All the major institutions of society are involved in bringing about social integration and regulation, largely through lifelong socialization. These integrating and regulating institutions include the family, the school, the mass media, and religious institutions. Typically, these familiar, everyday institutions are far more effective at controlling us informally than are formal institutions, including the police, courts, and prisons.

All of this brings us to the topic of "victimization" since the prevention of victimization is a central concern of all social control and, especially, a central concern of formal social control. **Victimization** can be defined as the singling out of an individual or group for subjection to crime, unfair treatment, or another wrong. Our interest in this chapter will mainly be on "victims of crime" because we can easily identify the harm done and the people harmed. Discussing "victims of crime" reminds us of the main reason we study social control and also the reason we have laws, police, courts, and prisons. Criminal victimization is harmful: we can identify the harm done and the people harmed.

In this area, as in other areas of sociology and **criminology**, numerous theories have been proposed to explain why some people are more likely to be victimized than other people, and why some people are more likely than others to be repeat victims.

Theories about Victims and Victimization

Four main theories are commonly used to explain why some groups of people are more likely to be victims of crime than others: routine activity theory, lifestyle theory, deviant place theory, and victim precipitation theory. We will consider each one in order. On another note, we will also discuss victim precipitation theory, or "blaming the victim."

Routine Activity Theory

First, **routine activity theory** posits that crime depends mainly on opportunities that are created through activity patterns. Developed by Lawrence E. Cohen and Marcus Felson (1979), this theory holds that a criminal offence is unavoidable if the following three elements are present:

1. A motivation to commit an offence
2. Vulnerability of a potential victim
3. A lack of protection to prevent crime

When these three aspects converge, a criminal offence takes place. Stated another way, the opportunity for a criminal offence arises whenever an offender is aware of the target's daily routine—a regular way of doing things in a particular order—that enables the offender to easily access the victim. This tells us, among other things, that people with well-known, unchangeable routines are at greater than average risk of victimization, especially if they frequent dangerous locales.

According to this theory, victimization results from the convergence of likely offenders and suitable targets in hot spots where capable guardians are absent. Since this terminology is unfamiliar, we should take a moment to examine each part of the theory. (See Table 10.1 for a brief summary of this terminology.)

Capable guardianship is an important element of routine activity theory. There are three key aspects of capable guardianship: (1) a willingness to supervise, (2) an ability to detect potential offenders, and (3) a willingness to intervene when necessary. The idea of "capable guardianship" is not without problems, however. Consider residential guardians, such as "Neighbourhood Watch"—informal agents of social control in a specific locality who may include self-appointed vigilantes. Sometimes, the very people charged with the responsibility of protecting us are the most likely to harm us: nowhere

Table 10.1 Elements of Routine Activity Theory

Term	Description
Capable guardian	• An individual who watches for potential crimes and is both capable and willing to intervene
Hot spot	• A location where crime is most likely to occur, usually due to lack of visibility and available help
Suitable target	• A person who, for demographic or other reasons, attracts the attention of likely offenders in hot spots

is this more evident than in cases of domestic violence, but it is evident in cases of police violence as well. And it is most evident in cases of vigilantism like the casual murder in 2012 of 17-year-old Trayvon Martin by self-styled neighbourhood protector George Zimmerman, in Sanford, Florida.

A second aspect of routine activity theory is *hot spots*. These are locations where the risks of crime are especially high (e.g., downtown entertainment districts, tourist attractions, dance halls, bars, and nightclubs). In these hot spots, young people are more likely to be victimized by violent crime than older people precisely because young people are much more likely to frequent hot spots. However, family homes are also hot spots for victimization. Here, likely offenders are often close to familiar, likely victims. Often, the so-called guardians are themselves the perpetrators.

Finally, a third aspect of routine activity theory is the presence of *suitable targets*. Suitable targets are people who are regularly exposed to crime or for other reasons have heightened vulnerability. Location aside, some people are more likely than others to be victimized. The risk of violent victimization is higher among certain demographic groups than others, for example, among people who are young (aged 15–24 years), single, live in an urban area, and have a low household income (Cohen, Kluegel, & Land, 1981). Accordingly, violent victimization is highest among Canada's most disadvantaged people (Sampson, Raudenbush, & Earls, 1997); this group includes people who self-identify as homosexual or Aboriginal or who have an activity limitation or physical handicap.

Three characteristics put some people at greater risk of victimization than others, according to routine activity theory:

1. *Target vulnerability:* That is, physical weakness or psychological distress
2. *Target gratifiability:* For example, the female gender for the crime of sexual assault
3. *Target antagonism*: For instance as an ethnic or racial identity that may spark hostility or resentment

As regards the third characteristic, members of certain groups are particularly inclined to attack or harass members of other specific groups.

Immigrants and ethnic minorities run a particularly high risk of victimization in the form of hate crimes (Allen, 2014). According to the Criminal Code of Canada (see http://laws-lois.justice.gc.ca/eng/acts/C-46/), a *hate crime* is committed in order to intimidate, terrify, or harm an entire group of people to which the victim belongs. The victims are targeted for who they are, not because they have done anything wrong. We cannot be certain how many hate crimes are committed each year since many victims are unwilling to come forward. Equally, we cannot say with certainty whether documented increases in the number of hate crimes reveal an increased incidence of such crimes or merely a greater willingness to report them.

In 2009, black people were the most victimized racial group, followed by Arabs and West Asians. Religious hate crimes are mostly committed against people of the Jewish and Muslim faiths (Dauvergne & Brennan, 2011). Hate crimes differ from other offences because of their unique form of aggression. Criminal acts based on hate serve both a symbolic and instrumental function for offenders. The instrumental goal is to hurt a member of the hated minority group. The symbolic goal is to convey an aggressive message to a hated community, neighbourhood, or minority group.

Causes of hate crime vary widely. However, the broad range of factors causing hate crimes includes (1) deep resentment of minority groups in general, (2) governmental decline in protection of civil rights, and (3) sense of economic competition and economic frustration (Craig, 2002).

Social Identity Theory

According to **social identity theory**, developed by Tajfel and Turner (1986), deep resentment and fear lie at the root of many hate crimes. According to this theory, people often act in ways intended to preserve a positive self-image of themselves and their group. As a result, people may commit hate crimes in order to distinguish themselves from, or feel superior to, their victims. Discriminating against an out-group (i.e., the victim's group) often increases the self-awareness of one's in-group (i.e., the perpetrator's group). Ironically, however, victims and offenders often live in the same neighbourhood (Sampson, Raudenbush, & Felton, 1997) and both may even belong to groups that equally experience social exclusion.

Hate crimes also occur because of an insufficient government effort to prevent them. Governmental protection of civil rights in the US, for example, began to decline in the 1980s. Harsh and market-oriented social policies came to dominate American political life after 1980 (and, to some degree, Canadian political life as well under Conservative Party governments). From this standpoint, we can say that the rise and persistence of hate crimes is a result of "neo-liberal" or dog-eat-dog ideology in North American political life. With this in mind, we might want to transform the question "Why do hate crimes occur?" into "Why don't hate crimes occur more frequently?" (Craig, 2002).

Lifestyle Theory

Another approach to understanding victimization that complements routine activity theory is **lifestyle theory**. This theory posits that, for lifestyle reasons, younger people, males, and singles are more likely than older people, females, and married people to spend their leisure time in public places outside the home, where security is low and the risk of crime is high (Hindelang, 1976). People who prefer to spend their evenings in public places, such as bars or clubs, rather than at home, are more exposed to high-risk situations and therefore are more vulnerable to criminal victimization. Men who regularly go to bars, for example, are much more likely to be victimized (e.g., assaulted) than men who spend their evenings at home watching television. Similarly, juveniles who engage in delinquent activities significantly increase their risks of victimization.

Deviant Place Theory

The fourth approach to understanding victimization is *deviant place theory*. Deviant place theory, an offshoot of social disorganization theory, refers to the risks associated with living in "bad areas of town." People who live in danger-ous (i.e., bad) areas are at higher-than-average risk of victimization, regardless of their routine activities or lifestyles. Because of the sheer volume of crime in their neighbourhood, they are at a higher-than-average risk of encountering criminals, no matter what they do. Typically, poverty, unemployment, social isolation, and a large number of young, poorly educated males characterize such high-risk areas (MacDonald, Shildrick, Webster, & Simpson, 2005).

Victim Precipitation Theory (or Blaming the Victim)

Finally, let's consider *victim precipitation theory*. According to this theory (Wolfgang, 1957), people often create their own risks of being victimized. A victim-precipitated crime is an offence that would not have occurred except for (real or perceived) provocative actions by the victim (Felson & Steadman, 1983). By this reasoning, victim-precipitated offenders differ from the other offenders because their crime is a spontaneous yet foreseeable response to the victim's provocative action (e.g., insults). In fact, some of the defendants have never before even considered committing a criminal offence, and the ones who do so finalize their decision only when provoked extensively by the victim. Some would put "honour killings" into this category.

Under the "right" conditions, insults and taunts may escalate into homi-cides or aggravated assaults. Likewise, under the "right" conditions—for example, when the victim is carelessly handling money or other valuables—someone will rob that person. And, under the "right" conditions—for exam-ple, when a young woman gets drunk at a fraternity party—a woman will be raped in "an episode ending in forced intercourse in which a female first agreed to sexual relations, or invited them verbally or through gestures, but then retracted before the act" (Curtis, 1974, as cited in Miethe, 1985).

Of course, that's how the perpetrator might tell the story: the "victim made me do it." The notion of "victim precipitation" has its supporters, in popular opinion and among law enforcers. No one condones homicide, robbery, or rape, but some people are ready to believe that the victim brought it on him- or herself.

Let's go with this idea for a while. Evidently, victim-precipitation can be intended or unintended, conscious or unconscious. It can result from an intentional action or from a failure to act. Also, the length of interval between the precipitator's action and the defendant's response helps to identify whether the committed crime was planned or spontaneous and impulsive: the longer the interval, the more likely we are to believe the offender's response was planned, not impulsive. However, even if we are sympathetic to this idea, it is impossible to accurately measure the degree of victim precipitation because the theory is complex and ambiguous. At worst, it is merely circular: "The victim *must* have caused me to hurt him/her, because that's what I did."

That said, there is the inconvenient fact that some people are victimized multiple times while other people are not victimized at all. This might make us think the victim must be doing something to cause so much victimization.

Now, let's put this in context by using an analogy. If we told you that 22-year-old George Smith was laid off his job earlier this year and is having trouble dealing with unemployment, you might be tempted to ask, "Why did George get laid off? What did he do to cause this?" In other words, you might be tempted to blame George for being unemployed. However, if we also told you that 15–25 per cent of men in George's age group were unemployed, you might think about George's situation in a different way. You might ask, "What's going wrong in our society that is leading to such high unemployment?"

Well, that's the situation we're facing with sexual assaults on young women. Officially endorsed data estimate that 15–25 percent of women currently studying in colleges and universities have been sexually assaulted. Typically, they were assaulted by a friend, acquaintance, or date and, in most cases, did not report this to institutional authorities. In the instances where they did report it, many complained that little support was offered and little help was given. So, in this context, you might not be inclined to blame Georgette Smith, who was reportedly raped on a college campus last week, for her own victimization. Author Jon Krakauer discusses this precise situation at length in a recent book about campus rapes, *Missoula: Rape and the Justice System in a College Town*, (2015).

However, not all cases are clear-cut. Consider a study of rape victimization in US colleges by Franklin (2010), which used survey data collected from a sample of colleges. Franklin notes that college women commonly experience sexual assault, verbal coercion, and threats of force or force resulting in attempted or completed rape. Sorority women, according to Franklin, are more likely than other college women to drink too much, and women who drink too much are more likely than other women to engage in risky sexual behaviours. Alcohol reduces their ability to assess and respond to danger cues, increasing their risk of victimization.

Does this mean they are to blame for being raped? Some recent media articles have said they are. One such article, entitled "College Women: Stop Getting Drunk," appeared as the headline in *Slate Magazine*. In this article (2013), writer Emily Yoffe put the burden of blame squarely on the shoulders of female university students who consumed excessive amounts of alcohol, thereby increasing their "chances" of getting raped. Yoffe writes that "the rise of female binge drinking has made campuses a prey-rich environment" and that when "[a woman] loses the ability to be responsible for [herself], [she] drastically increases the chances that [she] will attract the kinds of people who . . . don't have [her] best interest at heart."

Sentiments like this, in the press and in ordinary conversation, reveal disapproval of the victims of rape. Such sentiments may also discourage victims from reporting that they have been assaulted. Indeed, data from Statistics Canada indicate that roughly 88 per cent of women who have been sexually assaulted in the past 12 months do *not* report their assault to the police.

Increasingly, researchers find the line has blurred between consensual and non-consensual sex; also, between violent and non-violent sex. That is because non-physical (e.g., psychological) coercion is hard to measure—also it is, hard to prove in courts of law or sometimes even in victims' minds. According to the research, many young women drift into sexual activities they would prefer to avoid, if they are sufficiently threatened, shamed, or guilt-tripped into doing so. To circumvent these conceptual difficulties, more researchers are now talking about "unwanted sex." By definition, all unwanted sex is the result of coercion by some means or another; and the coercion may not be violent. Consent may be reluctantly given, or not given at all, yet compliance will take place.

Unwanted sex can have dire psychological consequences—for example, feelings of shame and guilt—and sometimes even long-term educational or occupational consequences, such as a reluctance or inability to interact with strangers at school or on the job, or even to leave the house (Blythe, Fortenberry, Temkit, Tu, & Orr, 2006). These, in fact, are common correlates of depression and post-traumatic stress disorder (PTSD), which some research has connected to unwanted sexual experiences.

To conclude this section, we should note that a majority of sexual assaults—81 per cent, according to victims interviewed in Canada's 2004 General Social Survey (the most recent available data)—are classified as Level 1 assaults, involving only unwanted sexual touching. Level 1 assault involves no physical injuries (or only minor injuries). Of these, 94 per cent go unreported to police, typically because the victim considered the incident to be not important enough (58 per cent say this), because the matter was dealt with in another way (54 per cent), or because the victim did not want to get involved with the police (41 per cent). The more serious sexual assaults, Levels 2 and 3, are attacks typically involving penetration, threat, injury, and in some cases even a weapon; these are much rarer and more traumatizing. Twenty-two per cent of sexual attacks (Levels 2 and 3) are reported to the police.

So, as we see, even the most serious forms of sexual assault are likely to go unreported and unpunished. However, most women's far-too-common experiences of sexual victimization are less likely to be violent, and to go unreported. We will next discuss women's experiences of victimization due to battering.

How Women Experience Battering: The Process of Victimization

It would be tempting to imagine that violated women eventually graduate from a situation of high victimization risk to one of lower risk; but sadly that is not the case. One of the most commonly studied forms of victimization is domestic abuse, and wife battering today is recognized as a widespread social problem.

Every nine seconds, somewhere in the United States, a woman is battered by someone she knows, and there is no reason to think that the frequencies are lower in Canada, although comparable data are unavailable. Each year, 1.5 to 2 million women in these abusive relationships require immediate medical attention as a result of domestic violence (Roberts, 2006). Such relationships rarely start out being abusive, however.

A battered woman, by definition, is someone who has been repeatedly assaulted emotionally, physically, and/or sexually by her intimate partner. As Stark (2007) points out, physical violence is only one element in an abusive relationship; other aspects of everyday behaviour also cause significant physical and emotional harm (Stark, 2007). For example, consider verbal abuse: studies have found that people who are verbally abusive also tend to be physically abusive toward their partners (Straus et al., 1980, as cited in Goodlin & Dunn, 2010).

In general, women run more serious risks of intimate partner violence than men. The National Violence against Women Survey (NVAWS) estimates that 25 per cent of women have experienced intimate partner violence at one time or another. As well, women are more likely than men to be abused in a variety of ways: verbally, emotionally, physically, and sexually. For many women, this comes as part of a long history of abuse. According to data from the National Crime Victimization Survey (NCVS), women who were sexually and physically abused in childhood are more likely to be abused in adulthood as well (Reyns, 2010), with the result that roughly 15 per cent of women experience repeated victimization over the course of their lives (Goodlin and Dunn, 2010).

The easily observable, physical consequences are horrible, but there are also less visible, psychological consequences. Some women lose consciousness during an assault and many battered women suffer from chronic headaches and brain injuries (Campbell & Soeken, 1999). Battered women also commonly report head and neck injuries, depression, mental disorders, miscarriages, abortions, alcohol and drug abuse, and suicide attempts (Roberts, 2006; Campbell & Soeken, 1999; Barnett, 2000).

Why don't these women leave their dangerous, abusive partners? Many battered women stay in abusive relationships because they cannot imagine leaving and living without their partner. They focus on all the difficulties of disentangling themselves from a violent relationship. As well, they fear they would feel guilty or ashamed, if they were to leave. As Ferraro and Johnson (1983) note, women's socialization emphasizes the primary value of being a good wife and mother, despite the associated costs and adversities. In addition, most cultures still place a high value on marriage. Though divorce is common and easy to accomplish, many may consider it a personal failure; and it is seldom undertaken without emotional upheavals. Many women do not leave after the first assault because they think the situation is temporary and may improve. As well, psychological abuse accompanying violence often creates feelings of shame and long-lasting feelings of inferiority in the victim (Ferraro & Johnson, 1983). These feelings of guilt and shame, at least in the early stages of battering, are mixed with a hope that things will get better.

According to Ferraro and Johnson (1983), battered women use six "techniques of neutralization" to rationalize the actions of their abuser as normal, acceptable, or at least justifiable. They are presented in Table 10.2.

Table 10.2 The Six Techniques of Neutralization

Technique	Description
Appeal to the salvation ethic	• Seeing the abuser as "sick" and reliant on the victim for support • Trying to save abusers from themselves
Denial of victimizer	• Blaming the abuse on factors outside of their control • Thinking the abuse is "natural" or "unavoidable"
Denial of injury	• Inability to accept that abuse is taking place • Quick return to routine as if nothing happened
Denial of victimization	• Blaming oneself for the abuse; exonerating the abuser • Thinking the victim caused the abuse, not that it is unjustified
Denial of options	• Practical options: lack of money, place to go, protection, etc. • Emotional options: fear of social isolation without the abuser
Appeal to higher loyalties	• Staying with the abuser due to religious beliefs about the sanctity of marriage

Some women who manage to escape an abusive household end up returning to their batterers or are dragged back against their will. Research has estimated that, on average, women leave and return five times before they permanently cut off all contact with their batterer (Barnett, 2000). If there is only emotional abuse in a relationship, it may be harder for the woman to leave because it is less tangible than physical abuse, therefore harder to use as evidence of the need to escape an abusive husband (Barnett, 2000). As well, if a woman has been psychologically abused, she may come to doubt her own judgment and ability to make decisions for herself. This form of self-control entraps women in their relationships with their abusers (Sabina & Tindale, 2008).

In cases where women summon up the resolve to leave their abusive partner, violence and even homicide sometimes erupts (Roberts, 2006; Sabina & Tindale, 2008). A study of cases where an abused woman was murdered by her partner showed that seventy-five per cent of the time the woman was trying to end the relationship when the murder occurred. However, many women are also driven to killing their abusive partner. An estimated 500 chronically battered women kill their partners each year in response to terrifying death threats, post-traumatic stress disorder (PTSD), and/or intrusive fears of their own death at the hands of the abuser (Roberts, 2006).

A lack of sufficient resources may keep some women from leaving abusive relationships. Often, battered women suffer from a shortage of resources—social capital, education, and income—that would make leaving easier. Reportedly, most chronically battered women have a low educational attainment—fewer than 20 per cent have a degree higher than a high school diploma. Women with low educational attainment are more likely to stay in a violent relationship because of their financial dependence on their partner. By contrast, battered women who leave their partner shortly after the violence begins are more likely to come from the middle- or upper-income class and have completed at least some post-secondary schooling (Roberts, 2006).

Having children also makes it difficult for women to leave an abusive relationship. Compared to women who are able to escape from short-term battering, women suffering from long-term battering (ranging from 4 to 40 years) are more often mothers of young children (Roberts, 2006). Their desire to be "good wives" and "good mothers" takes precedence over their leaving an abusive relationship.

To summon the courage to leave an abusive relationship, the battered woman must undergo several changes of attitude toward the relationship (Barnett, 2000). First, she must recognize that her relationship is an unhealthy one. The second stage is for her to realize that the relationship cannot be improved and that her situation is unlikely to get better. Third, a catalyst—some dramatic event—edges her toward deciding to leave. This catalytic event can include severe injury as well emotional distress brought on by a huge fight. Finally, she must accept that she has to leave the relationship even though doing so may not be final (Barnett, 2000).

Official statistics provide only a pale reflection of the numbers of women who suffer from domestic abuse. They provide an even paler reflection of the reasons women fail to report spousal violence to police, as we see in Figure 10.1.

To conclude, a great many abused women are reluctant and fearful about leaving an abusive partner, for a great many reasons, as we have seen. However, among these reasons we must include fear of being blamed by oneself and others for having failed to make the marriage work. As we see in Box 10.1, as in the case of unwanted sex, a tendency to blame the victim—to say the victim precipitated the abuse—remains all too common.

Victimization and Sex Workers

Like homeless men and women, sex workers—who are mainly women—run a continuing risk of violence throughout their lives. For instance, "Research

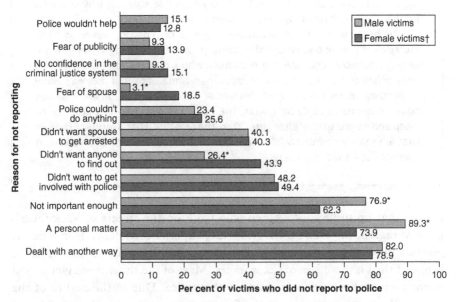

Figure 10.1 Reasons for Not Reporting Spousal Violence to Police, by Sex, in Canada, 2009

† reference category
* significantly different from reference category (p < 0.05)

Note: Includes legally married, common-law, same-sex, separated, and divorced spouses who experienced spousal violence within the previous five years and who indicated that the violence did not come to the attention of police. Figures do not add to 100 per cent due to multiple responses. Data from the Northwest Territories, Yukon, and Nunavut were collected using a different methodology and are therefore excluded.

Source: Statistics Canada. (2012, 20 December). *General social survey, 2009*. Retrieved from http://www.statcan.gc.ca/pub/85-224-x/2010000/ct003-eng.htm

Box 10.1   How to Reduce Victim Blaming

If we want to reduce victimization in our society, we need to reduce the public tendency to blame the victim. Only if we do so will victims feel bold enough to "out" their abusers and leave abusive relationships. But how might we go about changing these victim-blaming attitudes?

In 2011, Fox and Cook set out to study the effect on students of a "victimology" course about victim-blaming attitudes. They found that as they increased their knowledge about victimization, students became less likely to blame the victims of crimes for the victimization (Fox & Cook, 2011). As people gain more understanding of a social problem—are better able to put themselves in the shoes of the victims, for example—they are likely to adopt more enlightened views about the problem. However, what do we do about the attitudes of people who have not received this information and understanding? Perhaps, we can design new ways of distributing the information, as a type of public-health education (or health-promotion) strategy. A great many health promotion programs—for example, urging people to stop smoking or start exercising—have met with considerable success; why should a program aimed at reducing victim-blaming not succeed too?

The best way to reduce victim blaming is to help people realize that the lifestyles of people and groups that predispose them to being victimized are largely unchosen. Consider the prostitute who works the street corner in a poor neighbourhood, and the homeless man who sleeps in a doorway every night: they are both putting themselves at risk of victimization and may not have much choice to do otherwise. The homeless man has no safe place to sleep and no one to look after him. Often, the prostitute has a range of choices that are mainly or entirely bad. Consider the risky lifestyle of sex workers in present-day Canadian society.

reveals that up to 98% of women who work on the streets of Vancouver's poorest region, the Downtown East side, experience violence from clients, pimps and other sex-workers" (O'Doherty, 2011). For good reason, violence is one of the biggest fears of sex workers. Most of the time, these victimized women will not report their abuse to the police. Due to the nature of the activity they are engaged in, many fear that they will be further victimized in the justice system.

In Benoit and Millar's study of 200 sex workers in BC, "virtually all those interviewed expressed alienation from the protective services of the police and expressed a reluctance to report violence incidences or turn to the police for help" (Benoit & Millar, 2001, as cited in O'Doherty, 2011). Sex workers rarely receive much sympathy when they are victimized because they do not possess the attributes of an ideal victim: innocence, purity, and a lack of knowledge about relevant risks. Indeed, police may ignore their complaints of sexual abuse because sex work is known to be inherently risky (Doezema, 1998).

Many, if not most, street workers are impoverished women who enter sex work as a way of surviving (Shannon, Kerr, Allinott, Chettiar, Shoveller, & Tyndall, 2008). Many are also drug addicts and racial minorities (Nuttbrock, Rosenblum, Magura, Villano, & Wallace, 2004). They may lack the education and skills to compete for other, more respectable work opportunities. Many have a history of childhood and adult neglect, or even abuse. Women sex workers who walk the city streets in search of trade are at an especially high risk of assault, rape, murder, and other types of physical violence. The male perpetrators of these crimes include muggers, drug dealers, potential customers, and sometimes people passing by. They are also at risk of poor treatment and even violent abuse by the police.

Once again, routine activity theory helps us recognize the other factors that play a significant role. Street prostitutes are more likely to meet with harm since they roam the streets at night in search of customers. When working the streets, sex workers expose themselves to homeless people, people on drugs, and people out looking for trouble. Then, they provide sex in private or hidden places, without guardians around to protect them from danger.

Canadian laws regarding sex work have been in transition for the past few years. The way the criminal law has been enforced has encouraged violence against sex workers by forcing them to work under unsafe circumstances. In response to demands from the Supreme Court, the Conservative government of Stephen Harper proposed a law that goes after sex buyers, by criminalizing the buying of sex. The penalties include jail time—up to five years in some cases—and minimum cash fines that go up after a first offence. The bill doesn't say what constitutes a "sexual service," however, so the courts will have to draw the line. For example, lap dancing and masturbation in a massage parlour may count as a "sexual service," but not stripping or the production of pornography.

Sex workers also face penalties under this proposed bill. Specifically, it would be illegal for a sex worker to discuss the sale of sex in certain locales. It would also be illegal for a person to gain a "material benefit" from the sale of sexual services by anyone other than themselves. Anyone who "receives a financial or other material benefit, knowing that it is obtained by or derived directly or indirectly" from the sale of a "sexual service," faces up to 10 years in prison. Prime Minister Justin Trudeau has made it clear that he will announce a different way of dealing with the dangers that face sex workers, but the details are unknown at the time of this book's publication. Conceivably, the new bill will support decriminalization of sex work.

Some have proposed that decriminalization of prostitution is necessary to reduce the violence and victimization experienced by sex workers. According to this argument, prostitutes need to be able to protect themselves from the inherent risks of the sex industry by, for example, speaking to potential clients for long enough to evaluate how dangerous they are (Richards, 1979).

Some researchers also suggest that decriminalizing or legalizing prostitution merely perpetuates social and gender inequality and sexual exploitation (Farley, 2004). Fundamentally, decriminalization does not change beliefs in the superiority of men over women and the right of men to use women as sexual objects. Nowhere is this depersonalization and subordination of women sex workers more evident than in the case of Aboriginal sex workers. However, as we see in Box 10.2, the victimization of Aboriginal

Box 10.2   Victimization of Aboriginal People

In Canada, as in the United States and elsewhere, Aboriginal people are over-represented as victims of violence, even including intimate partner violence (Brzozowski et al., 2006). In fact, the victimization of Aboriginal people significantly exceeds the number of victims among non-Aboriginal people.

In 2009, Statistics Canada reported that more than one-third (37 per cent) of the Aboriginal population aged 15 years or older living in Canadian provinces has been victimized, in comparison to about one-quarter of non-Aboriginals. Figure 10.2 shows that the most common forms of victimization among the Aboriginal population include theft of personal property, physical assault, and sexual assault (Perreault, 2011a). They are also significantly more likely to be victims of homicide. Between 1997 and 2000, the homicide rate for Aboriginal people was seven times higher than the rate for non-Aboriginal people (Perreault, 2011b). No other minorities, immigrants, or native-born are at the same risk of victimization.

Location theory helps explain these high rates of Aboriginal victimization. Historically, Aboriginal people have continued to live in worse social and economic conditions than non-Aboriginal people, on average. Persistent social and economic inequalities surrounding Aboriginals have continued to involve them in criminal incidents either as victims or as offenders. Factors such as poor living conditions situated in crowded areas, unemployment, lack of education, and low income have continued to increase their exposure and proximity to crime (Reading & Wien, 2009; La Prairie, 2002). Also, Aboriginal people have continued to maintain high-risk life-styles that include drugs, alcohol, and "hanging out on the streets" (Brady, Dawe, & Richmond, 1998; Hunter, Hall, & Spargo, 1991; Perkins, Sanson-Fisher, Blunden, people, and especially women, goes well beyond the risks associated with prostitution.

Victimization of the Homeless

All of the theories about victims and victimization that we discussed earlier in this chapter predict that homeless people will be victimized more than any other group because of their location, their lifestyles, and their routine activities (Lee & Schreck, 2005; Fischer, 1992). Living on the street inevitably exposes homeless people to criminals and crimes. As well, many homeless people take part in risky activities, such as begging, prostitution, or selling drugs (Surrat & Inciardi, 2004). Occasionally, homeless people are also the victims of non-economic (hate) crimes committed by teenage

Lunnay, Redman, & Hensley, 1994). This especially applies to Aboriginal youth. As we have seen, high-risk lifestyles lead to high-risk situations, which increase the likelihood of victimization.

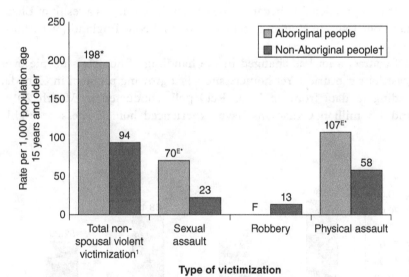

Figure 10.2 Rates of Victimization for Aboriginal vs. Non-Aboriginal People in Canada
Notes
† Reference category
* Significantly different from reference category (p < 0.05)
F too unreliable to be published
1. Includes robbery and excludes all incidents of spousal sexual and physical assault. Includes incidents that occurred during the 12 months preceding the survey.
Source: Statistics Canada, General Social Survey, 2009.

thrill-seekers (Gaetz, 2004). Victimization, unfortunately, is nothing new to homeless people. Many of the homeless carry a personal history of victimization into their current lives. For example, many homeless women report having experienced childhood physical or sexual abuse (Simons & Whitbeck, 1991).

As we can see in Figure 10.3, victimization is most common among the youngest Canadians, and a high proportion of people who are victimized in later life are repeating the experience of victimization they first suffered in earlier life. This is particularly true of homeless people, who, as a group, tend to have histories of childhood neglect, deprivation, and abuse.

Routine activity theory, discussed earlier in this chapter, is key to understanding the victimization of homeless people. Said simply, homeless people are available and suitable targets. They carry their property around with them and they are ignored or stigmatized by society, often shunned and held in low regard, if they are noticed at all. Homeless people also, for the most part, lack capable guardians, such as relatives, friends, and people in authority. Also, homeless people are continually exposed to potential offenders, such as addicts, ruffians, and street criminals. Because they are shunned and stigmatized, the homeless are still being "warned out" of the most public places—a practice that began in the sixteenth century as a result of Elizabethan Poor Laws in England and then colonial New England (Wachholz, 2005).

Of course, a lot has changed in the handling of homeless people over the past four centuries. Yet homelessness is a growing problem in Canada. According to data from an Ipsos Reid poll, conducted in March 2013, around 1.3 million Canadians have experienced homelessness or highly

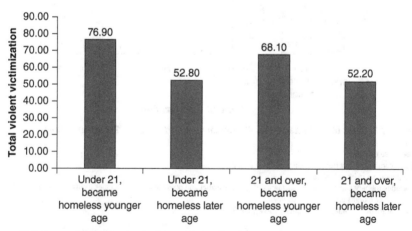

Figure 10.3 Rates of Victimization by Age, per 1000 People
Source: www.homelesshub.ca

insecure housing at some point in the past five years. Other research estimates that half (47.5 per cent) of the homeless population in Canada consists of single adult males, between the ages of 25 and 55. Aboriginal people (First Nations, Métis, and Inuit people) also make up a large percentage of the homeless. Youths account for about 20 per cent, followed by women and families—which is a growing concern in Canada (Gaetz et al., 2013). As Gaetz et al. (2013) point out, to date, the most effective strategy for combating homelessness has been the Housing First model because if you remove the homeless from their state of vulnerability, they are less likely to be victimized and more likely to improve their own circumstances. This idea follows logically from the routine activity and lifestyle theory of victimization.

However, the public is largely indifferent to homeless people and perhaps unwilling to pay the costs that housing the homeless would entail. It is not surprising that public sympathy to the homeless varies over time, and from place to place. After all, people are wrapped up in their own personal, social, and economic concerns. As well, people are inclined to conserve their sympathy by ignoring the plight of others worse off than themselves. To protect ourselves emotionally and morally, we tend to deny the problems of others and embrace what Swedish economist Gunnar Myrdal called the "convenience of ignorance" (Gaetz, Scott, & Gulliver, 2013). So, for reasons of self-protection, sympathy is an emotional response that is ritually and temporarily given, then taken away.

This is why people in our society mainly express sympathy for the homeless in December around Christmas, but not in February, after Christmas has long passed. We have only so much emotional energy, even though we live in a world filled with suffering. Similarly, as Bunis et al. (1996) point out, year after year, media coverage of homelessness increases in November, peaks in December, and declines in January. We see a similar pattern in charitable donations and volunteering by private citizens: they rise in November, peak in December, and decline in January. This is in keeping with what Durkheim said about the role of ritual activities in maintaining collective morality: people need these ritual expressions of sentiment. However, they couldn't live with the stress of feeling concern for unknown others throughout the year: to do so would be emotionally exhausting.

Conclusion

We have seen in this chapter that some people are victims of crime, and, for this, they deserve our protection and support.

Some types of victimization—for example, the victimization associated with sex work—can best be dealt with through harm-reduction strategies, such as decriminalizing and regulating sex work. Such strategies—tried and validated in other countries—would reduce victimization, although their implementation would require a change in the ways our federal government thinks about sex work. Such strategies might not seem as morally principled as strict rules and harsh punishments, perhaps, but they would be more effective in protecting sex workers and minimizing victimization.

Other types of victimization—for example, the victimization that results from domestic violence and sexual assault—require a wholesale change in our attitudes toward the victims of such violence. We will have to learn to stop "blaming the victim," and this will mean putting aside traditional, moralistic beliefs that the world is fair and people get what they deserve.

Finally, the victimization exemplified by homeless people and Aboriginal people—and the almost constant danger in which they live—can only be remedied through large-scale social reform. We are only beginning to collect needed data on the numbers and types of homeless people in Canada, let alone data on what they need to survive and what supports they would need to get off the street. Once we have the necessary data, we can begin to hope that public discussion and legislation will follow.

As for the problems facing Aboriginal people, we already have much or even most of the data we need, but we are far from having frank and open discussions about what comes next. In this respect, we have to contest former Canadian prime minister Harper's view that this is no time for sociological analysis, in respect to the many Aboriginal women who have been assaulted, raped, and murdered in recent years. On the contrary, this is *precisely* the time for sociological analysis because the criminal justice system has proven itself unsuited to the tasks of violence prevention and deterrence where Aboriginals and other minorities are concerned. Likely, the new Prime Minister will take this into account when dealing with unresolved Aboriginal issues.

Postscript

We began this book by posing the question, "Why is the study of social control so crucial to the study of social order?" We suggested that one cannot fully understand social inequality and social order, which are at the very root of the sociological enterprise, without first understanding the pervasiveness of social control. Social control, as we have seen, involves a combination of coercion, voluntary compliance with established norms, and personal commitment to a set of social values that, over time, become privileged in society. Moreover, social control involves both integrative and regulative forces. And, as we hope you have realized from our discussion of multiple social contexts, social control is present *all the time*.

This book, however, has significantly departed from mainstream conceptions of social control in the twenty-first century, which adopt as their primary focus *criminological forms* of social control, such as the use of laws and prisons to control and punish behaviour. While we devoted some space to this model, we also took a step back from this narrow focus and devoted a great deal of attention to *informal forms* of social control.

We have argued throughout this book that the most effective forms of social control are *not* those prescribed by laws and enforced by police and the prison system. Rather, the internalization of norms by members of a society and the unconscious ways in which we ourselves regulate our own behaviour and the behaviour of others are far more powerful and reache a larger audience. It is largely for this reason that, as a society, we need to devote more time and attention to inculcating a civic morality in Canada, through our schools, churches, and mass media. Other societies (in northern Europe especially) do this far better than we do.

Subsequent chapters have shown that informal social sanctions and rewards are unequally distributed across society. Said another way, mechanisms of social control all operate differently on different people. Knowing this gives us a deeper awareness of social inequality and its significance. Disadvantaged people are more likely to be desperate and cynical, for example, and therefore less deterred from rule-breaking than more comfortable members of Canadian society.

We also included an extensive discussion of how social control flows through key *social institutions*: families, schools, workplaces, religious bodies, governments, and corporal systems are all involved in exerting social control over individuals. These social structures all use inbuilt mechanisms and sanction systems to teach and enforce social control. Agencies like the government, mass media, and religious institutions all seek to control people in their own ways to ensure conformity with standards and values, and to ensure social order. Much of what goes on in these institutions is delivered in a very calculated way. In these and other settings, the essence of social control can be traced to *what people care about*, that is, their values and what they deem (or are told to deem) important in their lives.

In Canada, the messages about what we *should* care about are very clear, from birth onwards: we are supposed to care about status, wealth, beauty, honour, and respect, to name just a few dominant values. Through media and advertising and interactions with others around us, we are told what "beauty" means, what "justice" means, what we should consider to be "success," and what is "normal." And while we may sometimes imagine we have chosen these values and ways of seeing the world, in fact, forces much stronger than any one of us have forced them upon us.

We hope that, if nothing else, you take this main message away from reading this book: social control is effective mainly because people are *not* taught to watch out for it. Our ignorance and blindness keeps us (often mindlessly) following society's norms, in support of those with the power and authority to enforce social control: our parents, teachers, religious leaders, media outlets, governments, and law enforcement officials, chief among them.

We hope that this book has inspired you to pursue further studies in some of these topics. At the very least, we hope you have come to understand the centrality of *social control* in the sociological enterprise—especially, its importance in shaping social inequality and social order in our complex society.

Questions for Critical Thought

1. Why are private places even riskier than public places for most types of victimization? What are the implications of this for social policy?

2. Find at least one aspect of victimization not explained by the current theories about criminal victimization, and discuss the kind of research needed to study this aspect.

3. Would the Aboriginal population suffer less victimization if it were socially and economically integrated with the rest of the Canadian population? If yes, what is standing in the way of such integration?

Recommended Readings

Belanger, Y.D., Head, G.W., & Awosoga, O. (2012). *Assessing urban Aboriginal housing and homelessness in Canada.* Ottawa, Ontario: Final Report prepared for the National Association of Friendship Centres (NAFC) and the Office of the Federal Interlocutor for Métis and Non-Status Indians (OFI), Ottawa, Ontario.

A timely discussion of Aboriginal people's housing conditions in urban areas showing that urban Aboriginal homelessness is a major issue based on the overrepresentation of Aboriginal people among the national homeless population. National policies are needed to specifically aid urban Aboriginal renters and homeowners, and to reduce urban Aboriginal homelessness.

Erikson, K. (2004). *Wayward Puritans: A study in the sociology of deviance* (rev. ed.). Boston: Allyn and Bacon.

This book uses evidence from the Puritan Settlement in seventeenth-century Massachusetts as a setting to examine different ideas about deviant behaviour in society. Deviant behaviour is argued to be an effective way of providing a necessary point of contrast that helps maintain social order, but it can also produce victims.

Krakauer, J. (2015). *Missoula: Rape and the justice system in a college town.* New York: Doubleday.

A carefully reported account of numerous sexual assaults at the University of Montana in Missoula—a typical college town, with a highly regarded state university and a football team whose fans are willing to ignore and forgive just about anything.

Recommended Websites

Joint Center on Violence and Victim Studies
www.washburn.edu/academics/community-continuing-education/academic-outreach/jcvvs/index.html

This American inter-university collective brings together three victimization studies programs, located at Washburn University, California State University-Fresno, and the University of New Haven, in the hopes of further developing the field of victimology. The site provides a broad listing of resources for studying victimization issues, and it is also a useful resource for students considering advanced study in the field.

Policy Centre for Victim Issues
www.justice.gc.ca/eng/cj-jp/victims-victimes/
Run out of the federal Department of Justice, this site has many links to criminal justice publications, news agencies, legislative bodies, and victims' services. The Policy Centre for Victim Issues is helpful in understanding how the government attempts to address victims' needs.

Statistics Canada: Criminal Victimization in Canada (2009)
www.statcan.gc.ca/pub/85-002-x/2010002/article/11340-eng.htm
This Statistics Canada survey provides information on reported victimization in Canada. The study is helpful not only in understanding the ubiquity of violent and non-violent forms of victimization but in also showing how arrest rates and conviction rates vary by region.

World Society of Victimology (WSV)
www.worldsocietyofvictimology.org/
This body, which aims to develop the academic study of victimology, is a not-for-profit non-governmental organization (NGO) with a consultative status with the Economic and Social Council of the United Nations. The WSV's website provides links to resources in this burgeoning field of study and also provides a list of print publications and non-affiliated research bodies in the field.

Glossary

Agnosticism: The belief that truths about religion and the existence of a god are unknowable to human beings.

Anomie: The collapse of certain elements of informal social control in a society that causes individuals to act without regard for interpersonal ethics and general social disorganization.

Atheism: The lack of belief in a god or a religious dogma.

Authoritarian states: A type of state that forbids public opposition to the regime and exercises strong control over society with the co-operation of the military and other organizations.

Autonomous morality The ability to make moral decisions independently and to understand why certain behaviours are considered good or bad.

Civilizing process A theory by Norbert Elias, which claims that manners, civility, and the state all develop in unison. Traditions and formalities that started out in the ruling class trickle down to the rest of society and slowly become the norm.

Collective consciousness: Durkheim's concept for the sentiment or understanding of the world shared by a group of people. This includes the cognitive-moral system of shared beliefs, convictions, and symbols.

Collective efficacy: How the members of a group perceive the effectiveness of their collective actions, which in turn affects how likely they are to pursue collective actions.

Conceptual entrapment: Rome's theory that people interpret events exclusively within the framework imposed upon them by the mass media.

Conformity: The tendency to adopt the attitudes, beliefs, or values of a group as one's own and to mimic their practices.

Criminal lifestyle: A career in crime, often involving frequent association with other criminals.

Criminology: The study of crime and those who commit it, as well as the study of systems of deterrence, rehabilitation, and punishment.

Cultivation theory: A theory that suggests that long-term viewing of television programming socializes and "cultivates" the viewer's understanding of normal behaviours and appearances.

Cycle of disadvantage: A set of factors that perpetuate poverty and make it difficult to break out of. These factors can even be multigenerational.

Decriminalization: Eliminating a proscribed behaviour from the criminal code.

Deprivation theory: The theory that prisoners are united by their shared experience as inmates, lacking property, freedom, privacy, and romantic partners.

Deterrence theory: The theory that the primary goal of punishment is to use fear to prevent further rule-breaking.

Deviance: Behaviour that runs contrary to social norms and is therefore a target of social control.

Differential association theory: The theory that people commit deviant acts when exposed to a culture or community that is accepting of such acts. It suggests that deviance is learned behaviour.

Discipline: A system of regulation designed to coerce and control an individual's actions and movements. Discipline has the twofold effect of increasing an individual's efficiency and decreasing his or her disobedience.

Embeddedness: The degree to which a person's actions are constrained by the relationships and religious or political institutions that surround them.

Formal social control: Centred on written legal norms, regulations, or laws as well as the systems employed expressly to enforce them.

Globalization: The ever-increasing interconnectedness of the world, brought about through technological improvements. Globalization is the mixture of cultures, ideas, peoples, and goods that has become more fluid as countries have become more strongly linked.

Health behaviour theory: A theory that suggests that individuals are more likely to adopt a behaviour when it is shown to have positive consequences.

Ideological control: A system of beliefs and norms that justifies the social and economic relationships that constitute a society. Echoing the ideals and concerns of the ruling class, ideology serves to legitimize and validate their domination of other groups.

Importation theory: The theory that violent prison culture is imported from the disorganized, low-income communities the majority of prisoners come from.

Incapacitation: The use of imprisonment to keep offenders from committing even more crimes.

Indictable offences: Offences that constitute more serious charges (than summary offences) and that include such crimes as homicide, rape, and violent behaviour.

Informal social control: A collection of unspoken rules, guides, and standards of behaviour.

Innovation: Finding a new method or process to achieve a certain goal.

Institutions: The structures, customs, and rules that govern a society and organize interactions. Some examples include abstract ideas like the family and etiquette as well as more concrete ones like banks and the state.

Integration: The process by which individuals become accepted as members of a group, community, or society, and the relationships between members that define the group itself.

Interaction theory: The theory that power inequalities, both among prisoners and between the prisoners and the administration, are responsible for violence in prisons.

Internalization: The process by which one incorporates the ideas and values of others into one's own world view.

Liberal democracy: A system of government that aims to preserve the liberty of citizens through elected representatives of the people and protected individual rights.

Lifestyle theory: A theory of crime victimization that suggests that certain people who are engaged in certain lifestyles are more prone to become victims of crime due to situational factors, such as location, age, race, socio-economic status, etc.

Male gaze: Refers to anything that portrays women from the perspective of heterosexual men, thereby exaggerating masculinity, objectifying women, and perpetuating patriarchy.

Mass media: Organizations that use technology to facilitate the exchange of information on a massive scale.

Medicalization: The process by which a form of deviance becomes treated as a medical problem rather than a social one. The language used to discus and "treat" behaviour becomes more medical, and responsibility for the behaviour is lifted from the offender.

Moral community hypothesis: Stark's theory that says that religion is most likely to deter people from delinquent behaviour when the religious community shares the same beliefs as the individual.

Moral entrepreneurs: Individuals who establish behavioural norms in a society and label behaviours as good or bad, for altruistic or other reasons.

Negative socialization: The process by which individuals internalize and accept norms that encourage destructive behaviour.

Organized religion: The set of social institutions, groups, buildings, and resources that constitute a religious group.

Peer group: The group of individuals with whom an individual shares most characteristics, including age, values, and social class.

Prisonization theory: The theory that imprisonment tends to make prisoners more fixed in their criminal ways and more resistant to change and improvement.

Profane: See *sacred*.

Prosocial activity: Behaviour that reinforces the cohesion of a group or community.

Recidivism (the "revolving door"): A pattern of returning to criminal behaviour even after having suffered punishment for earlier crimes.

Reference group: People to whom an individual refers when evaluating his or her own thoughts and behaviour.

Regulation: The process by which members of a group enforce the rules, norms, and values that they hold.

Rehabilitation: Practices designed to turn convicted criminals into law-abiding members of society.

Restorative justice: Ways of punishing criminal behaviour that seek rehabilitation or restitution.

Retributive punishment: Ways of punishing criminal behaviour that exact revenge for harm done.

Routine activity theory: A theory of crime victimization that suggests that activity patterns create opportunities for crime, especially in situations when a likely offender, a suitable target, and a lack of capable guardians converge.

Sacred (vs. profane distinction): Two categories explicated by Émile Durkheim in relation to religion. Sacred objects are considered extraordinary and are given meaning beyond their physical existence. These are distinct from profane objects, which are part of everyday life.

Secularization theory: A theory about the process whereby, especially in modern industrial societies, religious beliefs, practices, and institutions lose social significance, at least when they are measured in traditional ways, such as through church attendance.

Self-concept: A set of perceptions that define each individual, based on how we see ourselves and how we think others see us. A self-concept is not static, but changes over time.

Sexuality: Encompasses erotic experiences and human reproduction, as well as spiritual and personal feelings of attraction. It is a broad term that can be used in relation to many topics, including sexual orientation and sexual designation.

Sick role: A social role that permits a person to fail to fulfill socially defined duties, with the proviso that this person must also seek treatment and try to become well again.

Social capital: The increased productivity resulting from a strong network of relationships and engagement.

Social contract theory: A group of theories in political philosophy that understands the authority of the state as being derived from the consent—either implicit or explicit—of the governed. In this view, citizens give up some of their freedom in order to receive protection from the state.

Social control: The ability of a group, community, or society to regulate its members.

Social identity theory: A theory put forward by Tajfel and Turner (1986) that suggests that people commit hate crimes in order to preserve a positive self-image of themselves and their group by distinguishing themselves from their victims.

Social learning theory: The theory that individuals will mimic the behaviour that they see in their social environment, especially as practised by role models.

Social management: A process of social control that influences behaviour by shaping the settings and norms within which people act.

Social networks: The web of different people individuals are acquainted with and the groups they are divided into.

Social norms: The collection of informal—often unspoken—rules, guides, and standards of behaviour that prevail in any society or organization.

Social order: Émile Durkheim defines social order as the shared cultural norms and values that serve to maintain societal cohesion. Alternatively, Karl Marx defines it as the outcome of power relations between classes, whereby one group is able to continuously dominate another.

Social sanctioning: A process of social control by administering rewards and punishments to encourage and discourage certain behaviour.

Social welfare: The various social services (unemployment insurance, old age pensions, health care) provided by a state to benefit its citizens.

Socialization: The process by which individuals internalize the customs and rules of a society and thereby become members of it.

Spirituality: A set of subjectively meaningful beliefs or actions that, although possibly shared, are not necessarily enacted in the presence of other people.

State: An organization that administers laws within a given territory.

Its ability to enforce its laws derives from its sovereign power, famously defined by Max Weber as "a monopoly on the legitimate exercise of force."

Summary offences: Typically, less serious offences that require the accused person to appear before a provincial court judge without the right to a jury trial and/or indictment.

Total institutions: Goffman's concept of places in which the inhabitants are isolated from the world at large and live a highly structured and administered life. Examples include prisons, nursing homes, and monasteries.

Totalitarian state: A type of state that practises total control over its population through a powerful, centralized authority and a given ideology. State and ideological activities permeate all aspects of life and make everything political.

Totemism: A concept expounded upon by Émile Durkheim that refers to the widespread use of natural objects and animals to symbolize spirituality. Special rituals and ceremonies are enacted around them and they reinforce group solidarity and shared beliefs in the community as a whole.

Victimization: The singling out of an individual or group for subjection to crime, unfair treatment, or another wrong. It makes the victimized individual feel powerless.

References

Abdelaziz, S. (2014). Ousted Egyptian President Mubarak, two sons sentenced for embezzlement. *Cable News Network*, May 21.

Abrums, M. (2000). "Jesus will fix it after awhile": Meanings and health. *Social Science and Medicine, 50*, 89–105.

Adams, M. (1998). *Sex in the snow: Canadian social values at the end of the millennium*. Toronto: Penguin.

Agnew, R. (1999). A general strain theory of community differences in crime rates. *Journal of Research in Crime and Delinquency, 36*(2), 123–55.

Aguilar, A., Stupans, I., Scutter, S., & King, S. (2012). Exploring professionalism: The professional values of Australian occupational therapists. *Australian Occupational Therapy Journal, 59*(3), 209–17.

Albas, D., & Albas, C. (1993). Disclaimers mannerism of students: How to avoid being labelled as cheaters. *Canadian Review of Sociology, 30*(4), 451–67.

Allen, M. (2014). Police-reported hate crime in Canada, 2012. *Juristat*. Retrieved from http://www.statcan.gc.ca/pub/85-002-x/2014001/article/14028-eng.htm

Ammerman, N.T. (2005). *Pillars of faith: American congregations and their partners*. Berkeley: University of California Press.

Andersen, M.L. (1997). *Thinking about women: Sociological perspectives on sex and gender*. Boston: Allyn and Bacon.

Andersen, R., & Fetner, T. (2008). Cohort differences in tolerance of homosexuality attitudinal change in Canada and the United States, 1981–2000. *Public Opinion Quarterly, 72*(2), 311–30.

Anderson, C.A., & Bushman, B.J. (2001). Effects of violent video games on aggressive behavior, aggressive cognition, aggressive affect, physiological arousal, and prosocial behavior: A meta-analytic review of the scientific literature. *Psychological Science, 12*, 353–59.

Anderson, C.A., Gentile, D.A., & Buckley, K.E. (2007). *Violent video game effects on children and adolescents*. New York: Oxford University Press.

Anderson, C.A., & Huesmann, L.R. (2003). Human aggression: A social-cognitive view. In M.A.A. Hogg & J. Cooper (Eds.), *The Sage handbook of social psychology* (pp. 296–323). Thousand Oaks, CA: Sage.

Anderson, E. (1999). *Code of the street*. New York: Norton.

Anderson, P., De Bruijn, A., Angus, K., Gordon, R., & Hastings, G. (2009). Impact of alcohol advertising and media exposure on adolescent alcohol use: A systematic review of longitudinal studies. *Alcohol and Alcoholism, 44*(3), 229–43.

Anderson, Tammy L. (2014). *Understanding deviance: Connecting classical and contemporary perspectives*. New York: Routledge.

Andrade, D.D. (2010). On norms and bodies: Findings from field research on cosmetic surgery in Rio De Janeiro, Brazil. *Reproductive Health Matters, 18*(35), 74–83.

Andreoni, J., & Petrie, R. (2008). Beauty, gender and stereotypes: Evidence from laboratory experiments. *Journal of Economic Psychology, 29*, 73–93.

Andrews, D.A. (1989). Recidivism is predictable and can be influenced: Using risk assessments to reduce recidivism. *Forum on Corrections Research, 1*(2), 11–18.

Aoki, Y., & Todo, Y. (2009). Are immigrants more likely to commit crimes? Evidence from France. *Applied Economics Letters, 16*(15), 1537–41.

Arnett, J.J., & Jensen, L.A. (1994). Socialization and risk behavior in two countries: Denmark and the United States. *Youth & Society, 26*(1), 3–22.

Arum, R. (2000). Schools and communities: Ecological and institutional dimensions. *Annual Review of Sociology*, 395–418.

Atkinson, M. (2004). Tattooing and civilizing processes: Body modification as self-control. *Canadian Review of Sociology and Anthropology, 41*(2), 125–46.

Bagdikian, B. (1990). *The media monopoly* (3rd ed.). Boston: Beacon.

Bahr, S.J., Hoffmann, J.P., & Yang, X. 2005. Parental and peer influences on the risk of adolescent drug use. *The Journal of Primary Prevention, 26*(6), 529–51.

Ball, T., & Bellamy, R. (2003). *The Cambridge history of twentieth-century political thought*, Vol. 4. Cambridge, UK: Cambridge University Press.

Ballard, M.E., & Lineberger, R. (1999). Video game violence and confederate gender: Effects on reward and punishment given by college males. *Sex Roles, 41,* 541–58.

Ballard, M.E., & Wiest, J.R. (1996). Mortal Kombat™: The effects of violent video game play on males' hostility and cardiovascular responding. *Journal of Applied Social Psychology, 26,* 717–30.

Bandura, A. (1986). *Social foundations of thought and action*. Englewood Cliffs, NJ: Prentice Hall.

Bangert-Drowns, R.L. (1988). The effects of school-based substance abuse education—A meta-analysis. *Journal of Drug Education, 18*(3), 243–64.

Barlett, C.P., Harris, R.J., & Baldassaro, R. (2007). The longer you play the more hostile you feel: Examination of first person shooter video games and aggression during video game play. *Aggressive Behavior, 33,* 486–97.

Barlett, C.P., Harris, R. J., & Bruey, C. (2008). The effect of the amount of blood in a violent video game on aggression, hostility, and arousal. *Journal of Experimental Social Psychology, 44,* 539–54.

Barnett, C. (2000). *Measurement of white-collar crime using uniform crime reporting (UCR) data*. US Department of Justice, Federal Bureau of Investigation, National Criminal Justice Reference Service.

Baron, J.N., & Peter, C. (1985). Same time, next year: Aggregate analysis of the mass media and violent behavior. *American Sociological Review, 50,* 347–63.

Barthes, R. (1973). *Mythologies*. London: Paladin.

Bartlett, C.P., Anderson, C.A., & Swing, E.L. (2009). Video-game effects confirmed, suspected, and speculative: A review of the evidence. *Simulation and Gaming, 40*(3), 377–403.

Bartlett, K.T. (1994). Only girls wear barrettes: Dress and appearance standards, community norms, and workplace equality. *Michigan Law Review, 92,* 2541–82.

Baumer, S. (2014, 8 August). Downtown robbery victims flee to ballpark village. *Kmov.com*.

Baumrind, D. (1966). Effects of authoritative parental control on child behavior. *Child Development, 37*(4), 887–907.

Baxter, R. L., Barbaree, H.E., & Marshall, W.L. (1986). Sexual responses to consenting and forced sex in a large sample of rapists and nonrapists. *Behavior Research and Therapy, 24*(1), 513–20.

Beccaria, C. (2009). *On crimes and punishments and other writings*. Toronto: University of Toronto Press.

Becker, H.S. (1963). *Outsiders: Studies in the sociology of deviance*. New York: The Free Press of Glencoe.

Beckett, K. (1994). Setting the public agenda: "Street crime" and drug use in American politics. *Social Problems, 41*(3), 425–47.

Beckett, K., Nyrop, K., & Pfingst, L. (2006). Race, drugs, and policing: Understanding disparities in drug delivery arrests. *Criminology, 44*(1): 105–37.

Beckford, J.A. & Richardson, J.T. (2007). Religion and regulation. In J.A. Beckford & J.T. Richardson (Eds.), *The Sage handbook of sociology of religion* (pp. 396–419). London: Sage Publications Ltd.

Beckwith, C.G., Zaller, N., & Rich, J.D. (2006). Addressing the HIV epidemic through quality correctional health care." *Criminology and Public Policy, 5*(1), 149–55.

Beekman, D. (2014, January 28). Ex-billionaire investor Alberto Vilar loses final appeal after defrauding $22m from clients. *NY Daily News*.

Begley, S., & Clifton, T. (2000, 11 September). The drug crusade. *Newsweek*.

Belenko, S. (2001). *Research on drug courts: A critical review, 2001 update*. New York: National Center on Addiction and Substance Abuse (CASA) at Columbia University.

Benard, A.A. (2007). The material roots of Rastafarian marijuana symbolism. *History and Anthropology, 18*(1): 89–99.

Bennett, L. (2008). The "spanking" law: Section 43 of the Criminal Code. Ottawa, ON: Parliament of Canada. Retrieved from http://www.parl.gc.ca/Content/LOP/researchpublications/prb0510-e.htm

Benson, M.L., & Moore, E. (1992). Are white-collar and common offenders the same? An empirical and theoretical critique of a recently proposed general theory of crime." *Journal of Research in Crime and Delinquency, 29*(3), 251–72.

Benson, P.L., Karabenick, S.A., & Lerner, R.M. (1976). Pretty pleases: The effects of physical attractiveness, race, and sex on receiving help. *Journal of Experimental Social Psychology, 12*, 409–15.

Berger, J. (1972). *Ways of seeing*. London: Pelican.

Berger, P., & Berger, B. (1976.) *Sociology: A biographical approach*. New York: Penguin.

Berkowitz, L., & Macauley, J. (1971). The contagion of criminal violence. *Sociometry, 34*, 238–60.

Bertrand, M-A. (1996). Women in prisons: A comparative study. *Caribbean Journal of Criminology and Social Psychology, 1*(1), 38–58.

Bhati, A.S., & Piquero, A.R. (2007). Estimating the impact of incarceration on subsequent offending trajectories: Deterrent, criminogenic, or null effect? *Journal of Criminal Law and Criminology, 98*(1), 207–53.

Bianchi, M., Buonanno, P., & Pinotti, P. (2012). Do immigrants cause crime? *Journal of the European Economic Association, 10*(6), 1318–47.

Bibby, R.W. (2002). *Restless gods: The renaissance of religion in Canada*. Toronto: Stoddart.

Billings, A.C., Halone, K.K., & Denham, B.E. (2002). "Man, that was a pretty shot": An analysis of gendered broadcast commentary surrounding the 2000 men's and women's NCAA Final Four basketball championships. *Mass Communications and Society, 5*(3), 295–315.

Black, D. (2010). *The behavior of law*. Bingley, UK: Emerald Group Publishing.

Blanchfield, M. (2012, September 4). Canada's spanking law must go, doctors say, calling it an excuse for poor parenting. *National Post News*.

Blass, E. & Kurup, A.S. (Eds.). (2010). *Equity, social determinants and public health programmes*. Geneva: World Health Organization.

Blau, P.M., & Schwartz, J.E. (1984). *Crosscutting social circles: Testing a macrostructural theory of intergroup relations*. New Brunswick, NJ: Academic Press.

Blickle, G., Schlegel, A., Fassbender, P., & Klein, U. (2006). Some personality correlates of business white-collar crime. *Applied Psychology: An International Review, 55*, 220–33.

Blythe, M.J., Fortenberry, J.D., Temkit, M.H., Tu, W., & Orr, D.P. (2006). Incidence and correlates of unwanted sex in relationships of middle and late adolescent women. *Archives of Pediatric & Adolescent Medicine, 160*(6), 591–5.

Boguslaw, R. (1965). *The new utopians: A study of system design and social change*. Englewood Cliffs, NJ: Prentice-Hall.

Botvin, G.G., & Kenneth, W. (2003). Drug abuse prevention curricula in schools. In Z. Sloboda, & W.J. Bukoski (Eds.), *Handbook of Drug Abuse Prevention Theory, Science, and Practice*. New York: Kluwer Academic/Plenum Publishers.

Botvin, G.J., Griffin, K.W., & Nichols, T.D. (2006). Preventing youth violence and delinquency through a universal school-based prevention approach. *Prevention Science, 7*(4): 403–8.

Bouchard, M., & Ouellet, F. (2011). Is small beautiful? The link between risks and size in illegal drug markets. *Global Crime, 12*(1), 70–86.

Bouchery, E.E., Harwood, H.J., Sacks, J.J., Simon, C.J., & Brewer, R.D. (2011). Economic costs of excessive alcohol consumption in the US, 2006. *American Journal of Preventive Medicine, 41*(5), 516–24.

Boxer, P., Huesmann, L.R., Bushman, B.R., O'Brien, M., & Moceri, D. (2009). The role of violent media preference in cumulative developmental risk for violence and general aggression. *Journal of Youth and Adolescence, 38*, 417–28.

Brady, M., Dawe, S., & Richmond, R. (1998). Expanding knowledge among Aboriginal service providers on treatment options for excessive alcohol use. *Drug and Alcohol Review, 17*(1), 69–76.

Brandt, M., & Carstens, A. (2005). The discourse of the male gaze: A critical analysis of the feature section "The beauty of sport" in *SA Sports Illustrated*. *Southern African Linguistics and Applied Language Studies, 23*(3), 233–43.

Branson, R. (2012, 7 December). War on drugs a trillion-dollar failure. *CNN*.

Brodbeck, T. (2010, 3 March). Re-offending rates are staggering. *Toronto Sun*.

Retrieved from http://www.toronto
sun.com/news/columnists/tom_brod-
beck/2010/03/02/13089631.html

Brown, A., & Dittmar, H. (2005). Think
"thin" and feel bad: The role of appearance schema activation, attention level,
and thin-ideal internalization for young
women's responses to ultra-thin media
ideals. *Journal of Social and Clinical
Psychology, 24*(8), 1088–113.

Bruckert, C., & Hannem, A. (2013).
Rethinking the prostitution debates:
Transcending structural stigma in sys-
temic responses to sex work. *Canadian
Journal of Law and Society, 28*(1), 43–63.

Brunet, J.R. (2002). Employee drug testing
as social control: A typology of normative justifications. *Review of Public
Personnel Administration, 22*(3), 193–215.

Brzozowski, J-A., Taylor-Butts, A., &
Johnson, S. (2006). Victimization and
offending among the Aboriginal population in Canada. *Statistics Canada, 26,* 3.

Buchanan, I. (2010). *Oxford dictionary of
critical theory.* Oxford, UK: Oxford
University Press.

Bureau of Justice Statistics. (n.d.). The justice system. *Bureau of Justice Statistics.*

Burris, S., Beletsky, L., Burleson, J.A.,
Case, P., & Lazzarini, Z. (2007).
Do criminal laws influence HIV risk
behavior? An empirical trial. *Arizona
State Law Journal* (Research Paper No.
2007–03).

Bursik, R.J., Jr., & Grasmick, H.G. (1993).
Economic deprivation and neighbor-
hood crime rates, 1960–1980. *Law and
Society Review, 27,* 263–84.

Bushman, B.J., & Anderson, C.A. (2001).
Media violence and the American
public: Scientific facts versus media
misinformation. *American Psychologist,
56*(6–7), 477–89.

Bushman, B.J., & Huesmann, L.R. (2006).
Short-term and long-term effects of
violent media on aggression in children
and adults. *Archives of Pediatrics and
Adolescent Medicine, 160,* 348–52.

Cahill, S.E., & Eggleston, R. (1995).
Reconsidering the stigma of physical dis-
ability: Wheelchair use and public kindness. *Sociological Quarterly, 36*(4), 681–98.

Campbell, J. C., & Soeken, K.L. (1999).
Forced sex and intimate partner violence
effects on women's risk and women's

health. *Violence against women, 5*(9),
1017–35.

Caplow, Theodore. (1984). "Rule enforcement without visible means: Christmas
gift giving in Middletown." *American
Journal of Sociology 89*(6): 1306–1323.

Carnagey, N.L., & Anderson, C.A. (2005).
The effects of reward and punishment in
violent videogames on aggressive affect,
cognition, and behavior. *Psychological
Science, 16,* 882–9.

Cattarin, J.A., Thompson, J.K., Thomas, C.,
& Williams, R. (2000). Body image, mood,
and televised images of attractiveness: The
role of social comparison. *Journal of Social
and Clinical Psychology, 19*(2), 220–39.

Cavendish, J.C., Welch, M.R., & Leege,
D.C. (1998). Social network theory and
predictors of religiosity for black and
white Catholics. *Journal for the Scientific
Study of Religion, 37,* 397–410.

Caudill, B.D., Crosse, S.B., Campbell, B.,
Howard, J., Luckey, B., & Blane, H.T.
(2006). High-risk drinking among
college fraternity members: A national
perspective. *Journal of American College
Health, 55*(3), 141–55.

Cavico, F.J., Muffler, S.C., & Mujtaba, B.G.
(2013). Appearance discrimination in
employment: Legal and ethical implications of "lookism" and "lookphobia."
Equality, Diversity and Inclusion, 32(1),
83–119.

CBC News. (2014, October 23). Michael
Zehaf-Bibeau, slain Ottawa shooter,
had criminal record in Quebec, BC.
Retrieved from http://www.cbc.ca/news/
canada/montreal/michael-zehaf-bibeau-
slain-ottawa-shooter-had-criminal-
record-in-quebec-b-c-1.2809562

Center for Disease Control and Prevention.
(2014, 17 April). Excessive drinking
costs US $223.5 billion. Retrieved from
http://www.cdc.gov/features/alcoholcon-
sumption/index.html

Cerda, M., Wall, M., Keyes, K.M., Galea,
S., & Hasin, D. (2012). Medical marijuana laws in 50 states: Investigating the
relationship between state legalization of
medical marijuana and marijuana use,
abuse and dependence. *Drug Alcohol and
Dependence, 120*(1–3), 22–7.

Chatwin, C. (2013). A critical evaluation of the European drug strategy:
Has it brought added value to drug

policy making at the national level? *International Journal of Drug Policy, 24*(3), 251–6.

Chesney-Lind, M. (1997). *The female offender: Girls, women and crime.* Thousand Oaks, CA: Sage.

Christie, N. (1986). Suitable enemy. In H. Bianchi & R. von Swaaningen (Eds.), *Abolitionism: Toward a non-repressive approach to crime* (pp. 42–54). Amsterdam: Free University Press.

Clark, D.B. (2006). Children at high risk for underage drinking and alcohol use disorders. *Frontlines.* Bethesda, MD: National Institute on Alcohol Abuse and Alcoholism.

Clawson, R.., & Trice, R. (2000). Poverty as we know it: Media portrayals of the poor. *Public Opinion Quarterly, 64*(1), 53–64.

Clemmer, D. (1950). Observations on imprisonment as a source of criminality. *Journal of Criminal Law and Criminology 41*, 311–19.

Cohen, L.E., & Felson, M. (1979). Social change and crime rate trends: A routine activity approach. *American Sociological Review, 44*(4), 588–608.

Cohen, L.E., Kluegel, J.R., & Land, K.C. (1981). Social inequality and predatory criminal victimization: An exposition and test of a formal theory. *American Sociological Review 46*(5), 505–24.

Cohen, S. (1980). *Folk devils and moral panics: The creation of the mods and rockers.* New York: St. Martin's Press.

Coleman, J.S. (1990). *Foundations of social theory.* Cambridge: Harvard University Press.

Coles, R. (1990). *The spiritual life of children.* Boston: Houghton Mifflin.

Collins, C. (2006, 13 April). *Substance abuse issues and public policy in Canada: I. Canada's federal drug strategy.* Ottawa: Government of Canada. Retrieved from http://www.parl.gc.ca/content/lop/researchpublications/prb0615-e.html

Collins, J.M., & Schmidt, F.L. (1993). Personality, integrity, and white collar crime: A construct validity study. *Personnel Psychology, 46*(2), 295–311.

Conference Board of Canada. (2014). How Canada performs: Income inequality. Retrieved from http://www.conferenceboard.ca/hcp/details/society/income-inequality.aspx

Conrad, Peter. 1979. Types of medical social control. *Sociology of Health and Illness, 1*, 1–11.

Conrad, P. (1992). Medicalization and social control. *Annual Review of Sociology, 18*(1), 209–32.

Conrad, P., & Schneider, J.W. (1992). *Deviance and medicalization: From badness to sickness: With a new afterword by the authors* (expanded ed.). Philadelphia: Temple University Press.

Cornwall, M. (1989). The determinants of religious behavior: A theoretical model and empirical test. *Social Forces, 68*(2), 572–92.

Correa-Vélez, I., & Onsando, G. (2009). Educational and occupational outcomes amongst African men from refugee backgrounds living in urban and regional southeast Queensland. *The Australian Review of African Studies, 30*(2), 114–27.

Cote, S. (2002). *Criminological theories: Bridging the past to the future.* Thousand Oaks, CA: Sage.

Craig, K.M. (2002). Examining hate-motivated aggression: A review of the social psychological literature on hate crimes as a distinct form of aggression. *Aggression and Violent Behavior, 7*(1), 85–101.

Crank, B.R., & Brezina, T. (2013). Prison will either make ya or break ya: Punishment, deterrence, and the criminal lifestyle. *Deviant Behaviour, 34*(10), 782–802.

Criminal Code of Canada. 2010. *Criminal Code.* Justice Laws Website. Ottawa, ON: Government of Canada. Retrieved from http://laws-lois.justice.gc.ca/eng/acts/C-46/

Crosse, S.B., Ginexi, E.M., & Caudill, B.D. (2006). Examining the effects of a national alcohol-free fraternity housing policy. *The Journal of Primary Prevention, 27*(5), 477–95.

Crossman, J., Vincent, J., & Speed, H. (2007). The times they are a-changin': Gender comparisons in three national newspapers of the 2004 Wimbledon Championships. *International Review for the Sociology of Sport, 42*(1), 27–41.

Culbert, I. (2013). Analysis: The 2013 Federal Budget from the public health perspective. *Canadian Public Health Association.* Retrieved from http://www.cpha.ca/en/about/media/budget20130321.aspx

Currie, J., & Tekin, E. (2012). Understanding the cycle: Childhood maltreatment and future crime. *Journal of Human Resources, 47*(2), 509–49.

Curry, D.G., & Spergel, I.A. (1992). Gang involvement and delinquency among Hispanic and African-American adolescent males. *Journal of Research in Crime and Delinquency, 29*(3), 273–91.

Dauvergne, M., & Brennan, S. (2011). Police-reported hate crime in Canada, 2009. *Juristat, 3,* 85–102.

Davis, J. (2011, 18 July). Prison costs soar 86% in past five years: Report. *National Post.* Retrieved from http://news.nationalpost.com/news/canada/prison-costs-soar-86-in-past-five-years

Davis, K. (2002). "A dubious equality": Men, women and cosmetic surgery. *Body and Society, 8*(1), 49–65.

Drug Enforcement Administration (DEA). (2014a). DEA/federal trafficking penalties. *Drug Info.* Retrieved from http://www.dea.gov/druginfo/ftp3.shtml

Drug Enforcement Administration (DEA). 2014b. Program overview. *Prevention.* Retrieved from http://www.dea.gov/prevention/overview.shtml

DeCew, J.W. (1994). Drug testing: Balancing privacy and public safety. *Hasting Center Report, 21,* 17–23.

Deflem, M. (2007, 22–23 November). *The concept of social control: Theories and applications.* Paper presented at the International Conference on Charities as Instruments of Social Control in Nineteenth-Century Britain, Université de Haute Bretagne, Rennes, France.

de Goede, M. (1996). Ideology in the US welfare debate: Neo-liberal representations of poverty. *Discourse and Society, 7*(3), 317–57.

Dellinger, K., & Williams, C.L. (1997). Makeup at work: Negotiating appearance rules in the workplace. *Gender and Society, 11*(2), 151–77.

Denham, B.E. (2008). Folk devils, news icons and the construction of moral panics. *Journalism Studies, 9*(6), 945–61.

Department of Justice Canada. (2013a). Where our legal system comes from. Ottawa: Government of Canada. Retrieved from http://www.justice.gc.ca/eng/csj-sjc/just/03.html

Department of Justice Canada. (2013b). Civil and criminal cases. Ottawa: Government of Canada. Retrieved from www.justice.gc.ca/eng/csj-sjc/just/08.html

Desimone, J. (2007). Fraternity membership and binge drinking. *Journal of Health Economics, 26*(5), 950–67.

Desimone, J. (2008). Fraternity membership and drinking behavior. *Economic Inquiry, 47*(2), 337–50.

Desrumaux, P., De Bosscher, S., & Leoni, V. (2009). Effects of facial attractiveness, gender, and competence of applicants on job recruitment. *Swiss Journal of Psychology, 68*(1), 1–10.

Diamond, S., Bermudez, R., & Schensul, J. (2006). What's the rap about Ecstasy? Popular music lyrics and drug trends among American youth. *Journal of Adolescent Research, 21*(3), 269–98.

Dixon, T.L., Azocar, C.L., & Casas, M. (2003). The portrayal of race and crime on television network news. *Journal of Broadcasting and Electronic Media, 47*(4), 498–523.

Dixon, T.L., & Linz, D. (2000a). Overrepresentation and underrepresentation of African Americans and Latinos as law-breakers on television news. *Journal of Communication, 50*(2), 131–54.

Dixon, T.L., & Linz, D. (2000b). Race and the misrepresentation of victimization on local television news. *Journal of Communication Research, 27,* 547–73.

Dobkin, C., & Nicosia, N. (2009). The war on drugs: Methamphetamine, public health, and crime. *American Economic Review, 99*(1), 324–49.

Doering-Silveira, E., Grob, C.S., Dobkin de Rios, M., Lopez, E., Alonso, L.K., Tacla, C., et al. (2005). Report on psychoactive drug use among adolescents using ayahuasca within a religious context. *Journal of Psychoactive Drugs, 37*(2), 141–4.

Doezema, J. (1998). Forced to choose: Beyond the voluntary v. forced prostitution dichotomy. In K. Kempadoo and J. Doezema (Eds.), *Global sex workers: Rights, resistance, and redefinition* (pp. 34–50). London: Routledge.

Donahue, G.A., Tichenor, P.J., & Olien, C.N. (1973). Mass media functions, knowledge and social control. *Journalism Quarterly, 50,* 652–59.

Donohue, J.J., Ewing, B., & Peloquin, D. (2011). *Rethinking America's illegal drug policy*. Yale University, New Haven, CT: Yale Center for the Study of Globalization.

Dowler, K. (2004). Comparing American and Canadian local television crime stories: A content analysis. *Canadian Journal of Criminology and Criminal Justice, 46*(5), 573–96.

Dowler, K., Fleming, T., & Muzzatti, S.L. (2006). Constructing crime: Media, crime, and popular culture. *Canadian Journal of Criminology and Criminal Justice, 48*(6), 837–50.

Duggan, S.J., & McCreary, D.R. (2004). Body image, eating disorders, and the drive for muscularity in gay and heterosexual men. *Journal of Homosexuality, 47*(3–4), 45–58.

Durkheim, É. (1979). *Suicide: A study in sociology* (J.A. Spaulding & G. Simpson, Trans.). New York: Macmillan. (Original work published 1897).

Durkheim, É., (1982). *The rules of sociological method* (S. Lukes, Ed.; W.D. Halls, Trans.) New York: Simon & Schuster. (Original work published 1895).

Durkheim, É., (1995). *The elementary forms of religious life*. New York: Free Press. (Original work published 1912).

Eastin, M.S., & Griffiths, R.P. (2006). Beyond the shooter game: Examining presence and hostile outcomes among male game players. *Communication Research, 33*, 448–66.

Edin, K., & Kefalas, M. (2005). *Promises I can keep*. Berkeley, CA: University of California.

Edmonds, A. (2007). "The poor have the right to be beautiful": Cosmetic surgery in neoliberal Brazil. *Journal of the Royal Anthropological Institute, 13*(2), 363–81.

Egley, A., & Major, A.K. (2002). Highlights of the 2002 National Youth Gang Survey. OJDP *Fact Sheet No. 1*. Washington, DC: Department of Justice.

Eitzen, D.S. (1992). Problem students: The sociocultural roots. *Phi Delta Kappan, 78*(8), 584.

Elias, N. (1978). *The history of manners: The civilizing process* (Vol. 1). New York: Pantheon.

Ellison, C.G. (1993). Religious involvement and self-perception among black Americans. *Social Forces, 71*, 1027–55.

Ellison, C.G. (1994). Religion, the life stress paradigm, and the study of depression.

In J.S. Levin (Ed.), *Religion in aging and health: Theoretical foundations and methodological frontiers*. Thousand Oaks, CA: Sage Publications.

Ellison, C.G., Boardman, J.D., Williams, D.R., & Jackson, J.S. (2001). Religious involvement, stress, and mental health: Findings from the 1995 Detroit Area Study. *Social Forces 80*(1): 215–49.

Ellison, C.G., & Sherkat, D.E. (1995). The "semi-involuntary institution" revisited: Regional variations in church participation among black Americans. *Social Forces, 73*(4), 1415–37.

Emerick, R.E. (1994). A conversation on classroom etiquette in introductory sociology courses. *Teaching Sociology, 22*(4), 341–4.

Ennett, S.T., Tobler, N.S., Ringwalt, C.L., & Flewelling, R.L. (1994). How effective is drug abuse resistance education? A meta-analysis of Project DARE outcome evaluations. *American Journal of Public Health, 84*(9), 1394–401.

Entman, R.M. (1989). *Democracy without citizens*. New York: Oxford University Press.

Entman, R.M. (1992). Blacks in the news: Television, modern racism, and cultural change. *Journalism Quarterly, 69*(2), 341–61.

Entman, R.M. (1994). Representation and reality in the portrayal of blacks on network television news. *Journalism Quarterly, 77*(3), 509–20.

Epstein, E.J. (1973). *News from nowhere*. New York: Random House.

Erikson, E. (1977). *Childhood and society*. St. Albans, UK: Triad/Paladin.

Erickson, P.G. (1993). The law, social control, and drug policy: Models, factors, and processes. *Substance Use and Misuse, 28*(12), 1155–76.

Erickson, P.G. (1996). The selective control of drugs. In B. Schisel & L. Mahood (Eds.), *Social control in Canada: A reader of the social constructions of deviance*. Toronto, ON: Oxford University Press.

Eriksson, M., Dahlgren, L., & Emmelin, M. (2009). Understanding the role of social capital for health promotion beyond Putnam: A qualitative case study from northern Sweden. *Social Theory & Health, 7*(4), 318–38.

Eron, L.D., Lefkowitz, M.M., Huesmann, L.R., & Walder, L.O. (1972). Does television violence cause aggression? *American Psychologist, 27,* 253–63.

Esbensen, F.-A., Deschenes, E.P., & Winfree, L.T. (1999). Differences between gang girls and gang boys: Results from a multisite survey. *Youth Society, 31*(1), 27–53.

Evans, W.P., Fitzgerald, C., Weigel, D., & Chvilicek, S. (1999). Are rural gang members similar to their urban peers? Implications for rural communities. *Youth & Society, 30*(3), 267–82.

Fagan, A.A. (2005). The relationship between adolescent physical abuse and criminal offending: Support for an enduring and generalized cycle of violence. *Journal of Family Violence, 20*(5), 279–90.

Farley, M. (2004). Bad for the body, bad for the heart: Prostitution harms women even if legalized or decriminalized. *Violence against Women, 10*(10), 1087–125.

Farrington, D.P., Gallagher B.L., Morley, L., St. Ledger, R.J., & West, D.J. (1986). Unemployment, school leaving, and crime. *The British Journal of Criminology, 26*(4), 35–56.

Federal Bureau of Investigation (FBI). 2012. Offence analysis. *Crime in the United States.* Retrieved from https://www.fbi.gov/about-us/cjis/ucr/crime-in-the-u.s/2012/crime-in-the-u.s.-2012/tables/7tabledatadecpdf/table_7_offense_analysis_united_states_2008-2012.xls

Felson, R.B., & Steadman, H.J. (1983). Situational factors in disputes leading to criminal violence. *Criminology, 21*(1), 59–74.

Ferguson, C.J. (2007). Evidence for publication bias in video game violence effects literature: A meta-analytic review. *Aggression and Violent Behavior,* 12(4), 470–82.

Fergusson, D.M., & Lynskey, M.T. (1997). Physical punishment/maltreatment during childhood and adjustment in young adulthood. *Child Abuse and Neglect,* 21(7), 617–30.

Fergusson, D., Swain-Campbell, N., & Horwood, J. (2004). How does childhood economic disadvantage lead to crime? *Journal of Child Psychology and Psychiatry,* 45(5), 956–66.

Ferraro, K.J., & Johnson, J.M. (1983). How women experience battering. *Social Problems, 30*(3), 325–39.

Feshbach, S., & Singer, R.D. (1971). *Television and aggression.* San Francisco: Jossey-Bass.

Fischer, P.J. (1992). The criminalization of homelessness. In M.J. Robertson & M. Greenblatt (Eds.), *Homelessness: A national perspective* (pp. 57–64). New York: Springer.

Fleming, M.J., & Rickwood, D.J. (2001). Effects of violent versus nonviolent video games on children's arousal, aggressive mood, and positive mood. *Journal of Applied Social Psychology,* 31, 2047–71.

Fleras, A. (1994). Media and minorities in a post-multicultural society: Overview and appraisal. In J.W. Berry & J.A. Laponce (Eds.), *Ethnicity and culture in Canada: The research landscape* (pp. 267–92). Toronto: University of Toronto Press.

Flew, A. (1954). The justification of punishment. *Philosophy, 29*(111), 291–307.

Florsheim, P., Tolan, P., & Gorman-Smith, D. (1998). Family relationships, parenting practices, the availability of male family members, and the behavior of inner-city boys in single-mother and two-parent families. *Child Development, 69*(5), 1437–47.

Foster, H., & Hagan, J. (2007). Imprisonment and intergenerational social exclusion. *Social Problems, 54*(4), 399–433.

Foucault, M. (1977). *Discipline and punish: The birth of the prison.* New York: Vintage Books.

Fox, K.A., & Cook, C.L. (2011). Is knowledge power? The effects of a victimology course on victim blaming. *Journal of Interpersonal Violence, 26*(17). doi:0886260511403752

Franklin, C.A. (2010). Physically forced, alcohol-induced, and verbally coerced sexual victimization: Assessing risk factors among university women. *Journal of Criminal Justice, 38*(2), 149–59.

Freeburg, B.W., & Workman, J.E. (2010). A method to identify and validate social norms related to dress. *Clothing Textiles and Research Journal, 28*(1), 38–55.

Freedman, J.L. (2002). *Media violence and its effect on aggression: Assessing the scientific evidence.* Toronto: University of Toronto Press.

Friedrich, L.K., & Stein, A.H. (1973). Aggressive and prosocial programs and the natural behavior of preschool children. *Monographs of the Society for Research in Child Development, 38*(4, Serial 151), 1–64.

Friedrichs, D.O. (2011). *Trusted criminals: White collar crime in contemporary society.* Belmont, CA: Wadsworth.

Fukuyama, F. (2004). *State-building: Governance and world order in the 21st century.* Ithaca, NY: Cornell University Press.

Gaetz, S. (2004). Safe streets for whom? Homeless youth, social exclusion, and criminal victimization. *Canadian Journal of Criminology and Criminal Justice, 46*(4), 423–56.

Gaetz, S., Scott, F., & Gulliver, T. (Eds.). (2013). *Housing First in Canada: Supporting communities to end homelessness.* Toronto: Canadian Homelessness Research Network Press.

Galli, N., & Reel, J.J. (2009). Adonis or Hephaestus? Exploring body image in male athletes. *Psychology of Men and Masculinity, 10*(2), 95–108.

Gamson, W.A., Croteau, D., Hoynes, W., & Sasson, T. (1992). Media images and the social construction of reality. *Annual Review of Sociology, 18*, 373–93.

Gans, H.J. (1979). *Deciding what's news.* New York: Random House.

Garland, D. (2001a). *The culture of control: Crime and social order in present-day society.* Chicago: The University of Chicago Press.

Garland, D. (2001b). Introduction: The meaning of mass imprisonment. Punishment and Society, 3(1), 5–7.

Garofalo, J., & McLeod, M. (1989.) The structure and operations of neighborhood watch programs in the United States. *Crime and Delinquency, 35*(3), 326–44.

Gavin, T. (2014, June 13). Globe and Mail editorial board endorsement of Kathleen Wynne; vetoed by editor-in-chief. *Canadaland.* Retrieved from http://www.haliburtonnews.ca/2014/06/13/globe-and-mail-editorial-board-endorsement-of-kathleen-wynne-vetoed-by-editor-in-chief/

Gazso, A. (2004). Women's inequality in the workplace as framed in news discourse: Refracting from gender ideology. *Canadian Review of Sociology, 41*(4), 449–73.

Geller, A., Garfinkel, I., Cooper, C.E., & Mincy, R.B. (2009). Parental imprisonment and child well-being: Implications for urban families. *Social Science Quarterly, 90*(5), 1186–1202.

Gerber, J., Jensen, E.L., Schreck, M., & Babcock, G.M. (1990). Drug testing and social control: Implications for state theory. *Present-day Crises, 14*, 243–58.

Gerbner, G. (1995). Television violence: The power and peril. In G. Dines & J. Humez (Eds.), *Gender, Race, and Class in Media (pp. 547–57).* Thousand Oaks, CA: Sage Publications, Inc.

Gerbner, G., Gross, L., Morgan, M., & Signorielli, N. (1994). Growing up with television: The cultivation perspective. In J. Bryant, & D. Zillman (Eds.), *Media effects.* Hillsdale, NJ: Lawrence Erlbaum Associates.

Gilens, M. (1999). *Why Americans hate welfare.* Chicago: The University of Chicago Press.

Gilliom, J. (1994). *Surveillance, privacy, and the law: Employee drug testing and the politics of social control.* Ann Arbor: University of Michigan Press.

Goffman, E. (1961). *Asylums: Essays on the social situation of mental patients and other inmates.* New York: Doubleday.

Golembeski, C., & Fullilove, R. (2005.) Criminal (in)justice in the city and its associated health consequences. *American Journal of Public Health, 95*(10), 1701–6.

Goode, E., & Ben-Yehuda, N. (1994). Moral panics: Culture, politics, and social construction. *Annual Review of Sociology, 20*(1), 149–71.

Goodlin, W.E., & Dunn C.S. (2010). Three patterns of domestic violence in households: Single victimization, repeat victimization, and co-occurring victimization. *Journal of Family Violence, 25*(2), 107–22.

Gordon, R.A. (1990). Attributions for blue-collar and white-collar crime: The effects of subject and defendant race on simulated juror decisions. *Journal of Applied Social Psychology, 20*(12), 971–83.

Gordon, R.A., Bindrim, T.A., McNicholas, M.L., & Walden, T.L. (1988). Perceptions of blue-collar and white-collar crime: The effect of defendant race on simulated juror decisions. *Journal of Social Psychology, 128*(2), 191–7.

Gorman, D.M. (2014). Is Project Towards No Drug Abuse (Project TND) an evidence-based drug and violence prevention program? A review and reappraisal of the evaluation studies. *The Journal of Primary Prevention, 35*(4), 217–32.

Gottfredson, M., & Hirschi, T. (1990). *A general theory of crime.* Stanford, CA: Stanford University Press, 1990.

Gottfredson, M., and Hirschi, T. (1995). National crime control policies. *Society, 32*(2), 30–6.

Gould, M. (2008, 3 October). Girls choosing camera lenses over microscopes. *The Guardian.* Retrieved from http://www.theguardian.com/education/2008/oct/03/science.choosingadegree

Government of Canada. (2012). 2012 corrections and conditional release statistical overview. Retrieved from http://www.publicsafety.gc.ca/cnt/rsrcs/pblctns/2012-ccrs/index-eng.aspx

Government of Canada. (2014a, 23 June). Controlled Drugs and Substances Act (S.C. 1996, C. 19). *Justice Laws Website.* Retrieved from http://laws-lois.justice.gc.ca/eng/acts/C-38.8/index.html

Government of Canada. (2014b, 5 August). Criminal Code (R.S.C., 1985, C. C-46). *Justice Laws Website.* Retrieved from http://laws-lois.justice.gc.ca/eng/acts/C-46/

Government of Canada. (2015, 16 July). Narcotic Control Regulations (C.R.C., c. 1041). *Justice Laws Website.* Retrieved from http://laws-lois.justice.gc.ca/eng/regulations/C.R.C.%2C_c._1041/

Graham, S., Furr, S., Flowers, C., & Burke, M.T. (2001). Religion and spirituality in coping with stress. *Counseling and Values, 46*(1), 2–15.

Gramsci, A. (1978). *Selections from political writings (1921–1926)* (Vol. 1). New York: International Publishers.

Granovetter, M. (1992). Economic institutions as social constructions: A framework for analysis. *Acta Sociologica, 35*(1), 3–11.

Gray, M.R., & Steinberg, L. (1999). Unpacking authoritative parenting: Reassessing a multidimensional construct. *Journal of Marriage and the Family, 61*(3), 574–87.

Greenhouse, S. (2003, 13 July). Looks aren't everything—unless you want a job. *The Miami Herald,* p. 21A.

Griffin, K.W., Botvin, G.J., Nichols, T.R., & Doyle, M.M. (2003). Effectiveness of a universal drug abuse prevention approach for youth at high risk for substance use initiation. *Preventive Medicine, 36*(1), 1–7.

Groesz, L., Levine, M.P., & Murnen, S.K. (2002). The effect of experimental presentation of thin media images on body satisfaction: A meta-analytic review. *International Journal of Eating Disorders, 31*(1), 1–16.

Grogan, S., Evans, R., Wright, S., & Hunter, G. (2004). Femininity and muscularity: Accounts of seven women body builders. *Journal of Gender Studies, 13*(1), 49–61.

Gruber, A.J. (2007). A more muscular female body ideal. In K.J. Thompson & G. Cafri (Eds.), *The muscular ideal: Psychological, social, and medical perspectives* (pp. 217–34). Washington, DC: American Psychological Association.

Gruber, E.L., Thau, H.M., Hill, D.L., Fisher, D.A., & Grube, J.W. (2005). Alcohol, tobacco and illicit substances in music videos: A content analysis of prevalence and genre. *Journal of Adolescent Health, 37*(1), 81–3.

Gunter, B. (2008). Media violence. Is there a case for causality? *American Behavioral Scientist, 51*(8), 1061–122.

Gusfield, J.R. (1963). *Symbolic crusade.* Urbana-Champaign: University of Illinois Press.

Hagan, J., & McCarthy, B. (1998). *Mean streets: Youth crime and homelessness.* Cambridge, UK: Cambridge University Press.

Hagan, J., & Peterson, R.D. (Eds.). (1995). *Crime and inequality.* Stanford, CA: Stanford University Press.

Hagell, A., & Newburn, T. (1994). *Young offenders and the media: Viewing habits and preferences.* London: Policy Studies Institute.

Hall, W., & Degenhardt, L. (2007). Adverse health effects of non-medical cannabis use. *Lancet, 374:* 1383–91.

Halpern, D. (2001). Moral values, social trust and inequality: Can values explain crime? *British Journal of Criminology, 41*(2), 236–51.

Hannah-Moffat, K., & O'Malley, P. (Eds). (2007). *Gendered risks.* London, UK: Routledge.

Hanson, F.A. (1993). *Testing: Social consequences of the examined life.* Berkeley: University of California Press.

Harding, D.J. (2009). Violence, older peers, and the socialization of adolescent boys in disadvantaged neighborhoods. *American Sociological Review, 74*(3), 445–64.

Harding, D.J., Wyse, J.J.B., Dobson, C., & Morenoff, J.D. (2011). Making ends meet after prison. *Journal of Policy Analysis and Management, 33*(2), 440–70.

Harell, A., & Soroka, S. (2010). *Race of recipient and support for welfare in Canada* (Working Paper 2010s-42). CIRANO Scientific Studies.

Hartley, L. (2001). A science of beauty? Femininity, fitness and the nineteenth-century physiognomic. *Women: A Cultural Review, 12*(1), 19–34.

Hartley, R.E., & Phillips, R.C. 2001. Who graduates from drug courts? Correlates of client success. *American Journal of Criminal Justice, 26*(1), 107–19.

Health Canada. (2014). Drug and alcohol use statistics. *Health concerns.* Retrieved from http://www.hc-sc.gc.ca/hc-ps/drugs-drogues/stat/index-eng.php

Hecht, M.L., Marsiglia, F.F., Elek, E., Wagstaff, D.A., Kulis, S., Dustman, P., et al. (2003). Culturally grounded substance use prevention: An evaluation of the *keepin' it R.E.A.L.* curriculum. *Prevention Science, 4*(4), 233–48.

Hecker, S., & Kaplan, M.S. (1989). Workplace drug testing as social control. *International Journal of Health Services, 19*, 693–707.

Hedley, R.A. (1999). Transnational corporations and their regulation: Issues and strategies. *International Journal of Comparative Sociology, 40*(1): 215–230.

Heimer, K. (1997). Socioeconomic status, subcultural definitions, and violent delinquency. *Social forces, 75*(3), 799–833.

Hennigan, K.M., Del Rosario, M., Heath, L., Cook, T.D., Wharton, J.D., & Calder, B.J. (1982). Impact of the introduction of television on crime in the United States: Empirical findings and theoretical implications. *Journal of Personality and Social Psychology, 42*, 461–77.

Henry, F., Hastings, P., & Freer, B. 1(996). Perceptions of race and crime in Ontario: Empirical evidence from Toronto and the Durham Region. *Canadian Journal of Criminology, 38*, 469–76.

Herman, E.S., & Chomsky, N. (1988). *Manufacturing consent.* New York: Pantheon.

Hildebrandt, A. (2014). Routes to decriminalization: A comparative analysis of the legalization of same-sex sexual acts. *Sexualities, 17*(1–2), 230–53.

Hindelang, M.J. (1976). *Criminal victimization in eight American cities: A descriptive analysis of common theft and assault.* Cambridge, MA: Ballinger Publishing.

Hindman, D.B, Littlefield, R., Preston, A., & Neumann, D. (1999). Structural pluralism, ethnic pluralism, and community newspapers. *Journalism and Mass Communication Quarterly, 76*, 250–63.

Hingson, R., Heeren, T., Winter, M., & Wechsler, H. (2005). Magnitude of alcohol-related mortality and morbidity among US college students ages 18–24: Changes from 1998 to 2001. *Annual Review of Public Health, 26*(1), 259–79.

Hirschi, T. (1969). *Causes of delinquency.* Los Angeles, CA: University of California Press.

Hobbes, T. (1969). *Leviathan.* Menston, UK: The Scholar Press Ltd. (Original work published 1651).

Hochschild, A.R. (1979). *The managed heart: The commercialization of human feeling.* Berkley, CA: The University of California Press.

Holley, L.C., Kulis, S., Marsiglia, F.F., & Keith, V.M. (2006). Ethnicity versus ethnic identity: What predicts substance use norms and behaviors? *Journal of Social Work Practice in the Addictions, 6*(3), 53–79.

Hosada, M., Stone-Romero, E.F., & Coats, G. (2003). The effects of physical attractiveness on job-related outcomes: A meta-analysis of experimental studies. *Personnel Psychology, 56*(2), 431–62.

HuffPost Living Canada. (2011, September 2). Sexualizing girls in media can cause long-term harm; Parents must take charge, expert says. In *Huffington Post Canada.* Retrieved from http://www.huffingtonpost.ca/2011/08/29/fashion-taking-it-too-far_n_940469.html

Hughes, C.E., Lancaster, K., & Spicer, B. (2011). How do Australian news media depict illicit drug issues? An analysis of print media reporting across and between illicit drugs, 2003–2008.

International Journal of Drug Policy,
22(4), 285–91.

Hunt, J. (1985). Police accounts of normal force. *Journal of Contemporary Ethnography, 13*(4), 315–41.

Hunter, E.M., Hall, W., & Spargo, R.M. (1991). *Distribution and correlates of alcohol consumption in a remote Aboriginal population* (Vol. 12). Sydney, AU: National Drug and Alcohol Research Centre.

Hurwitz, J., & Peffley, M. (1997). Public perceptions of race and crime: The role of racial stereotypes. *American Journal of Political Science,* 41(2), 375–401.

Hustad, J.T.P., Barnett, N.P., Borsari, B., & Jackson, K.M. (2010). Web-based alcohol prevention for incoming college students: A randomized controlled trial. *Addictive Behaviors, 35*(3), 183–9.

Hyde, K.E. (1990). *Religion in childhood and adolescence.* Birmingham, AL: Religious Education Press.

Ives, D.E. (2004). Inequality, crime and sentencing: Borde, Hamilton and the relevance of social disadvantage in Canadian sentencing law. *Queen's Law Journal, 30,* 114.

Ivory, J.D., & Kalyanaraman, S. (2007). The effects of technological advancement and violent content in video games on players' feelings of presence, involvement, physiological arousal, and aggression. *Journal of Communication, 57,* 532–55.

Jacobsen, M.H. (Ed.). (2008). *Encountering the everyday: An introduction to the sociologies of the unnoticed.* New York: Palgrave Macmillan.

The jail where every prisoner gets a flatscreen TV and private shower. (2012, 21 May). *The Week.* Retrieved from http://theweek.com/articles/475370/jail-where-every-prisoner-gets-flatscreen-tv-private-shower

James, E. (2013, 25 February). The Norwegian prison where inmates are treated like people. *The Guardian.* Retrieved from http://www.theguardian.com/society/2013/feb/25/norwegian-prison-inmates-treated-like-people

James, H.R. (2008). If you are attractive and you know it, please apply: Appearance based discrimination and employer discretion. *Valparaiso University Law Review, 42,* 629–677.

Janowitz, M. (1975). Sociological theory and social control. *American Journal of Sociology, 81,* 82–108.

Jargowsky, P.A. (1996). Take the money and run: Economic segregation in US metropolitan areas. *American Sociological Review, 61*(6), 984–98.

Johnson, N.B. (1982). Education as environmental socialization: Classroom spatial patterns and the transmission of sociocultural norms. *Anthropological Quarterly, 55*(1), 31–43.

Johnston, J., & Taylor, J. (2008). Feminist consumerism and fat activists: A comparative study of grassroots activism and the Dove Real Beauty Campaign. *Signs: Journal of Women in Culture and Society, 33*(4), 941–66.

Kallendorf, C.W. (Ed.). (2010). *A companion to the classical tradition.* New York: John Wiley & Sons.

Kane, J., & Wall, A.D. (2006). *The 2005 National Public Survey on White Collar Crime.* Fairmont, VA: National White-Collar Crime Center.

Katz, E., & Lazarsfeld, P.F. (1955). *Personal influence.* New York: The Free Press.

Keenan, E. (2014, 8 August). Brampton mayor Susan Fennell's spectacular expenses bring public ire down on all good works. *The Star.* Retrieved from http://www.the-star.com/news/insight/2014/08/08/brampton_mayor_susan_fennells_spectacular_expenses_bring_public_ire_down_on_all_good_works.html

Keery, H., Boutelle, K., van den Berg, P., & Thompson, J.K. (2005). The impact of appearance-related teasing by family members. *Journal of Adolescent Health, 37*(2), 120–7.

Kelly, M. (2010). Regulating the reproduction and mothering of poor women: The controlling image of the welfare mother in television news coverage of welfare reform. *Journal of Poverty, 14*(1), 76–96.

Kerr, T., Small, W., & Wood, E. (2005). The public health and social impacts of drug market enforcement: A review of the evidence. *International Journal of Drug Policy, 16*(4), 210–20.

Kessler, D., & Levitt, S.D. (1998). *Using sentence enhancements to distinguish between deterrence and incapacitation*

(No. w6484). Cambridge, MA: National Bureau of Economic Research.

Kilmer, J.R., Walker, D.D., Lee, C.M., Palmer, R.S., Mallet, K.A., & Larimer, M.E. (2006). Misperceptions of college student marijuana use: Implications for prevention. *Journal of College Student Development, 44*, 204–16.

Kilvington, J., Day, S., & Ward, H. (2001). Prostitution policy in Europe: A time of change? *Feminist Review, 67*, 78–93.

King, L.W. (2014). *The code of Hammurabi.* Netlancers Inc.

Knight, J.R., Wechsler, H., Kuo, M., Seibring, M., Weitzman, E.R., & Schuckit, M.A. (2002). Alcohol abuse and dependence among US college students. *Studies on Alcohol, 63*, 263–70.

Koch, J.R., Roberts, A.E., Armstrong, M.L, & Owen, D.C. (2007). Frequencies and relations of body piercing and sexual experience in college students. *Psychological Reports, 101*(1), 159–62.

Kramer, R.C. (2000). Poverty, inequality, and youth violence. *The Annals of the American Academy of Political and Social Science, 567*(1), 123–39.

Krause, N. (2003). Religious meaning and subjective well-being in late life. *Journal of Gerontology: Social Sciences, 58*(3), 160–70.

Kreager, D.A., Rulison, K., & Moody, J. (2011). Delinquency and the structure of adolescent peer groups. *Criminology, 49*(1), 95–127.

Krivo, L.J., & Peterson, R.D. (1996). Extremely disadvantaged neighbourhoods and urban crime. *Social Forces, 75*(2), 619–48.

Kross, K. (1997, Spring). TV sees welfare only as a debate. *Nieman Reports*, 44–45.

Kubrin, C.E., & Ishizawa, H. (2012). Why some immigrant neighborhoods are safer than others: Divergent findings from Los Angeles and Chicago. *The Annals of the American Academy of Political and Social Science, 644*(1), 148–73.

Kubrin, C.E. (2013). Immigration and crime. In F.T. Cullen & P. Wilcox (Eds.), *The Oxford handbook of criminological theory* (pp. 440–55). New York: Oxford University Press.

Kumar, R., O'Malley, P.M., Johnston, L.D., Schulenberg, J.E., Bachman, J.G. (2002). Effects of school-level norms on student substance use. *Prevention Science, 3*(2), 105–24.

Kwan, S., & Trautner, M.N. (2009). Beauty work: Individual and institutional rewards, the reproduction of gender, and questions of agency. *Sociology Compass, 3*(1), 49–71.

Langton, L. (2012, August). Victimizations not reported to the police, 2006–2010. *National Crime Victimization Survey.* US Department of Justice. Retrieved from http://www.bjs.gov/content/pub/pdf/vnrp0610.pdf

LaPrairie, C. (2002). Aboriginal over-representation in the criminal justice system: A tale of nine cities. *Canadian Journal of Criminology, 44*, 181.

Lareau, A. (2002). Invisible inequality: Social class and childrearing in black families and white families." *American Sociological Review*, 747–76.

Lareau, A. (2011). *Unequal childhoods: Class, race, and family life.* Berkeley, CA: University of California Press.

Larimer, M.E., Turner, A.P., Anderson, B.K., Fader, J.S., Kilmer, J.R., Palmer, R.S., & Cronce, J.M. (2001). *Evaluating a brief alcohol intervention with fraternities, 62*, 3.

Laslett, A., Room, R., Ferris, J., Wilkinson, C., Livingston, M., & Mugavin, J. (2011). Surveying the range and magnitude of alcohol's harm to others in Australia. *Addiction, 106*(9), 1603–11.

Latendresse, S.J., Rose, R.J., Viken, R.V., Pulkkinen, L., Kaprio, J., & Dick, D.M. (2008). Parenting mechanisms in links between parents' and adolescents' alcohol use behaviors. *Alcoholism: Clinical and Experimental Research, 32*(2), 322–30.

Laub, J.H., & Sampson, R.J. (1993). Turning points in the life course: Why change matters to the study of crime. *Criminology, 31*(3), 301–25.

Lazarsfeld, P.F., Berelson, B., & Gaudet, H. (1944). *The people's choice: How the voter makes up his mind in a presidential campaign.* New York: Columbia University Press.

Lee, B.A., & Schreck, C.J. (2005). Danger on the streets marginality and victimization among homeless people. *American Behavioral Scientist, 48*(8), 1055–81.

Leit, R.A., Gray, J.J., & Pope, H.G. (2002). The media's representation of the ideal male body: A cause for muscle dysmorphia? *International Journal of Eating Disorders, 31*(3), 334–8.

Lens, V. (2002). Welfare reform, personal narratives and the media: How welfare recipients and journalists frame the welfare debate. *Journal of Poverty, 6*(2), 1–20.

Leve, M., Rubin, L., & Pusic, A. (2011). Cosmetic surgery and neoliberalisms: Managing risk and responsibility. *Feminism and Psychology, 22*(1), 122–41.

Levine, D.U., & Ornstein, A.C. (1981). Education, socialization, and sex. *The High School Journal, 64*(8), 337–42.

Lichter, D.T., Parisi, D., & Taquino, M.C. (2012). The geography of exclusion: Race, segregation, and concentrated poverty. *Social Problems, 59*, 364–88.

Lippi, G., Franchini, M., Favaloro, E., & Targher, G. (2010). Moderate red wine consumption and cardiovascular disease risk: Beyond the "French paradox." *Seminars in Thrombosis and Hemostasis, 36*(1), 59–70.

Lipset, S.M. (1991). *Continental divide: The values and institutions of the United States and Canada.* New York: Psychology Press.

Liquor Control Board of Ontario. (n.d.). About the LCBO. Retrieved from http://www.lcbo.com/content/lcbo/en/corpo rate-pages/about.html

Litt, M.D., Kadden, R.M., & Stephens, R.S. (2005). Coping and self-efficacy in marijuana treatment: Results from the Marijuana Treatment Project. *Journal of Consulting and Clinical Psychology, 73*, 1015–25.

Lochner, L., & Moretti, E. (2004). The effect of education on crime: Evidence from prison inmates, arrests, and self-reports. *American Economic Review, 94*, 155–89.

Locke, J. (2013). *Two treatises on government: A translation into modern English* (Vol. 5). Industrial Systems Research. (Original work published 1965).

Lorenzo, G.L., Biesanz, J.C., & Human, L.J. (2010). What is beautiful is good and more accurately understood: Physical attractiveness and accuracy in first impressions of personality. *Psychological Science, 21*(12), 1777–82.

Lyons, C.J., Velez, M.B., & Santoro, W.A. (2013). Neighborhood immigration, violence, and city-level immigrant political

opportunities. *American Sociological Review, 78*(4), 604–32.

MacDonald, R., Shildrick, T., Webster, C., & Simpson, D. (2005). Growing up in poor neighbourhoods: The significance of class and place in the extended transitions of "socially excluded" young adults. *Sociology, 39*(5), 873–91.

Macdonald, S., and Wells, S. (1994). The impact and effectiveness of drug testing programs in the workplace. In S. Macdonald & P. Roman (Eds.), *Drug testing in the workplace: Research advances in alcohol and drug problems* (pp. 121–42). New York: Plenum.

MacIver, R.M. (2012). *Community: A sociological study, being an attempt to set out native & fundamental laws.* London: Routledge. (Original work published 1970).

Mackrael, K. (2013, 7 January). Prison work programs fail inmates and the public, documents show. *The Globe and Mail.*

Mahoney, A., Pargament, K.I., Murray-Swank, A., & Murray-Swank, N. (2003). Religion and the sanctification of family relationships. *Review of Religious Research, 44*, 220–36.

Manchikanti, L. (2007). National drug control policy and prescription drug abuse: Facts and fallacies. *Pain Physician, 10*, 399–424.

Mannheim, Karl. (1940). *Man and society in an age of reconstruction.* London: Kegan Paul.

Manning-Miller, C.L. (1994). Media discourse and the feminization of poverty. *Explorations in Ethnic Studies*, 79–88.

Manson, D. (1986). *Tracking offenders— white-collar crime.* Bureau of Justice Statistics. Washington: United States Government.

Marcuse, H. (1964). *One-dimensional man: Studies in the ideology of advanced industrial society.* Boston: Beacon.

Martin, P.Y., & Hummer, R.A. (1989). Fraternities and rape on campus. *Gender & Society, 3*(4), 457–73.

Martinez, R., Lee, M.T., & Nielsen, A.L. (2004). Segmented assimilation, local context and determinants of drug violence in Miami and San Diego: Does ethnicity and immigration matter? *International Migration Review, 38*(1), 131–57.

Mascharka, C. (2001). Mandatory minimum sentences: Exemplifying the law of unintended consequences (2000–2001). *Florida State University Law Review, 28,* 935–75.

Massey, D.S., & Denton, N.A. (1993). *American apartheid: Segregation and the making of the underclass.* Cambridge, MA: Harvard University Press.

Mathios, A., Avery, R., Bisogni, C., & Shanahan, J. (1998). Portrayal on prime-time television: Manifest and latent message. *Studies on Alcohol, 59*(3), 305–10.

McCabe, D., & Trevino, L.K. (2002). Honesty and honor codes. *Academe, 88*(1), 37–41.

McCreary, D.R., & Sasse, D.K. (2000). An exploration of the drive for muscularity in adolescent boys and girls. *Journal of American College Health, 48*(6), 297–304.

McCullough, M.E., & Smith, T.B. (2003). Religion and health: Depressive symptoms and mortality as case studies. In M. Dilon (Ed.), *Handbook of the sociology of religion,* (pp. 190–204). Cambridge, UK: Cambridge University Press.

McDonald, D. (2014, April). *Outrageous fortune: Documenting Canada's wealth gap.* Canadian Centre for Policy Alternatives. Retrieved from https://www.policyalternatives.ca/sites/default/files/uploads/publications/National%20Office/2014/04/Outrageous_Fortune.pdf

McGee, J.P., & DeBernardo, C.R. (2002). The classroom avenger. In N.G. Ribner (Ed.), *The California School of Professional Psychology handbook of juvenile forensic psychology* (pp. 230–52). San Francisco: Jossey-Bass.

McIntosh, W.A., Sykes, D., & Kubena, K.S. (2002). Religion and community among the elderly: The relationship between the religious and secular characteristics of their social networks. *Review of Religious Research, 44*(2), 109–25.

McLanahan, S., & Percheski, C. (2008). Family structure and the reproduction of inequalities. *Annual Review Sociology, 34,* 257–76.

McLeod, J.M., Atkin, C.K., & Chaffee, S.H. (1972). Adolescents, parents and television use: Adolescent self-report measures from Maryland and Wisconsin samples. In G.A. Comstock & E.A. Rubinstein (Eds.), *Television and social behavior, Vol. 3. Television and adolescent aggressiveness* (pp. 173–238). Washington, DC: Government Printing Office.

Mcnulty, T.L., Bellair, P.E., & Watts, S.J. (2012). Neighborhood disadvantage and verbal ability as explanations of the black-white difference in adolescent violence: Toward an integrated model. *Crime and Delinquency, 59*(1), 140–60.

Mead, G.H. (1925). The genesis of the self and social control. *International Journal of Ethics, 35*(3), 251–77.

Mead, G.H. (1934). *Mind, self and society from the standpoint of a social behaviorist* (C.W. Morris, Ed.). Chicago: University of Chicago.

Mechoulan, S. (2011). The external effects of black male imprisonment on black females. *Journal of Labor Economics, 29*(1), 1–35.

Merton, R.K. (1938). Social structure and anomie. *American Sociological Review, 3*(5), 672–82.

Miethe, T.D. (1985). The myth or reality of victim involvement in crime: A review and comment on victim-precipitation research. *Sociological Focus,* 209–20.

Milkie, M.A. (1999). Social comparisons, reflected appraisals, and mass media: The impact of pervasive beauty images on black and white girls' self-concepts. *Social Psychological Quarterly, 62*(2), 190–210.

Miller, J. (2001). *One of the guys: Girls, gangs, and gender.* New York: Oxford University Press.

Millhorn, M., Monaghan, M., Montero, D., Reyes, M., Roman, T., Tollasken, R., et al. (2009). North Americans' attitudes toward illegal drugs. *Journal of Human Behavior in the Social Environment, 19*(2): 125–41.

Miron, J.A. (2003). The effect of drug prohibition on drug prices: Evidence from the markets for cocaine and heroin. *Review of Economics and Statistics, 85*(3), 522–30.

Moiseyenko, O. (2005). Education and social cohesion. *Journal of Education, 80*(4), 89–104.

Morris, L. (1997). Globalization, migration and the nation-state: The path to a post-national Europe? *British Journal of Sociology, 48*(2): 192–209.

Morris, S.Z., & Gibson, C.L. (2011). Corporal punishment's influence on children's aggressive and delinquent behavior. *Criminal justice and behavior, 38*(8), 818–39.

Muir, J. (2011). Bridging and linking in a divided society: A social capital case study from Northern Ireland. *Urban Studies, 48*(5), 959–76.

Mulder, J., Ter Bogt, T.F.M., Raaijmakers, Q.A.W., Gabhainn, S.N., Monshouwer, K., & Vollebergh, W.A.M. (2009). The soundtrack of substance use: Music preference and adolescent smoking and drinking. *Substance Use and Misuse, 44*(4), 514–31.

Mulvey, L. (1975). Visual pleasure and narrative cinema. *Screen, 16*(3), 6–18.

Murphy, Emily. F. (1926). *The Black Candle.* Toronto: Thomas Allen.

Murray, J. (2005). The effects of imprisonment on families and children of prisoners. In A. Liebling & S. Maruna (Eds.), *The effects of imprisonment* (pp. 442–92). New York: Routledge.

Murray, R.K., & Swatt, M.L. (2013). Disaggregating the relationship between schools and crime: A spatial analysis. *Crime and Delinquency, 59*(2), 163–90.

Murray, S.B., Rieger, E., Karlov, L., & Touyz, S.W. (2013). Masculinity and femininity in the divergence of male body image concerns. *Journal of Eating Disorders, 1*(11), 1–8.

Murthy, D. (2012). "Towards a sociological understanding of social media: Theorizing Twitter. *Sociology, 46*(6), 1059–73.

Nally, J., Lockwood, S., Knutson, K., & Ho, T. (2012). An evaluation of the effect of correctional education programs on post-release recidivism and employment: An empirical study in Indiana. *Journal of Correctional Education, 63*(1), 69–88.

National Institute of Justice. (2014, 16 July). Drug courts. *Office of Justice Programs.* Retrieved from http://www.nij.gov/topics/courts/drug-courts/Pages/welcome.aspx

National Institute on Alcohol Abuse and Alcoholism (NIAAA). (2013, July). College drinking. Retrieved from http://pubs.niaaa.nih.gov/publications/CollegeFactSheet/CollegeFact.htm

National Survey on Drug Use and Health (NSDUH). (2013). Results from the 2012 National Survey on Drug Use and Health: Summary of national findings.

Neckerman, K.M., & Torche, F. (2007). Inequality: Causes and consequences. *Annual Review of Sociology, 33,* 335–57.

Neighbors, C., Geisner, L.M., & Lee, C.M. (2008). Perceived marijuana norms and social expectations among entering college student marijuana users. *Psychology of Addictive Behaviors, 22,* 433–38.

Neuman, W.R. (1991). *The future of the mass audience.* New York: Cambridge University Press.

Nolan, J., Jr. (2001). *Reinventing justice: The American drug court movement.* Princeton, NJ: Princeton University Press.

Normand, J., Lempert, R.O., & O'Brien, C.P. (Eds.). (1994). *Under the influence? Drugs and the American work force.* Washington, DC: National Academy Press.

Nuttbrock, L.A., Rosenblum, A., Magura, S., Villano, C., & Wallace, J. (2004). Linking female sex workers with substance abuse treatment. *Journal of Substance Abuse Treatment, 27*(3), 233–39.

Nuwer, H. (2001). *Wrongs of passage: Fraternities, sororities, hazing, and binge drinking.* Bloomington: Indiana University Press.

O'Brien, P. (2013). Medical marijuana and social control: Escaping criminalization and embracing medicalization. *Deviant Behavior, 34,* 423–43.

O'Doherty, T. (2011). Victimization in off-street sex industry work. *Violence against Women, 17*(7). doi:1077801211412917.

Oetting, E.R., and Beauvais, F. (1990). Adolescent drug use: Findings of national and local surveys. *Journal of consulting and clinical psychology, 58*(4), 385.

Okon, E.E. (2012). Religion as instrument of socialization and social control. *European Scientific Journal, 8*(26), 136–42.

Olivardia, R., Pope, H.G., Borowiecki, J.J., & Cohane, G.H. (2004). Biceps and body image: The relationship between muscularity and self-esteem, depression, and eating disorder symptoms. *Psychology of Men and Masculinity, 5*(2), 112–20.

Osgood, D.W., & Anderson, A.L. Unstructured socializing and rates of delinquency. *Criminology, 42*(3), 519–50.

Oswald, M.E., Hupfeld, J., Klug, S.C., & Gabriel, U. (2002). Lay-perspectives on criminal deviance, goals of punishment, and punitivity. *Social Justice Research, 15*(2), 85–98.

Page, T.N. (1905). *The Old South: Essays social and political.* New York: C. Scribner's Sons.

Parsons, T. (1951). Illness and the role of the physician: A sociological perspective. *American Journal of Orthopsychiatry, 21*(3), 452–60.

Paschall, M.J., Grube, J.W., & Kypri, K. (2009). Alcohol control policies and alcohol consumption by youth: A multi-national study. *Addiction, 104*(11), 1849–55.

Payne, B.K. (2012). *White-collar crime: A text/reader.* Los Angeles: Sage.

Pederson, P.M., & Whisenant, W.A. (2003). Examining stereotypical written and photographic reporting on the sports page: An analysis of newspaper coverage of interscholastic athletics. *Women in Sport and Physical Activity Journal, 12*(1), 67–75.

Peguero, A.A., Popp, A.M., Latimore, T.J., Shekarkhar, Z., & Koo, D.J. (2011). Social control theory and school misbehavior: Examining the role of race and ethnicity. *Youth Violence and Juvenile Justice, 9*(3): 259–75.

Perkins, H.W., Meilman, P.W., Leichliter, J.S., Cashin, J.R., & Presley, C.A. (1999). Misperceptions of the norms for the frequency of alcohol and other drug use on college campuses. *College Health, 47*, 253–8.

Perkins, J.J., Sanson-Fisher, R.W., Blunden, S., Lunnay, D., Redman, S., & Hensley, M.J. (1994). The prevalence of drug use in urban Aboriginal communities. *Addiction, 89*(10), 1319–31.

Perreault, S. (2009). The incarceration of Aboriginal people in adult correctional services. *Juristat, 29*(3), 9.

Perreault, S. (2011a). Violent victimization of Aboriginal people in the Canadian provinces, 2009. *Juristat, 30*(4), 1–35.

Perreault, S. (2011b). Common menu bar links. *Impaired Driving in Canada, 2011. Juristat.* Retrieved from http://www.statcan.gc.ca/pub/85-002-x/2013001/article/11739-eng.htm

Pettit, B., & Western, B. (2004). Mass imprisonment and the life course: Race and class inequality in US imprisonment. *American Sociological Review, 69*(2), 151–69.

Phillips, D.P. (1983). The impact of mass media violence on US homicides. *American Sociological Review, 48*, 560–8.

Phillips, D.P., & Hensley, J.E. (1984). When violence is rewarded or punished: The impact of mass media stories on homicide. *Journal of Communication, 34*(3), 101–16.

Piaget, J. (1932). *The moral judgment of the child.* London: Routledge.

Pinker, S. (2011). *The better angels of our nature: Why violence has declined.* New York: Viking.

Platt, M. (2012, 28 February). Canada's criminal sitting pretty as price tag for prisoners soars. *Calgary Sun.* Retrieved from http://www.torontosun.com/2012/02/28/canadas-criminal-sitting-pretty-as-price-tag-for-prisoners-soars

Poortinga, E., Lemmen, C., & Jibson, M.D. (2006). A case control study: White-collar defendants compared with defendants charged with nonviolent theft. *Journal of the American Academy of Psychiatry and the Law, 34*(1), 82–9.

Pope, H.G., Olivardia, R., Gruber, A., & Borowiecki, J. (1998). Evolving ideas of male body image as seen through action toys. *International Journal of Eating Disorders, 26*(1), 65–72.

Pope, H.G., Phillips, K.A., & Olivardia, R. (2000). *The Adonis complex.* New York: Touchstone.

Primack, B.A., Dalton, M.A., Carroll, M.V., Agarwal, A.A., & Fine, M.J. (2008). Content analysis of tobacco, alcohol, and other drugs in popular music. *Archives of Pediatrics and Adolescent Medicine, 162*(2), 169–75.

Public Safety Canada. (2014, March 4). *A statistical snapshot of youth at risk and youth offending in Canada.* Government of Canada. Retrieved from http://www.publicsafety.gc.ca/cnt/rsrcs/pblctns/ststclsnpsht-yth/index-eng.aspx

Putnam, R. (2000). *Bowling alone: The collapse and revival of American community.* New York: Touchstone.

Quinney, R. (1974). *The social reality of crime.* Boston, MA: Little Brown.

Ragatz, L.L., Fremouw, W., & Baker, E. (2012). The psychological profile of white-collar offenders: Demographics, criminal thinking, psychopathic traits, and psychopathology. *Criminal Justice and Behaviour, 39*(7), 978–97.

Rasul, J.W., Rommel, R.G., Jacquez, G.M., Fitzpatrick, B.G., Ackleh, A.S., Simonsen, N., et al. (2011). Heavy episodic drinking on college campuses: Does changing the legal drinking age make a difference? *Study of Alcohol and Drugs, 72*, 15–23.

Reading, C.L., & Wien, F. (2009). *Health inequalities and the social determinants of Aboriginal peoples' health.* Prince George, BC: National Collaborating Centre for Aboriginal Health.

Rehm, J., Baliunas, D., Borges, G.L.G., Graham, K., Irving, H., Kehoe, T., et al. (2010). The relation between different dimensions of alcohol consumption and burden of disease: An overview. *Addiction, 105*(5), 817–43.

Reyns, B.W. (2010). A situational crime prevention approach to cyberstalking victimization: Preventive tactics for Internet users and online place managers. *Crime Prevention & Community Safety, 12*(2), 99–118.

Richards, D.A.J. (1979, May). Commercial sex and the rights of the person: A moral argument for the decriminalization of prostitution. *University of Pennsylvania Law Review,* 1195–1287.

Ringwalt, C.L., Paschall, M.J., & Gitelman, A.M. (2011). Alcohol prevention strategies on college campuses and student alcohol abuse and related problems. *Journal of Drug Education, 41*(1), 99–118.

Riniolo, T.C., Johnson, K.C., Sherman, T., & Misso, J.A. (2006). Hot or not: Do professors seen as physically attractive receive higher student evaluations? *The Journal of General Psychology, 133*(1), 19–35.

Robers, S., Kemp, J., Rathbun, A., Snyder, T.D., & Morgan, R.E. (2013). Indicators of school crime and safety: 2013. *National Center for Education Statistics.* Institute of Education Science.

Roberts, A.R. (2006). Classification typology and assessment of five levels of woman battering. *Journal of Family Violence, 21*(8), 521–7.

Roberts, J.V. (2007). Public confidence in criminal justice in Canada: A comparative and contextual analysis. *Canadian Journal of Criminology and Criminal Justice. 49*(2), 153–84.

Roberts, R.E., Deleger, S., Strawbridge, W.J., & Kaplan, G.E. (2003). Prospective association between obesity and depression: Evidence from the Alameda County Study. *International Journal of Obesity, 27*(4), 514–21.

Robertson, J.C. (1990). Sex addiction as a disease: A neurobehavioral model. *American Journal of Preventive Psychiatry and Neurology, 2*(3), 15–18.

Robinson, J., & Bachman, J. (1972). Television viewing habits and aggression. In G.A. Comstock & E.A. Rubinstein (Eds.), *Television and social behavior, Vol. 3, Television and adolescent aggressiveness* (pp. 372–82). Washington, DC: Government Printing Office.

Rome, D. (2004). *Theory: UCR, racial bias, public policy, and the mass media. Black demons: The media's depiction of the African American male criminal.* Westport: Prager.

Rose, A.M., & Myrdal, G. (1964). *The Negro in America: The condensed version of Gunnar Myrdal's* An American Dilemma. New York: Harper & Row.

Ross, Edward A. (1926). *Social control: A survey of the foundations of order.* New York: Macmillan. (Original work published 1921).

Rutter, M., Giller, H., & Hagell, A. (1998). *Antisocial behavior by young people: A major new review.* Cambridge, UK: Cambridge University Press.

Sabina, C., & Tindale, R.S. (2008). Abuse characteristics and coping resources as predictors of problem-focused coping strategies among battered women. *Violence against Women, 14*(4), 437–56.

Sale, E., Sambrano, S., Springer, J.F., & Turner, C.W. (2003). Risk, protection, and substance use in adolescents: A multi-site model. *Journal of Drug Education, 33*(1), 91–105.

Saltz, R.F., Paschall, M.J., Mcgaffigan, R.P., & Nygaard, P.M. (2010). Alcohol risk management in college settings. *American Journal of Preventive Medicine, 39*(6), 491–9.

Sampson, R.J. (1987). Urban black violence: The effect of male joblessness and family disruption. *American Journal of Sociology,* 348–82.

Sampson, R.J., Raudenbush, S.W., & Earls, F. (1997). Neighborhoods and violent crime: A multilevel study of collective efficacy. *Science, 277*(5328), 918–24.

Sanderson, C.A., Darley, J.M., & Messinger, C.S. (2002). I'm not as thin as you think I am: The development and consequences of feeling discrepant from the thinness norm. *Personality and Social Psychology Bulletin, 28*(2), 172–83.

Saouli, A. (2011). Hizbullah in the civilising process: Anarchy, self-restraint and violence. *Third World Quarterly, 32*(5): 925–42.

Saucier, M.G. (2004). Midlife and beyond: Issues for aging women. *Journal of Counseling and Development, 82*(4), 420–5.

Schiefenhovel, W., & Macbeth, H.M. (2011). *Liquid bread: Beer and brewing in cross-cultural perspective.* New York: Berghahn.

Schieman, S. (2010). Socioeconomic status and beliefs about God's influence in everyday life. *Sociology of Religion, 71*(1), 25–51.

Schieman, S., & Bierman, A. (2007). Religious activities and changes in the sense of divine control: Dimensions of social stratification as contingencies. *Sociology of Religion, 68*(4), 361–81.

Schieman, S., & Pudrovsaka, T. (2003). "It's in God's hands": Socioeconomic status and the sense of divine control among black and white elderly. *American Sociological Association, IX*(3), 1, 4.

Schieman, S., Pudrovska, T., & Milkie, M.A. (2005). The sense of divine control and the self-concept: A study of race differences in late-life. *Research on Aging, 27,* 165–96.

Schiller, H.I. (1989). *Culture, Inc.* New York: Oxford University Press.

Schlesinger, T. (2005). Racial and ethnic disparity in pretrial criminal processing. *Justice Quarterly, 22*(2): 170–92.

Schmidt, L.A., Mäkelä, P., Rehm, J., & Room, R. (2010). Alcohol: Equity and social determinants. In E. Blas & A.S. Kurup (Eds.), *Equity, social determinants and public health programmes* (pp. 11–29). Geneva, Switzerland: World Health Organization.

Schooler, D., Ward, M.L., Merriwether, A., & Caruthers, A. (2004). Who's that girl: Television's role in the body image development of young white and black women. *Psychology of Women Quarterly, 28*(1), 38–47.

Schram, S.F., Fording, R.C., & Soss, J. (2008). Neo-liberal poverty governance: Race, place and the punitive turn in US welfare policy. *Cambridge Journal of Regions, Economy and Society, 1*(1), 17–36.

Schur, E.A., Sanders, M., & Steiner, H. (2000). Body dissatisfaction and dieting in young children. *International Journal of Eating Disorders, 27*(1), 74–82.

SexyTypewriter. (2011, August 11). Unattainable beauty. *Toronto Sun.* Retrieved from http://www.torontosun.com/2011/08/09/unattainable-beauty

Shannon, K., Kerr, T., Allinott, S., Chettiar, J., Shoveller, J., & Tyndall, M.W. (2008). Social and structural violence and power relations in mitigating HIV risk of drug-using women in survival sex work. *Social Science & Medicine, 66*(4), 911–21.

Shaver, F.M. (2011). Prostitution. In *The Canadian Encyclopedia.* Retrieved from http://www.thecanadianencyclopedia.com/en/article/prostitution/

Shaw, C.R., & McKay, H.D. (1942). *Juvenile delinquency and urban areas.* Chicago: University of Chicago Press.

Shaw, C.R., & McKay, H.D. (1969). *Juvenile delinquency and urban areas* (rev. ed.). Chicago: University of Chicago Press.

Shaw, C.R., & McKay, H.D. (2014). Juvenile delinquency and urban areas. In T.L. Anderson (Ed.), *Understanding deviance: Connecting classical and contemporary perspectives.* New York: Routledge.

Shaw, D.L., & Martin, S.E. (1992). The function of mass media agenda setting. *Journalism and Mass Communication Quarterly, 69*(4), 902–20.

Shelden, R.G. (2010). *Our punitive society: Race, class, gender and punishment in America.* Long Grove, IL: Waveland Press.

Sherkat, D.E. (2002). African-American religious affiliation in the late 20th century: Cohort variations and patterns of switching, 1973–1988. *Journal for the Scientific Study of Religion, 41,* 485–93.

Sherkat, D.E. (2003). Religious socialization: Agents of influence and influences of agency. In M. Dilon (Ed.), *Handbook of the sociology of religion* (pp. 151–63). Cambridge: Cambridge University Press.

Shewan, D., & Dalgarno, P. (2005). Evidence for controlled heroin use? Low levels of negative health and social outcomes among non-treatment heroin users in Glasgow (Scotland). *British Journal of Health Psychology, 10*(1), 33–48.

Shrum, H. (2004). No longer theory: Correctional practices that work. *Journal of Correctional Education, 55*(3), 225–35.

Shulman, D., & Silver, I. (2003). The business of becoming a professional sociologist: Unpacking the informal training of graduate school. *American Sociologist, 34*(3), 56–72.

Siegel, K., Anderman, S.J., & Schrimshaw, E.W. (2001). Religion and coping with health-related stress. *Psychology and Health, 16*, 631–53.

Siegel, L.J. (2004). *Criminology: Theories, patterns, and typologies* (8th ed.). Belmont, CA: Wadsworth.

Simon, R.J., & Sikich, K.W. (2007). Public attitudes toward immigrants and immigration policies across seven nations. *International Migration Review, 41*(4), 956–62.

Simons, R.L., & Whitbeck, L.B. (1991). Sexual abuse as a precursor to prostitution and victimization among adolescent and adult homeless women. *Journal of Family Issues, 12*(3), 361–79.

Slevec, J., & Tiggemann, M. (2010). Attitudes toward cosmetic surgery in middle-aged women: Body image, aging anxiety, and the media. *Psychology of Women Quarterly, 34*, (1), 65–74.

Smeeding, T.M. (2005). Public policy, economic inequality, and poverty: The United States in comparative perspective. *Social Science Quarterly, 86*(s1), 955–83.

Smith, C. (2000). "Healthy prisons": A contradiction in terms? *The Howard Journal of Criminal Justice, 39*(4), 339–53.

Smith, C. (2003). Theorizing religious effects among American adolescents. *Journal for the Scientific Study of Religion, 42*, 17–30.

Smith, K.C., Twum, D., & Gielen, A.C. (2009). Media coverage of celebrity DUIs: Teachable moments or problematic social modeling? *Alcohol and Alcoholism, 44*(3), 256–60.

Sniderman, P.M., & Piazza, T. (1993). *The scar of race.* Cambridge, MA: Harvard University Press.

Snyder, L.B., Milici, F.F., Slater, M., Sun, H., & Strizhakova, Y. (2006). Effects of alcohol advertising exposure on drinking among youth. *Archives of Pediatrics and Adolescent Medicine, 160*(1), 18–24.

Somers, M.R., & Block, F. (2005, April). From poverty to perversity: Ideas, markets, and institutions over 200 years of debate. *American Sociological Review,* 260–87.

Sorensen, J., Wrinkle, R., Brewer, V., & Marquart, J. (1999). Capital punishment and deterrence: Examining the effect of executions on murder in Texas. *Crime and Delinquency, 45*(4), 481–93.

Sotirovic, M. (2001). Media use and perceptions of welfare. *Journal of Communication, 51*(4), 750–74.

Spilka, B., Hood, R.W., Hunsberger, B., & Gorsuch, R. (2003). *The psychology of religion.* New York: Guildford Press.

Spitzer, B.L., Henderson, K.A., & Zivian, M.T. (1999). Gender differences in population versus media body sizes. *Sex Roles, 40*, 545–65.

Stansfield, R., Akins, S., Rumbaut, R.G., & Hammer, R.B. (2013). Assessing the effects of recent immigration on serious property crime in Austin, Texas. *Sociological Perspectives, 56*(4), 647–72.

Stark, E. (2007). *Coercive control: How men entrap women in personal life.* New York: Oxford University Press.

Stark, R. (1996). Religion as context: Hellfire and delinquency one more time. *Sociology of Religion, 57*, 163–73.

Stark, R., & Finke, R. (2000). *Acts of faith: Explaining the human side of religion.* Berkeley, CA: University of California Press.

Statistics Canada (2006, 2 May). Study: Who's religious? *The Daily.* Retrieved from http://www.statcan.gc.ca/daily-quotidien/060502/dq060502a-eng.htm

Statistics Canada. (2009). Household income and victimization in Canada, 2004. Canadian Centre for Justice Statistics Profile Series (No. 20, catalogue number 85F0033M). Retrieved from http://www.statcan.gc.ca/pub/85f0033m/2009020/c-g/c-g3-eng.htm.

Statistics Canada. (2012, 12 October). Adult correctional statistics in Canada, 2010/2011. *Juristat.* Retrieved from http://www.statcan.gc.ca/pub/85-002-x/2012001/article/11715-eng.htm

Statistics Canada. (2013). Section D—Eating disorders. *Health state descriptions for*

Canadians. Retrieved from http://www
.statcan.gc.ca/pub/82-619-m/2012004/
sections/sectiond-eng.htm

Statistics Canada. (2014). Police-reported
crime statistics in Canada, 2013.
Juristat.
Retrieved from http://www.statcan.gc.ca/
pub/85–002-x/2014001/article/14040–
eng.htm

Steedman, M. (1997). *Angels of the workplace: Women and the construction of
gender relations in the Canadian clothing
industry, 1890–1940.* Toronto: Oxford
University Press.

Stenning, P., & Roberts, J.V. (2001). Empty
promises: Parliament, the Supreme
Court, and the sentencing of Aboriginal
offenders. *Saskatchewan Law Review, 64,*
137–68.

Stern, S.R. (2005). Messages from teens
on the big screen: Smoking, drinking,
and drug use in teen-centered films.
Journal of Health Communication, 10(4),
331–46.

Stevens, D.J. (1994). The depth of imprisonment and prisonization: Levels of security and prisoners' anticipation of future
violence. *Howard Journal of Criminal
Justice, 33*(2), 137–57.

Stokes, C.E. & Regnerus, M.D. (2008).
When faith divides family: Religious
discord and adolescent reports of parent-
child relations. *Social Science Research,
38*(1), 155–67.

Strang, J., Babor, T., Caulkins, J., Fischer, B.,
Foxcroft, D., & Humphreys, K. (2012).
Drug policy and the public good:
Evidence for effective interventions. *The
Lancet, 379*(9810), 71–83.

Straus, M.A. (1991). Discipline and deviance: Physical punishment of children
and violence and other crime in adulthood. *Social Problems,* 133–54.

Stroope, S. (2012). Social networks and
religion: The role of congregational
social embeddedness in religious belief
and practice. *Sociology of Religion,
73*(3), 273–98.

Stuntz, W.J. (1998). Race, class, and
drugs. *Columbia Law Review, 98*(7),
1795–842.

Surratt, H.L., & Inciardi, J.A. (2004). HIV
risk, seropositivity and predictors of infection among homeless and non-homeless
women sex workers in Miami, Florida,
USA. *AIDS Care, 16*(5), 594–604.

Sutherland, E.H. (1939). *Principles of
criminology* (3rd ed.). Philadelphia: J.B.
Lippincott.

Sutherland, E.H. (1940). White-collar
criminality. *American Sociological Review,
5*(1), 1–12.

Sutherland, E.H. (1945). Is "white collar
crime" crime? *American Sociological
Review, 10*(2), 132–9.

Sutherland, E.H. (1947). *Principles of
criminology.* Chicago: JB Lippincott
Company.

Sutherland, E.H. (1973). *On analyzing crime.*
Chicago: University of Chicago Press.

Sutherland, E.H. (2002). Is "white collar crime" crime?" In S. Cote (Ed.),
*Criminological theories: Bridging the past
to the future.* Thousand Oaks, CA: Sage
Publications.

Tajfel, H. & Turner, J.C. (1986). The social
identity theory of intergroup behavior.
In S. Worchel & W.G. Austin (Eds.),
Psychology of intergroup relations (pp.
7–24). Chicago: Nelson-Hall.

Tamer, C. (2012). Toddlers, tiaras, and
pedophilia? The "borderline child pornography" embraced by the American
public. *Texas Review of Entertainment and
Sports Law, 85,* 85–101.

Taylor, S.E. (1983). Adjustment to threatening events: A theory of cognitive adaption.
American Psychologist, 38(11), 1161–73.

Taylor, S. (2008). Outside the outsiders:
Media representations of drug use.
Probation Journal, 55(4), 369–87.

Thibault, E. (2014, 18 March). Federal
inmate cost soars to $117Gs each
per year. *Edmonton Sun.* Retrieved
from http://www.edmontonsun.
com/2014/03/18/federal-inmate-cost-
soars-to-177gs-each-per-year

Thompson, F.J., Riccucci, N.M., & Ban, C.
(1991). Drug testing in the federal workplace: An instrumental and symbolic
assessment. *Public Administration Review,
51,* 515–25.

Thompson, K.J., Heinberg, L.J.,
Altabe, M., & Tantleff-Dunn, S. (1999).
*Exacting beauty: Theory, assessment
and treatment of body image distur-
bance.* Washington, DC: American
Psychological Association.

Thompson, K.J., & Stice, E. (2001). Thin-
ideal internalization: Mounting evidence
for a new risk factor for body-image dis-
turbance and eating pathology. *Current*

Directions in Psychological Science, 10(5), 181–3.

Thornberry, T.P., Moore, M., & Christenson, R.L. (1985). The effect of dropping out of high school on subsequent criminal behavior. *Criminology, 23*(1), 3–18.

Thorogood, N. (1992). Sex education as social control. *Critical Public Health, 3*(2), 43–50.

Thrasher, F.M. (1927). *The gang: A study of 1,313 gangs in Chicago.* Chicago: University of Chicago Press.

Tiggemann, M. (2004). Body image across the adult life span: Stability and change. *Body Image, 1*(1), 29–41.

Tobler, N.S. (1986). Meta-analysis of 143 adolescent drug prevention programs: Quantitative outcome results of program participants compared to a control or comparison group. *Drug Issues, 16*(4), 537–67.

Uggen, C., & Piliavin, I. (1998). Asymmetrical causation and criminal desistance. *Journal of Criminal Law and Criminology, 88,* 1399–422.

United Nations. (1997). International drug control programme. *World Drug Report,* 124.

United States Government. (2013). *Summary of performance and financial information (fiscal year 2013).* Department of Labour. Retrieved from http://www.dol.gov/_sec/media/reports/2013summary/FY2013PerformanceSummary.pdf

Valentino, N.A. (1999). Crime news and the priming of racial attitudes during evaluations of the president. *Public Opinion Quarterly, 63,* 293–320.

Vander Ven, T. (2011). *Getting wasted: Why college students drink too much and party so hard.* New York: New York University Press.

Velez, M.B. (2009). Contextualizing the immigration and crime effect: An analysis of homicide in Chicago neighborhoods. *Homicide Studies, 13*(3), 325–35.

Vermeer, P. (2009). Denominational schools and the (religious) socialisation of youths. A changing relationship. *British Journal of Religious Education, 31*(3), 201–11.

Vermeer, P. (2010). Religious education and socialization. *Religious Education, 105*(1), 103–16.

Visher, C., Debus, S., & Yahner, J. (2008, 20 October). Employment after prison: A longitudinal study of releases in three states. *Urban Institute, Justice Policy Center.* Retrieved from http://www.urban.org/research/publication/employment-after-prison-longitudinal-study-releasees-three-states

Wachholz, S. (2005). Hate crimes against the homeless: Warning-out New England style. *Journal of Sociology & Social Welfare, 32,* 141.

Wacquant, L.J. (1993). Urban outcasts: Stigma and division in the black American ghetto and the French urban periphery. *International Journal of Urban and Regional Research, 17*(3), 366–83.

Walda, I.C., Tabak, C., Smit, H.A., Räsänen, L., Fidanza, F., Menotti, A., et al. (2002). Diet and 20–year chronic obstructive pulmonary disease mortality in middle-aged men from three European countries. *European Journal of Clinical Nutrition, 56*(7), 638–43.

Walker, D.D., Neighbors, C., Rodriguez, L.M., Stephens, R.S., & Roffman, R.A. (2011). Social norms and self-efficacy among heavy using adolescent marijuana smokers. *Psychology of Addictive Behavior, 25*(4), 727–32.

Wallack, L., Grube, J.W., Madden, P.A., & Breed, W. (1990). Portrayals of alcohol on prime-time television. *Studies on Alcohol, 51*(5), 428–37.

Walmsley, R. (2013). World prison population list (10th ed.). *International Centre for Prison Studies.* Retrieved from http://www.prisonstudies.org/sites/default/files/resources/downloads/wppl_10.pdf

Walzer, M., & Miller, D. (2007). *Thinking politically: Essays in political theory* (D. Miller, Ed.). New Haven, CT: Yale University Press.

Warhol-Down, R., & Herndl, D.P. (1997). *Feminisms: An anthology of literary theory and criticism* (rev. ed.). New Brunswick, NJ: Rutgers University Press.

Warr, M. (2002). *Companions in crime: The social aspects of criminal conduct.* Cambridge, UK: Cambridge University Press.

Weatherspoon, F.D. (2004). Racial profiling of African-American males: Stopped, searched, and stripped of constitutional protection. *John Marshall Law Review, 38,* 439–59.

Weber, M. (2009). *From Max Weber: Essays in sociology.* New York: Routledge.

Weber, M., & Whimster, S. (2004). *The essential Weber: A reader.* New York: Psychology Press.

Weinstein, I. (2003). Fifteen years after the federal sentencing revolution: How mandatory minimums have undermined effective and just narcotics sentencing. *American Criminal Law Review, 40,* 87–132.

Wenzel, M., & Thielmann, I. (2006). Why we punish in the name of justice: Just desert versus value restoration and the role of social identity. *Social Justice Research, 19*(4), 450–70.

Western, B. (2006). *Punishment and inequality in America.* New York: Russell Sage Foundation.

Western, B. (2007). The prison boom and the decline of American citizenship. *Society, 44*(5), 30–6.

White, K.M., & Holman, M. (2012). Marijuana prohibition in California: Racial prejudice and selective-arrests. *Race, Gender and Class, 19*(3), 75–92.

White House. (2013, 7 July). A drug policy for the 21st century. Retrieved from https://www.whitehouse.gov/ondcp/drugpolicyreform

Wiegman, O., & van Schie, E.G.M. (1998). Video game playing and its relations with aggressive and prosocial behaviour. *British Journal of Social Psychology, 37,* 367–78.

Wildeman, C. (2010). Paternal imprisonment and children's physically aggressive behaviors: Evidence from the Fragile Families and Child Wellbeing Study. *Social Forces, 89*(1), 285–309.

Williams, R.R. (2010). Space for God: Lived religion at work, home, and play. *Sociology of Religion, 71*(3), 257–79.

Willits, D., Broidy, L., & Denman, K. (2013). Schools, neighborhood risk factors, and crime. *Crime and Delinquency, 59*(2), 292–315.

Wilson, W.J. (1987). *The truly disadvantaged: The inner city, the underclass, and public policy.* Chicago: The University of Chicago Press.

Wilson, W.J. (1997). *When work disappears: The world of the new urban poor.* New York: Vintage.

Wingood, G.M., Diclemente, R.J., Bernhardt, J.M., Harrington, K.,

Davies, S.L., Robillard, A., et al. (2003). A prospective study of exposure to rap music videos and African American female adolescents' health. *American Journal of Public Health, 93*(3), 437–9.

Wolfgang, M.F. (1957). Victim precipitated criminal homicide. *Journal of Criminal Law and Criminology, 48*(1): 1–11.

Wolfson, S. (2000). Students' estimates of the prevalence of drug use: Evidence for a false consensus effect. *Psychology of Addictive Behaviors, 14,* 295–8.

Wood, E., Kerr, T., Small, W., Li, K., Marsh, D.C., Montaner, J.S.G., et al. (2004). Changes in public order after the opening of a medically supervised safer injecting facility for illicit injection drug users. *Canadian Medical Association Journal, 171*(7), 731–4.

World Health Organization. (2014). Global status report on alcohol and health 2014. Retrieved from http://www.who.int/substance_abuse/publications/global_alcohol_report/en/

Worobey, J., & Worobey, H.S. (2014). Body-size stigmatization by preschool girls: In a doll's world, it's good to be "Barbie." *Body Image, 11*(2), 171–4.

Wortley, S. (2003). Hidden intersections: Research on race, crime, and criminal justice in Canada. *Canadian Ethnic Studies, 35*(3), 99–117.

Wortley, S., & Tanner, J. (2004). Social groups or criminal organizations? The extent and nature of youth gang activity in Toronto. In J. Phillips & B. Kidd (Eds.), *Enforcement and prevention to civic engagement: Research on community safety* (pp. 59–80). Toronto: Centre of Criminology.

Yamamoto, M. (2011). Mass media as a macrolevel source of social control: A new direction in the community structure model. *Mass Communication and Society, 14,* 820–37.

Yoffe, E. (2013, October 15). College women: Stop getting drunk. *Slate.com.* Retrieved from http://www.slate.com/articles/double_x/doublex/2013/10/sexual_assault_and_drinking_teach_women_the_connection.html

Zaller, J. (1992). *The nature and origins of mass opinion.* Cambridge: Cambridge University Press.

Index

Aboriginal peoples: legal system and, 157–8, 159, 174, 175, 202; missing and murdered women, 202; social assistance and, 108; victimization of, 198–9
Abrums, Mary, 92–3
academic integrity, 72–3
academic success: parenting styles and, 69
Adams, Michael, 95–6
adolescents: American vs. Danish, 77; appearance concerns of girls, 26, 28; drug use and, 57; sexuality and, 73–4
"Adonis complex," 27
advertising and mass media, 107
advice columns, 22–3
African-Americans: historic treatment of, 112–13; in inner cities, 149–50; media depictions of criminal behaviour, 110–13; media depictions of welfare use, 108; religiosity of, 91, 94
agnosticism, 88, 98
Aguilar, A., et al., 76
Albanese, P., 80
Albas, Daniel, and Cheryl Albas, 72
alcohol advertising, 47
alcohol use and abuse: by celebrities, 47; costs of, 44; deaths from, 43, 44; drinking patterns, 44; in fraternities, 79; portrayal in mass media, 46–8; recreational use of, 50; regulating vs. prohibiting use, 50–1; women rape victims and, 191
Alternative project, 180
altruistic suicide, 6
American Psychology Association (APA), 31
Andreoni, J., and R. Petrie, 23
Andrews, D.A., 178
anomic suicide, 6
anomie theory, 147
anorexia, 35
appearance: judging, 22–3
appearance norms: challenges to, 37–9; early socialization and, 29–31; gendered, 28, 29–30; mass media and beauty ideals, 23–9; racial variation in, 28, 29; stigmatized appearance, 34–7; in the workplace, 31–4; see also deviant appearances
appearance patterns and anxieties, 30
appearance subcultures, 37–8
approval of others, 64–5; see also social norms
atheism, 88, 98
athletes, female, 26–7
Atkinson, Michael, 38
attachment, 11–12
attractive people: biases in favour of, 23, 31, 33, 34; character traits and, 23, 30

authoritarian parenting, 67, 68
authoritarian states, 128–9
authoritative parenting, 67, 68, 153
authority: types of, 126
autonomous morality, 65
ayahuasca, 46

Baer, D.E., 140
Bagdikian, B., 106
Barthes, R., 106
Bashevkin, S., 140
battered women: failure to report abuse, 195; reasons for not leaving abuser, 193–5; types of abuse, 192
Baudrillard, Jean, 102, 103
Baumrind, Diana, 67
Beaman, L.G., and P. Beyer, 100
beauty contests, 24, 31
beauty ideals: advice columns on, 22–3; internalization of, 22, 27; mass media and, 23–9; racial variation in, 28, 29; Western societies, 21–2
Beccaria, Cesare, 168
Becker, Howard, 51
Becker, Howard, et al., 81
behavioural change, 19; legislation and, 42–3
"behaviour problems," 3
Belanger, Y.D., et al., 204
belief (in values), 12
Benjamin, Walter, 102
Benoit, C., and A. Millar, 196
Bentham, Jeremy, 18
Berger, John, 102
Berger, P., and B. Berger, 85
Bertrand, M-A., 176
Bibby, R.W., 96
Black, D., 51
Black, R., 40
black Canadians: hate crimes and, 188; legal system and, 157
black communities: crime and, 149–50
"black markets," 52
blaming the victim, 189–92; reducing, 196
body dissatisfaction: girls and, 30, 36; homosexual vs. heterosexual men, 28; men and, 27, 28; obesity and, 36; women and, 26, 36
body image: black girls and women, 28, 29; female athletes, 26
body size and weight: changes in, 36; girls and, 36; ideal vs. actual, 24–5; teasing and, 30
Boguslaw, Robert, 63
bonding social capital, 137

Freedman, J., 119, 121
free trade: *see* globalization
Frey, J., 59
Friedrichs, D.O., 161
fundamentalist religions, 99

Gaetz, S., et al., 201
Gamson, W.A., et al., 105, 107
gangs, 152, 158–9
Gans, Herbert, 105–6, 107
Gazso, A., 108
gender and gangs, 158
gender-role expectations, 31–2; schools and, 71
gender socialization, 65, 77, 79; flight attendants, 66
General Social Survey, 191
Gerbner, G., 118
Gilliom, J., 52
Gini Index, 146
girls: fashion for, 104; socialization of, 30; teasing and, 30
globalization, 133, 134; impact on nation-states, 135
God: role in individuals' lives, 91–2, 92–3
Goffman, Erving, viii, 18, 20, 34, 72
gossip, 14; honour killings and, 15
goths and punks, 37
Gottfredson, Michael, and Hirschi, Travis, 12, 56
Gottschalk, M., 183
governmentality, 8
government and politics, 123–41
Gramsci, Antonio, x, 132
gratification: deferred vs. immediate, 12
Gruber, A.J., 26
guilt, 14
Gunter, Barrie, 118

Habermas, J., and J. Ratzinger, 100
Hagan, J., and B. McCarthy, 157
Hagan, J., and R.D. Peterson, 146–7, 148
hair, 22
Halpern, David, 145–6, 147
Hammurabi, Code of, 166, 167
Handel, G., 81
Hannah-Moffat, K., and P. O'Malley, 176
Hanson, F.A., 52
Harding, D.J., et al., 176
Harell, A., and S. Soroka, 108
Harper, Stephen, 136, 197
Hartley, R.E., and R.C. Phillips, 55
hate crimes, 188
healing rituals, 88
health: beauty ideals and, 25–6, 27, 36; drugs and, 43; imprisonment and, 175, 176; religion and, 92–4
health behaviour theory, 47

health-care system: distrust of, 93–4
height norms, 22
Herman, E.S., and N. Chomsky, 107
heroin, 51; health issues, 43; socio-economic traits of users, 48
Hezbollah, 129
hierarchy: in religious institutions, 86
Hirschi, Travis, 10–12
Hitler, Adolf, 127
HIV infection and transmission, 139
Hobbes, Thomas, 124
Hochschild, Arlie, 65
homeless people, 157; sympathy for, 201; victimization of, 199–201
homicide: battered women and, 194
homosexuality, 131
honour killings, 15, 189
Hosada, M., et al., 31
hot spots, 187
Housing First, 201
Hunt, Jennifer, 170
hygiene, 23
hyperreality, 102–3; creating, 104–17

ideal societies, 63
ideological control, 16–17
ideology: definition of, 132; social control and, 123–41
illegal drugs, 42–3; costs of controlling and persecuting, 54; deaths from, 44; decriminalization, 52, 53; efforts to control, 51–3; informal social control of use, 51; legalization, 53; recreational use of, 50; trends in use, 58
illness: coping with, 92–4
immigrants: hate crimes and, 188; religiosity of, 96; rights and freedoms, 139; in urban centres, 150–1
impaired driving, 44, 47
importation theory, 178
"impression management," 72
imprisonment, 17–18; Aboriginal peoples and, 157–8, 174, 175; costs of, 178–80; health and safety issues, 175, 176; impact on family life, 159, 175; incarceration rates, 13, 172–3, 180; life after, 176–7, 179–80; as lifestyle turning point, 159; perceptions of, 169; prison subculture, 177; of racial minorities, 156–8, 173–5; recidivism rates, 165, 176, 178, 179, 180; rethinking support for, 178–82; as retributive punishment, 170–7; women, 175–6
incapacitation, 168
income inequality: incentives to commit crime and, 145–56
indictable offences, 171
inductive socialization, 68